Equal Citizenship and Public Reason

Published in the Series:

Equal Citizenship and Public Reason

A Feminist Political Liberalism

LORI WATSON AND CHRISTIE HARTLEY

OXFORD
UNIVERSITY PRESS

OXFORD
UNIVERSITY PRESS

Oxford University Press is a department of the University of Oxford. It furthers the University's objective of excellence in research, scholarship, and education by publishing worldwide. Oxford is a registered trade mark of Oxford University Press in the UK and certain other countries.

Published in the United States of America by Oxford University Press
198 Madison Avenue, New York, NY 10016, United States of America.

© Oxford University Press 2018

CIP data is on file at the Library of Congress
ISBN 978-0-19-068303-0 (pbk.)
ISBN 978-0-19-068302-3 (hbk.)

For Thomas, Matthew, Charlie, William, and Josephine, in the hopes that they inherit a better world than they entered.

Contents

Preface

THIS BOOK IS the result of over a decade of collaboration. Although we knew each other in graduate school and realized we had common philosophical interests then, it was not until we saw each other at a Pacific APA meeting in March of 2006 that we decided to work together on a paper. One paper led to another and another and another and, eventually, to this book. Most important, our collaboration led to an amazing friendship and a shared sense of comfort in doing this work with someone who understands one's most deeply held views about equality and justice because she too has them.

This book is co-equally authored. We have broken protocol with alphabetizing our names only because all our shared articles lead with Hartley's name, and in an effort to embody fairness (or erase the moral luck of one's last name) we simply reverse our names here. However, that should not be read as an indication of priority of authorship; we are equal authors. Every chapter, except chapters 7 and 8, are fully co-equally authored. Watson is the sole author of chapter 7. Hartley is the sole author of chapter 8.

We have many people to thank, individually and together. Watson's acknowledgments are first, followed by Hartley's, and then our shared acknowledgments.

Watson's Acknowledgments

First, I would like to thank Christie Hartley for everything. We began writing together over a decade ago, and neither of us could have predicted how, from an initial idea for one paper, we would create a body of work culminating in this book. Nor could we have predicted what an amazing friendship and partnership would grow out of our shared work. I feel very lucky on both counts.

Books like this don't happen quickly, and they don't happen without a lot of support. Thankfully, my support network is both broad and deep. Thanks are owed, though not sufficient to acknowledge the tremendous amount of support given to me by the following individuals: my parents, Billie and Larry Watson; my sister, Marti Watson; my brother, Barrett Watson; and Amy Baehr, Elizabeth Barnes, Susan Brison, Brian Clack, John Corvino, Remy Debes, Anne Eaton, Liz Goodnick, Lori Gruen, Carol Hay, Michael Kelly, Rebecca Kukla, Alice MacLachlan, Sarah Clark Miller, Blain Neufeld, Noelle Norton, Susanne Sreedhar, and Matt Zwolinski.

The intellectual debt owed to my teachers and mentors, without each of whom I would not have achieved whatever level of success I have, is enormous. John Christman made me a philosopher. Tony Laden taught me how to read Rawls. Charles Mills and Martha Nussbaum both acted as generous mentors over the years. And then there is Catharine MacKinnon. It would take an entire book in its own right to thank her properly. I first "met" her as an undergraduate reading *Toward a Feminist Theory of the State*, though I never dreamed I would actually meet the person. And then I did. Since that original meeting in 1999, she has been a constant presence in my life. Beyond her enormous intellect, she is one of the most generous, loving, and loyal persons I have ever known. My friendship with her is one of the most important of my life. Thank you, Cat, for everything you are.

Finally, I would like to thank my wife, Michelle Watson, whose tolerance for my constantly saying "I have to write" is superhuman. Without her love and support, this book would never have been written.

The University of San Diego has provided generous support in the form of research grants, but also in offering an intellectual climate in which I have been able to flourish. One could not hope for better colleagues than I am fortunate to have in the philosophy department and the law school.

Hartley's Acknowledgments

First, I'd like to thank Lori for being an amazing coauthor and friend. I have learned so much from her in our collaboration, and I am so lucky that we began this journey together. She makes everything fun, including our disagreements, and I can't thank her enough for her understanding, support, and encouragement throughout our partnership.

I've discussed the topics of this book with so many people over so many years that I can't begin to name them all here. In this past several years, though, I have had numerous conversations with some colleagues and students to whom I owe an incredible debt of gratitude. Amy Baehr and Blain Neufeld each provided sharp and insightful feedback that added so much to the final product. I have benefited tremendously from conversations with my colleagues in social and political philosophy at Georgia State University. In particular, I thank my colleagues, Andrew Altman, Andrew I. Cohen, Andrew J. Cohen, Sandy Dwyer, Bill Edmundson, Peter Lindsay, and George Rainbolt, and I thank those students who worked on topics closely related to the ideas covered in this book, including Jeffrey Carroll, Garrison Claremont, Mercer Gary, Stephen Herman, Kathryn Joyce, Mandy Long, Meagan Malone, and Pierce Randall. I was also extremely fortunate to have had two fantastic mentors in graduate school—Elizabeth Anderson and Stephen Darwall—from whom I learned so much and to whom I will always be grateful for their support.

Finally, I am extremely grateful to my parents, Jim and Patricia Hartley, my sister, Carrie, and my spouse, Scott Brown, for their love, support and encouragement as this project grew and grew and grew. And I thank my favorite distractions—Thomas and Matthew—for reminding me what is important every day.

Joint Debts

Amy Baehr and Blain Neufeld deserve our joint acknowledgment and deep gratitude. Each read numerous versions of nearly every chapter in the book and provided incredible constructive feedback that challenged us to sharpen our view and clarify our arguments. They happily went way beyond what is fair to ask of any colleague and have been sources of encouragement and insight for years. Every good story needs a villain, and we thank Kevin Vallier for playing that role for us. We thank him for being a generous critic and for challenging us to sharpen our arguments.

An earlier version of chapter 2 was presented as part of the political theory workshop at the University of California San Diego. We thank participants for helpful comments. A very early version of what is now some of the material in chapter 4 and some of the material in chapter 5 was presented at the Bowling Green State University Workshop in Applied Ethics and Public Policy on Religious Exemptions. We thank workshop participants for helpful feedback and stimulating presentations on this topic. The revised chapter 9 was presented at Loyola University and Furman University, and we are grateful for comments from audience participants.

Cheshire Calhoun, series editor for Studies in Feminist Philosophy, and Peter Ohlin, at Oxford University Press, provided guidance and support as we prepared our manuscript. Two anonymous referees provided detailed and generous feedback that greatly contributed to the final product.

Three chapters in this book are revised versions of previously published material. Chapter 5 is a revised version of "Political Liberalism and Religious Exemptions" in *Religious Exemptions*, edited by Kevin Vallier and Michael Weber (Oxford: Oxford University Press, 2017): 97–119. We thank Oxford University Press for permission to reprint material from that volume in this book. Chapter 6 is a revised version of "Is a Feminist Political Liberalism Possible?," *Journal of Ethics and Social Philosophy* 5 (2010), www.jesp.org. We gratefully acknowledge the publication of material from that article in our chapter. Chapter 9 is a revised version of "Political Liberalism, Marriage and the Family," *Law and Philosophy* 31 (2012): 185–212. We thank *Law and Philosophy* for permission to reprint material from that article here.

Abbreviations of Works by John Rawls

Rawls's works are cited in footnotes with the following abbreviations:

IPRR   "The Idea of Public Reason Revisited." In *John Rawls: Collected Papers*. Ed. Samuel Freeman, 573–615. Cambridge: Harvard University Press, 1999.

JF   *Justice as Fairness: A Restatement*. Ed. Erin Kelly. Cambridge: Harvard University Press, 2001.

LP   *The Law of Peoples*. Cambridge: Harvard University Press, 1999.

PL   *Political Liberalism*, expanded edition. New York: Columbia University Press, 2005.

RTH   "Reply to Habermas." In *Political Liberalism*, expanded edition. New York: Columbia University Press, 2005.

TJ   *A Theory of Justice*, rev. ed. Cambridge: Harvard University Press, 1999.

Equal Citizenship and Public Reason

Introduction

WE HAVE ARRIVED at a time in which nearly everyone explicitly values equality. Those who argue for the unequal or subordinated status of women and racial minorities are labeled "fringe," "extremists," or sometimes "hate groups." And while it may be more common for gays, lesbians, bisexuals, trans persons, gender nonconforming persons and persons with disabilities to encounter explicit claims that challenge their status as equal citizens, there are encouraging social movements in liberal states demanding equality for members of these groups. Yet, despite our general agreement over the value of equality, we (even in liberal democracies) are far from realizing this ideal in substance as many persons are still subordinated on the basis of group membership. There is significant disagreement about what equality is and what it requires.

While women, as a group, do have formal political equality as a result of years of activism, piecemeal legislation, and some landmark judicial decisions, the promise of substantive equality remains unfulfilled. A range of facts bare out the substantive equality gap between women and men as groups: Women do not earn as much as men. They earned just 81% of men's median weekly earnings in 2015.[1] Women are more likely to be poor. In 2015 they were "35% more likely to live in poverty than men."[2] Compared to men, women disproportionately care for children and other dependents.[3] They are underrepresented in the most powerful positions in the labor market and in the political sphere. In 2017, women

---

[1] U.S. Bureau of Labor Statistics, "Women in the Labor Force."

[2] Tucker and Lowell, "National Snapshot."

[3] U.S. Bureau of Labor Statistics, "Time Use Survey (2016)."

held 25.1% of executive/senior-level official and manager positions at S&P 500 Companies;[4] the number of women CEOs at Fortune 500s was a pitiful record high of 32.[5] Women earned half of law school degrees, but in 2017 they were only 20% of the equity partners at firms.[6] In that same year, women held 21% of the seats in the U.S. Senate and 19.3% of the seats in the House of Representatives. Furthermore, women continue to be terrorized by sexual and domestic violence at an alarming rate. Recent statistics reveal that one in five women report experiencing rape in their lifetime. One in 20 women report forms of sexual violence other than rape. Young women (age being another vector of inequality) are especially vulnerable to sexual violence: 37.4% of rape victims report first being raped between the ages of 18 and 24.[7] According to data from the National Domestic Violence Hotline, "From 1994 to 2010, about 4 in 5 victims of intimate partner violence were female."[8] Being young and a woman are risk factors for domestic and sexual violence. When women are members of groups subordinated on the basis of race, ethnicity, religion, disability status, sexuality, or gender identity, the layered structure of obstacles to the enjoyment of substantive equality are all the more solidified.

Given the disparity between liberalism's theoretical promise of equality and the inequality that characterizes actual liberal democracies, such as the inequality in the United States, some feminists, critical race theorists, and others argue that if equality is our goal, liberalism just doesn't have the goods to deliver. Some critics claim the problem is that liberals offer an impoverished view of equal citizenship and place too much emphasis on choice, which leaves the view unable to deliver more than mere formal equality and results in group-based inequalities that effectively undermine free and equal citizenship for some members of society. This criticism gains further purchase when we acknowledge liberalism as such doesn't have a theory of gender or race per se. Importantly, it is not liberal theory but different types of feminist theory and critical race theory that have explained and made clear the nature of group-based subordination—both its structure and its particularities.

---

[4] Catalyst, *Pyramid.*

[5] McGregor, "The Number of Women CEOs."

[6] Olson, "A Bleak Picture."

[7] U.S. Centers for Disease Control and Prevention. "Sexual Violence."

[8] National Domestic Violence Hotline. "Get the Facts and Figures."

Given these considerations, one might think those concerned with equal citizenship and systematic practices of social subordination on the basis of group membership such as sex and race should abandon liberalism as a framework for theorizing about justice. While we appreciate the critical impulse driving this claim, we think that liberalism is well worth defending. However, our aim in the book is not to defend liberalism generally over other rival political theories (republicanism, socialism, and the like). Rather, we want to explore whether a particular version of liberalism has the internal resources to secure substantive equality for women, racial minorities, and other socially subordinated groups. In particular, we are interested in whether political liberalism can deliver on the promise of equal citizenship for all.

For those familiar with different varieties of liberal theory, political liberalism may seem like a surprising orientation for our project. It is the theory developed by John Rawls in his canonical work, *Political Liberalism,* and in some of his later writings.[9] Central to the view is the fact of reasonable pluralism, or the idea that under free institutions, reasonable people will accept diverse and irreconcilable yet reasonable comprehensive doctrines.[10] This is to say that reasonable people will reasonably disagree about the good life. What's more, a view is not unreasonable, according to political liberals, simply because it includes beliefs about gender difference or even gender hierarchy as appropriate for certain aspects of life. (It depends upon the particular views about gender.) Furthermore, political liberals accept a restrictive view of public reason for matters of basic justice and constitutional essentials. In particular, political liberals claim that in the public, political sphere persons should limit the justifications they offer for laws and policy related to matters of basic justice and constitutional essentials to those reasons shared by persons as free and equal citizens. Hence, in the justification of relevant law and policy, for example, feminists can't appeal to their full egalitarian views of the good life which stretch beyond persons' interests as free and equal citizens, but neither can religious persons justify restrictions on contraception (supposing such is central to fundamental health care) on the grounds it is contrary to God's law.

---

[9] PL and IPRR.

[10] PL, p. 36.

Some may worry that political liberalism's restrictions on public reason will preclude feminists from appealing to the arguments needed to justify the reforms necessary to secure equal citizenship for women. The aim of this book is to show that this isn't the case. Indeed, we defend political liberalism as a feminist liberalism. We argue that political liberalism's core commitments restrict all reasonable conceptions of justice to those that secure genuine, substantive equality for women and other marginalized groups. We aim to develop a feminist political liberalism for two reasons. First, we are both convinced that political liberalism is the most promising account of political morality. In this book, we don't advance an argument for that claim, and we don't defend political liberalism as superior to other forms of liberalism. Rather, we aim to explore the power and limits of political liberalism. Second, we are both feminists. We think any account of political morality that fails to deliver equal freedom to women is fatally flawed. If it could be shown that political liberalism can't secure substantive sex equality, then that is a sufficient reason to reject the theory.

Our target audience for the book is quite diverse. We not only aim to show skeptical feminists the power of political liberalism to deliver substantive sex equality; we also aim to highlight for liberal theorists the egalitarian commitments of political liberalism and its distinctive and appealing vision of democratic society.

We develop the overall argument of the book in two parts and divide the book accordingly. In the first part, we aim to articulate and defend a novel interpretation of political liberalism. In the course of making our case, we engage with commentators on a range of hotly debated and divisive issues in political theory, including, for example, methodological questions about the role of ideal versus nonideal theory for theorizing about justice, substantive questions about the appropriate criteria for publicly justified laws, norms for public deliberation and the connection between public justification and public deliberation, the issue of whether restrictive accounts of public reason threaten the integrity of some religiously oriented citizens, and the matter of whether there should be religious exemptions from publicly justified laws.

In the second half of the book, we make the case that our interpretation of political liberalism is a feminist liberalism, with the necessary theoretical apparatus to identify and rectify substantive inequalities that women and other socially subordinated groups continue to face. Here we demonstrate the power of public reason arguments for law and policy to address historical sites of women's subordination to advance equality; for example, we develop public reason arguments concerning the state regulation of prostitution, state regulation of cultural practices of gender inequality, and state recognition of the institution of marriage. Below we provide chapter overviews to direct readers with specific interests to particular parts of the book.

Part One: Equal Citizenship and Public Reason
Chapter 1: The Role of Ideal Theory

In this chapter, we consider whether a commitment to ideal theory, in a particular form, makes political liberalism especially ill-suited for theorizing about justice for socially subordinated groups. Some feminists and critical race theorists argue that those interested in justice for subordinated groups should reject ideal theory in favor of nonideal theory, for they claim the latter is designed to address questions of domination, inequality, and group-based injustice. These critics charge that, insofar as the project of political liberalism aims at defending a conception of justice, or a family of such conceptions, appropriate for an ideal, liberal society, the project effectively dismisses concerns about racial and gender justice from the start.

We clarify the commitment to ideal theory of political liberals and respond to such criticisms. We advance several important claims in this chapter: (1) One may reject some of Rawls's idealizations as presented in his particular defense of justice as fairness and remain a political liberal. Political liberals need not endorse Rawls's specific methodology or argument for justice as fairness. (2) Nevertheless, the project of political liberalism is centrally motivated by two concerns: (a) the legitimate use of political power should be justifiable, in some sense, to all reasonable persons as free and equal citizens, and (b) in a liberal democratic state that protects certain freedoms, reasonable pluralism among citizens is inevitable. Given these motivating concerns, political liberals aim to provide an account of public justification that respects the challenge posed by the fact of reasonable pluralism. However, the way in which one understands how the fact of *reasonable* pluralism arises shapes whether one is likely to think that some commitment to ideal theory is a necessary part of the project of political liberalism.

We think, and will make clear in what follows, that the fact of *reasonable* pluralism and the problem it raises for thinking about public justification arises only in the context of an ideal, liberal polity. And so it is within ideal theory that the central organizing question of political liberalism arises, namely, "How is it possible for there to exist over time a just and stable society of free and equal citizens who still remain profoundly divided by reasonable religious, philosophical, and moral doctrines?"[11] (3) We argue that a commitment to ideal theory does not entail assuming away race or gender as social categories that give rise to concerns about justice. In other words, we argue that even within a politically liberal well-ordered (ideal) society, racial or gender inequalities may arise due to the role that beliefs about race or gender play in some persons' comprehensive doctrines. Thus, political liberals must theorize about racial and gender inequality from within ideal theory; such work is not merely "nonideal" theorizing. Finally, (4) we claim that ideal theory provides important guidance for correcting injustices on the basis of gender and race in nonideal societies.

Chapter 2: The Moral Foundation of Public Justification and Public Reason

In this chapter we offer an account of the moral foundation of public justification and begin to develop our account of public reason for political liberalism. We begin by contrasting two views of liberal democracies and their distinctive accounts of public justification. We claim that political liberals view liberal democracies as a shared project among persons with the end of living on terms of mutual respect with others whom they view as free and equal citizens and whom they take to share interests with them as such. This view gives rise to the shared reasons account of public reasons as necessary to satisfy a principle of public justification. In this chapter we hope to show what is unique and compelling about political liberalism's account of public justification and suggest its superiority to convergence accounts of public justification currently defended by some leading scholars. To this end, we argue against convergence accounts on several grounds, including (1) convergence accounts of public reason fail to capture what is distinctive about democratic decision-making, namely,

---

[11] PL, p. 4.

that it represents a kind of collective willing, and (2) convergence accounts lack normative stability. Political liberalism offers both.

Chapter 3: Exclusive Public Reason

This chapter concerns public deliberation, and, to fully explain our view, we address some important disagreements among political liberals related to public reason. In particular, we address the disagreement among political liberals about the scope of public reason, that is, the range of principles, laws, and policies to which the idea of public reason applies and their disagreement about the norms for public deliberation within the idea of public reason. We argue that the moral foundation for political liberalism delimits a narrow scope for the idea of public reason, such that public reasons are required only for matters of constitutional essentials and basic justice. With respect to norms for public discussion within the idea of public reason, some political liberals permit persons to draw upon their comprehensive doctrines in the context of discussing laws and policies—not to justify laws or policies but for other purposes, such as strengthening the stability of an overlapping consensus of reasonable comprehensive doctrines or even strengthening the ideal of public reason itself. We argue that arguments for these claims are not convincing. Furthermore, we argue that appealing to one's comprehensive doctrines where the idea of public reason applies is contrary to properly respecting persons as free and equal citizens. Hence, the most defensible idea of public reason is an exclusive one, according to which citizens have a moral duty to never appeal to their comprehensive doctrines when engaged in public reasoning.

Chapter 4: Integrity and the Case for Restraint

Some may think our account of public reason privileges secular worldviews and raises concerns about the ability of some religious persons to participate in public, political debate as equals or on fair terms. They may think that our account is just too demanding for some religiously oriented citizens and threatens or undermines their integrity. In this chapter, we consider various accounts of integrity that might underwrite such criticisms. We argue that purely formal accounts of integrity that do not distinguish between the integrity of reasonable and unreasonable persons, as specified within political liberalism, cannot underwrite integrity challenges that should concern political liberals. Simply put, political liberals are not concerned with preserving the integrity of unreasonable persons. However, if we limit our inquiry to conceptions of integrity that can distinguish between reasonable and unreasonable persons, the supposed burdens persons of faith face are not unjustifiable burdens different from the burdens of social cooperation that all citizens face equally. Thus, although critics frame their challenge to political liberalism in terms of concerns over the integrity of religious believers, the objection is really best understood as a challenge to the account of public justification and the account of public reason as a moral ideal. We think the defense of public justification and public reason offered in chapters 2 and 3 offers a powerful response to these kinds of criticisms.

Chapter 5: Religious Exemptions

In this chapter, we continue our discussion of potential challenges to political liberalism that might be raised by theorists concerned with the interests of persons of faith. In particular, we consider whether political liberals can recognize exemptions from generally applicable laws when those laws substantially burden living in accordance with a religious comprehensive doctrine. We argue that in some cases political liberals can recognize religious accommodations or exemptions. However, political liberals cannot single out religion, in particular, for special treatment; when other commitments function in the same way, those commitments should enjoy the same status as religious commitments. Nevertheless, political liberals cannot recognize exemptions or accommodations on any basis when a law is needed to secure and protect the equal standing of all persons as free and equal citizens. Since such laws are justified on the basis of public reasons, which are shared by persons as free and equal citizens, exemptions from or accommodations to them are contrary to properly respecting persons as free and equal citizens. Of course, some cases are complex, as our discussion will show.

Part Two: Feminist Political Liberalism
Chapter 6: Is a Feminist Political Liberalism Possible?

In this chapter we start to make our case that political liberalism is a feminist liberalism. We argue that political liberalism's ideas of reciprocity and equal citizenship limit reasonable political conceptions of justice to only those that include principles that yield substantive equality for all, including women (and other marginalized groups). To this end, we claim that the criterion of reciprocity calls for (1) the eradication of social conditions of domination and subordination relevant to democratic deliberation among free and equal citizens and (2) the provision of the social conditions of recognition respect. As a result we claim that the criterion of reciprocity limits reasonable political conceptions of justice to those that provide genuine equality for women along various dimensions of social life central to equal citizenship. We close this chapter by addressing the worry that some might think our view amounts to a comprehensive liberalism. We argue that while our view commits us, as political liberals, to the normative priority of citizenship, this commitment does not transcend the limits of a political, as opposed to comprehensive, liberalism.

Chapter 7: Public Reason and Prostitution

Feminists have long argued that prostitution is a primary site of the social subordination of women, both the women in prostitution and all women insofar as the practice of prostitution is premised on the belief that women should sexually service men. However, more recently, some feminists have challenged this analysis of prostitution. These feminists prefer to call such practices "sex work" and defend "sex work" as a voluntary practice of sexual agency. In this chapter, we critically engage with the "sex work" approach to prostitution and argue that treating "sex work" like any other form of work is neither possible nor compatible with valuing the freedom and equality of women as citizens.

Many liberals, too, are fond of pro–"sex work" arguments. Such liberals often claim, erroneously, that liberalism's commitment to a kind of neutrality among competing conceptions of the good life and its commitment to antipaternalism requires either decriminalization or legalization of prostitution. They think there just aren't good arguments against legalization or decriminalization that are consistent with liberalism's commitment to tolerating a wide range of ways of living.

While we agree that arguments that rest on a particular conception of the "good" of sex or of the role of sex in a broader conception of the good are illegitimate grounds for state policy, there are, nonetheless, good public reason arguments against decriminalization or legalization of prostitution. Public reason arguments require appealing to the value of free and equal citizenship and offering an interpretation of what, in a particular case, such freedom and equality requires.

We give a sex equality argument against decriminalization and legalization (often thought to be the quintessential liberal positions) and, instead, argue in favor of what is known as "the Nordic model"— understood broadly as a state policy which fully decriminalizes the selling of sex yet criminalizes the buying of sex while adopting substantive social supports to enable persons in prostitution to exit prostitution.[12] We craft our arguments drawing on a rich body of empirical data concerning different models of regulation and facts about the conditions of persons living in prostitution. In this sense, this entire argument is an exercise in nonideal theory. However, as many of our arguments concern the intrinsic features of prostitution, they equally apply in any politically liberal well-ordered society. The normative basis for our argument is the particular account of free and equal citizenship we have argued for thus far. We give what we take to be powerful public reason arguments both against legalization and full decriminalization and in favor of the Nordic model.

Chapter 8: Social Norms, Choice, and Work

In modern liberal democracies, the gendered division of labor is partially the result of men and women making different choices about work and family life, even if such choices stem from social norms about gender. The choices that women make relative to men's disadvantage them in various ways: such choices lead them to earn less, enjoy less power and prestige in the labor market, be less able to participate in the political sphere on an equal basis, make them to some degree financially dependent on others, and leave them at a bargaining disadvantage and vulnerable in certain personal relationships. In this chapter, we consider if and when the state can intervene to address women's disadvantage and inequalities that are the result of gender specialization.

---

[12] A brief description of the Nordic model as a sex equality model can be found on Equality Now's website. Catharine A. MacKinnon pioneered a full defense of the Nordic model as a sex equality model, as she developed the legal model. See her early formulation of the central ideas in "Prostitution and Civil Rights," in *Women's Lives, Men's Laws*, pp. 151–161, and her most recent and developed defense in "Trafficking, Prostitution, and Inequality," pp. 277–278.

Chapter 9: Political Liberalism and Marriage

In this chapter we consider whether political liberals can and should recognize and otherwise support legal marriage as a matter of basic justice. We offer a general account of how political liberals should evaluate the issue of whether the legal recognition of marriage is a matter of basic justice. We develop and examine some public reason arguments that, given the fundamental interests of citizens, could justify various forms of legal marriage in some contexts. Indeed, we argue that there are strong public reasons that can be given in support of some forms of legal marriage in some contexts. In particular, in certain conditions, the recognition of some form of legal marriage may be the best way to protect the fundamental interests of women as equal citizens in freely chosen associations. Or it may be that, in certain conditions, to secure the social conditions necessary for gays, lesbians, and bisexuals to be free and equal citizens, some form of legal marriage can or should be recognized. We think a much underappreciated point about political liberalism is that the particular institutions that are justifiable or required as a matter of basic justice depend in part on the conditions of a particular politically liberal society, as societies characterized by reasonable pluralism can be quite diverse. Finally, we consider whether political liberals must recognize some forms of polygamous marriage where they recognize monogamous marriages. We argue that political liberals have good reason to refuse legal recognition to structurally inegalitarian forms of polygamy, but we claim that egalitarian forms of plural marriage must be treated equally with monogamous marriages where the state recognizes such marriages. Hence, the actual implications of political liberalism for marriage law cannot be worked out in advance of information about a particular politically liberal society, since the social policy needed to secure equal citizenship in a given society must be context-sensitive to be effective.

By the end of the book, we take ourselves to have offered a powerful defense of a feminist political liberalism. Our hope is to have provided a sound defense of the core normative commitments of political liberals as entailing a commitment to substantive equality for all citizens; of course, we are especially interested in persuading political liberals of their commitment to substantive sex equality. And we hope to have given feminists skeptical of liberalism generally, or political liberalism specifically, reason to rethink their view. Liberal political theory holds out the great values of freedom and equality; but, as we know from history, liberal political practice hasn't come close to delivering on the promise of equal freedom for all. Yet, we think it can. We need the political will to get us there. This book has the modest hope of providing one additional impetus to find that shared will.

PART ONE

Equal Citizenship and Public Reason

1

The Role of Ideal Theory

Sound political theories must be capable of representing normatively relevant political facts. If they can't represent certain injustices, then they can't help us identify them. If they can't represent the causes of certain injustices, then they can't help us identify solutions.

—ELIZABETH ANDERSON, *"Toward a Non-Ideal, Relational Methodology for Political Philosophy"*

I. Introduction

In the first half of this book, we develop an interpretation of the key commitments of political liberalism from which we defend a unique account of public reason. In the second half of the book, we argue that this account of political liberalism is a kind of feminist liberalism. We claim that our view offers important resources and direction for redressing the injustices that women and racial and other minorities continue to endure in liberal democracies under nonideal conditions. Indeed, we think that given the liberal, democratic ideal of equal freedom for all citizens, liberal political theory must provide the resources for redressing social inequalities that threaten or thwart a person's status as a free and equal citizen. If political liberals cannot provide such resources, then political liberalism should be rejected.[1]

Although we argue that political liberalism has the internal resources to guarantee substantive equality to all citizens and, so, to redress forms of social subordination based on group membership that undermine equal citizenship, considerable doubt has been expressed

---

[1] However, as will become clear later in this chapter, we argue that some forms of racial or gender inequality may persist even in ideal societies—societies in which the basic structure is ordered by liberal principles of justice. When such inequalities threaten to undermine equal citizenship, we argue that the politically liberal state must intervene.

about this claim.[2] Some critics argue that political liberalism's method-ological commitment to ideal theory and to certain idealizations make it especially ill-suited and, perhaps, incapable of providing the theoretical resources necessary for recognizing patterns of injustice faced by his-torically subordinated groups.[3] Thus, these critics charge that insofar as the project of political liberalism includes a defense of a conception of justice—or a family of such conceptions—appropriate for an ideal, lib-eral society, the project effectively dismisses concerns about racial and gender justice from the start. Further, they charge, if political liberalism cannot provide the tools with which one can properly diagnose cases of unjust social subordination, then surely it doesn't provide the tools to correct them.

Given these criticisms, one might think those committed to developing a feminist political liberalism would reject ideal theory and recast political liberalism as a kind of nonideal theory. However, we argue that a methodo-logical commitment to some of the features of ideal theory underwrites the very project of political liberalism. Moreover, we think this project is of great value to developing a normative vision of a just society and to articulating the normative basis for mutual respect and cooperation among citizens who are deeply divided by their views of the good. Hence, despite criticisms that a methodological commitment to ideal theory results in a flawed approach to redressing injustices, we don't think that retaining such a commitment precludes political liberals from being able to properly diagnose and redress the kinds of social subordination that compromise equal citizenship.

The structure of our argument in this chapter is as follows: First, we set out the project of political liberalism. In doing so, we clarify that the motivating question of political liberalism arises only in the context of ideal theory. That question is "How is it possible that there may exist over time a stable and just society of free and equal citizens profoundly di-vided by reasonable though incompatible religious, philosophical, and

---

[2] See, e.g., Okin, "Political Liberalism, Justice and Gender," "Justice and Gender," and "'Forty Acres and a Mule' for Women"; Abbey, "Back toward a Comprehensive Liberalism?"; Chambers, *Sex, Culture and Justice*, pp. 159–201.

[3] See, e.g., Mills, "'Ideal Theory' as Ideology" and "Schwartzman vs. Okin"; Pateman and Mills, *Contract and Domination*, especially chapter 3; Schwartzman, *Challenging Liberalism*, "Non-Ideal Theorizing," and "Feminism, Method, and Rawlsian Abstraction,"; Anderson, "Toward a Non-Ideal, Relational Methodology."

moral doctrines?"[4] While this is a limited philosophical project, it is not so limited that it leads us away from proper concern with various forms of injustice, including injustice resulting from group-based inequalities. Next, we explore which features of ideal theory and which idealizations that are part of "justice as fairness" must be retained in political liberalism. Following this, we reply to critics of political liberalism's methodological commitment to ideal theory who charge that such a commitment makes political liberalism particularly ill-suited to both theorize about and redress historical forms of subordination on the basis of group membership. Finally, we begin to develop our account of reasonable political deliberation, which we further develop throughout the first half of the book. Here we aim to establish how the account of public reason, which we view as an interpretation of the respect equal citizens owe one another as persons engaged in the project of finding shared terms of social cooperation reasonably acceptable to each in their capacity as citizens, provides powerful grounds for criticizing the inequalities that members of subordinated groups face.

II. The Project of Political Liberalism

We begin by explaining our view of the aims of political liberalism. Rawls says in the introduction to *Political Liberalism* that his aim is to "resolve a serious problem internal to justice as fairness."[5] That problem concerns the account of stability as presented in part III of *Theory*. The problem becomes apparent with the recognition of the fact of reasonable pluralism, which is the fact that "a plurality of reasonable yet incompatible comprehensive doctrines is the normal result of the exercise of human reason within the framework of the free institutions of a constitutional democratic regime."[6] Importantly, this is not simply a statement about mere pluralism or the diversity of beliefs and values in the modern world. It is the fact of *reasonable* pluralism, the fact of a plurality of *reasonable* comprehensive doctrines. Reasonable pluralism, as such, arises only in the

---

[4] PL, p. xviii.

[5] PL, pp. xv–xvi. For a detailed account of the role that the problem of stability plays in the move from *A Theory of Justice* to *Political Liberalism*, see Weithman, *Why Political Liberalism* and *Rawls, Political Liberalism and Reasonable Faith*.

[6] PL, p. xvi.

specific context of a liberal, democratic state that secures the conditions of freedom for citizens.

Recognition of the fact of reasonable pluralism led Rawls to think the account of the well-ordered society in *Theory* was "unrealistic," for it assumed that all persons accepted the same *philosophical* justification for justice as fairness, which was based on the same (partially) comprehensive doctrine. This justification required acceptance of a kind of Kantian autonomy as an essential part of a person's good and as expressing our "free and rational nature." This assumption poses problems for the account of stability offered for justice as fairness in *Theory*. There such stability was predicated on a deeper agreement than is possible given the fact of reasonable pluralism, which, again, makes clear that no single reasonable comprehensive doctrine is affirmed by all citizens, nor should we expect one such doctrine to ever be affirmed by all reasonable citizens.[7]

To address the stability problem, Rawls thought it was necessary to recast "justice as fairness" as a *political* conception of justice, which would not require, nor expect, that citizens accept any particular reasonable comprehensive doctrine. This led Rawls to pose the fundamental question that drives *political* liberalism, which, again, is "How is it possible that there may exist over time a stable and just society of free and equal citizens profoundly divided by reasonable though incompatible religious, philosophical, and moral doctrines?"[8] So when Rawls recast justice as fairness as a political conception of justice, he was not merely engaging in a defensive project, but, rather, he revised his understanding of the positive project facing liberal theorists. Demonstrating that the liberal project is a coherent one requires addressing how citizens may find stable, shared terms of social cooperation, given that the fact of reasonable pluralism is the "normal result of the exercise of human reason" under conditions of freedom as secured by liberal, constitutional democracies.

This way of understanding the project of political liberalism is reflected in Jonathan Quong's reading of political liberalism as trying to solve a problem *internal* to liberal theory itself. Quong distinguishes between two views of the project of political liberalism: the internal conception and the external conception.[9] The internal conception takes the fact of *reasonable*

---

[7] PL, p. xvi.

[8] PL, p. xviii.

[9] Quong, *Liberalism without Perfectionism*, pp. 138–145.

pluralism to be a fact that follows from liberal institutions, and so it is a problem internal to liberal theory. As such, it raises the question of how liberal political theory can accommodate this fact and remain internally consistent.[10]

On the internal conception, political liberals are concerned with the fact of reasonable pluralism because such pluralism occurs in a well-ordered society. As originally understood by Rawls, such a society was one in which, inter alia, a) "everyone accepts, and knows that everyone else accepts, the very same principles of justice," and b) "citizens have a normally effective sense of justice" and strictly comply with the principles of justice.[11] In the following section, we argue this understanding of a well-ordered society requires revision as a result of the move to political liberalism. For now what is important are certain assumptions that constitute the description of a well-ordered society that support calling pluralism *reasonable* in a very particular sense. Reasonable pluralism, as opposed to pluralism as such, arises in the context of a society in which persons desire fair terms of social cooperation for their own sake and persons accept that political power must be justified to all who share this desire (those who are reasonable). Hence, reasonable pluralism arises in a context in which persons accept some basic liberal norms. Rawls's concern is that if such persons, so described, cannot find agreement over political principles, then the liberal project is incoherent.

The external conception of political liberalism understands the project of political liberalism much more ambitiously. On the external conception, the fact of pluralism is a fact about the world, much like the fact of the moderate scarcity of resources, which any account of justice must address.[12] It aims for the justification of liberalism to some persons who do not accept "any liberal norms or values."[13] Those with this view think that political liberals must justify liberalism to those who may not accept the idea of society as a fair system of cooperation as a limiting feature for theorizing about justice or those who do not accept the fundamental democratic ideal that political power must be justified to all reasonable persons.

---

[10] Quong, *Liberalism without Perfectionism*, p. 139.

[11] See TJ, p. 4; JF, pp. 8–9; Quong, *Liberalism without Perfectionism*, p. 139.

[12] Quong, *Liberalism without Perfectionism*, pp. 138–139.

[13] Quong, *Liberalism without Perfectionism*, pp. 139–140.

On this reading of the aims of political liberalism, there are no shared normative commitments that are initially available from which to justify the liberal project. Thus, to attempt to provide such a justification requires justifying liberalism all the way down. So it would require at least providing a philosophical justification of the values of freedom and equality. This is an ambitious project. However, it's not Rawls's project. While some think that an external justification of liberalism is ultimately needed, we think that the more limited Rawlsian project is a very valuable project nonetheless—for it both aims to establish the internal coherence of liberalism and provides a powerful account of equal citizenship.

On either conception of political liberalism an account of public justification is fundamental. However, the nature of public justification varies considerably on these accounts. On the internal conception, the problem the account of public justification aims to solve is this: what kinds of arguments can citizens (idealized as reasonable in a specific sense) offer to one another as grounds for political principles and public policy that are consistent with respecting one another as cooperators in a shared enterprise and as free and equal citizens whose deeper value commitments are not universally or publicly shared. On the external conception, the problem an account of public justification must solve is finding mutually acceptable terms of cooperation for persons who are deeply divided about values, the normative priority of competing values, and much else having to do with ethical orientation. In short, the persons for whom an account of public justification is addressed, on the external view, are much like the (nonidealized) persons who occupy current liberal democracies. In Quong's words, "We might say the aim is to find principles or laws that can be justifiable to, or acceptable to, the *widest possible constituency* within liberal societies, that is, to search for the least controversial ideals available."[14]

A crucial difference between these conceptions concerns what *kinds* of reasons will count as public reasons in political deliberation. If one understands the problem political liberals are attempting to solve to be what kinds of (public) reasons reasonable citizens may legitimately offer to one another consistent with respecting their equal standing as free and equal citizens (that is, consistent with respecting the criterion of

---

[14] Quong, *Liberalism without Perfectionism*, p. 141.

reciprocity),[15] then public reasons will be limited to those reasons that are justified to persons with a particular normative status substantively understood as liberal citizens. On the internal conception of political liberalism, working out the details of this account of public, political deliberation is the primary task. On the other hand, if one understands the problem political liberals are trying to solve as working out a theory of public, political deliberation for nonidealized persons (citizens "as they are"), then additional work will have to be done to explain how such a view is both moral (normative) and purely political. Quong has articulately elaborated further objections to the external reading of political liberalism,[16] which we won't rehash here, for our interest is less in defending the internal reading over the external reading as the project of political liberalism and more with identifying our project and exploring the richness of the internal conception for addressing the injustices faced by socially subordinated groups. Having made clear our reading of the aims of political liberalism, we turn to consider the role of ideal theory in the view.

III. Ideal Theory and Nonideal Theory

Despite Rawls's recognition of the need both to substantially revise the presentation of justice as fairness as a political conception of justice and to restate the overall theory as a political rather than comprehensive liberalism, he did not extend such revisions to his account of the well-ordered society nor to his account of ideal theory. We think both ideas stand in need of revision in light of the project of political liberalism. In this section, we argue for a revised understanding of a well-ordered society consistent with the acknowledgment that reasonable pluralism is not just a fact about comprehensive doctrines and conceptions of the good but also a fact about reasonable political conceptions of justice.

---

[15] A central aim of this book is to defend a specific interpretation of the criterion of reciprocity that entails that relationships of domination and subordination grounded in group identities that undermine equal citizenship must be eliminated in a politically liberal state. The criterion of reciprocity as articulated by Rawls is the requirement that "when those terms are proposed as the most reasonable terms of fair cooperation, those proposing them must also think it at least reasonable for others to accept them, as free and equal citizens, and not as dominated or manipulated, or under the pressure of an inferior social position" (IPPR, p. 578).

[16] Quong, *Liberalism without Perfectionism*, pp. 145–153.

To begin, we consider Rawls's account of ideal theory as originally expressed, which is unique and complex. Ideal theory, according to Rawls, concerns developing an account of justice for a well-ordered society under favorable conditions.[17] A well-ordered society is one in which "everyone accepts and knows that the others accept the same principles of justice"[18] and in which "the basic social institutions generally satisfy and are generally known to satisfy these principles."[19] Moreover, a well-ordered society is one in which there is *strict compliance* by all citizens with the principles of justice.[20] Favorable circumstances or reasonably favorable conditions are those that "make a constitutional regime possible" in the presence of a political will, and these conditions include the "historical, economic and social conditions" needed for "effective political institutions."[21]

Rawls's assumptions certainly limit his inquiry. However, he aims to examine "how far in our world . . . a democratic regime can attain complete realization of its appropriate political values—democratic perfection, if you like."[22] That is, a central aim of his project is to explore whether democratic ideals are *realistically utopian.* Are they coherent? Are they sufficient to sustain justice over time? Importantly, by limiting the scope of his inquiry and making certain idealizations, conceptions of justice can be compared on their own terms, without the introduction of various other causes for their success or failure.[23] This latter claim is analogous to restricting the introduction of certain variables in scientific investigation so as to test competing hypotheses. The assumptions of ideal theory preclude the introduction of certain variables that themselves threaten justice, like widespread noncompliance.

---

[17] TJ, p. 216.

[18] Yet this specification of a well-ordered society is too narrow for Rawls once he endorses political liberalism. In Rawls's later work, he recognizes that reasonable citizens within a well-ordered society will not all endorse the same reasonable political conception of justice. Citizens may endorse different yet reasonable political conceptions of justice, though all reasonable political conceptions share certain features. We will turn to this point shortly.

[19] TJ, p. 4.

[20] TJ, p. 8.

[21] JF, pp. 101, 47.

[22] JF, p. 13.

[23] Rawls says, "The suitability of a conception of justice for a well-ordered society provides an important criterion for comparing political conceptions of justice" (JF, p. 9). See, also, Simmons, "Ideal and Nonideal Theory."

In contrast to ideal theory, nonideal theory has to do with the development of principles concerning "less happy conditions."[24] Specifically, nonideal theory is concerned with principles for two sorts of conditions: (1) "natural limitations and historical contingencies" and (2) "injustice." The latter includes, for example, punishment, just war and civil disobedience, and principles for compensatory justice.[25] On Rawls's view, ideal theory—what justice demands in a well-ordered society under favorable conditions—offers a normative guide in less favorable conditions.[26] This includes diagnosing present injustices. Moreover, it is worth emphasizing that nowhere does Rawls conclude that having an account of justice for a well-ordered society entails that policies or proposals appropriate for that society ought to directly apply to our nonideal circumstances. We will need intermediate policies, given facts about our less than ideal conditions, to address particular contingencies and to move us closer to the ideal. Affirmative action policies are a prime example of such intermediate policies insofar as they redress social inequalities that act as barriers for members of groups (women and racial minorities, among others) to enjoy fair equality of opportunity and access to employment and educational opportunities previously denied them.

Rawls stresses two reasons ideal theory is needed for nonideal theory. Zofia Stemplowska and Adam Swift label these as the "target role" and the "urgency role" of ideal theory.[27] With respect to the former, Rawls claims that we need ideal theory to do nonideal theory because nonideal theory needs an object for guidance.[28] With respect to the latter, Rawls claims ideal theory helps us to identify urgent moral needs: "The reason for beginning with ideal theory is that it provides . . . the only basis for the systematic grasp of these more pressing problems [those of nonideal theory or partial compliance theory]."[29] He clarifies this claim further by adding, "The discussion of civil disobedience, for example, depends on

---

[24] TJ, p. 216.

[25] TJ, p. 216.

[26] TJ, p. 216.

[27] Stemplowska and Swift, "Ideal Theory and Nonideal Theory," p. 376.

[28] LP, p. 90: "For until the ideal is identified . . . nonideal theory lacks an objective, an aim, by reference to which its queries can be answered."

[29] TJ, p. 8.

it."[30] Thus, Rawls thinks, at least at the time of *Theory*, that determining appropriate responses to injustice requires an ideal theory of justice from which assessment of injustices can begin. He makes the point more cautiously in *Justice as Fairness*, when he writes, "Nevertheless, the idea of a well-ordered society *should* also provide *some* guidance in thinking about nonideal theory, and so about difficult cases of how to deal with existing injustices. It *should* also help to clarify the goal of reform and to identify which wrongs are more grievous and hence more urgent to correct."[31] Yet, in *Political Liberalism*, he emphasizes the stronger point: "Thus ideal theory, which defines a perfectly just basic structure, is a necessary complement to nonideal theory without which the desire for change lacks aim."[32] What is clear is that Rawls thinks ideal theory is a necessary companion to nonideal theory.

We do not think that those who theorize about justice must do ideal theory in the Rawlsian sense before doing any form of nonideal theory.[33] It depends on one's aim(s) and one's project. Sometimes one simply aims to determine more just circumstances in a certain context, and knowing what a perfectly just society would be like is not necessary for this.[34] For example, one doesn't need an ideal theory of justice to condemn slavery and to argue for its abolition. However, examining whether liberal theory can realize its own aims, and with that evaluating whether its conception of

---

[30] TJ, p. 8.

[31] JF, p. 13. Italics in quote are our emphasis.

[32] PL, p. 285.

[33] Tommie Shelby disagrees. Shelby argues that nonideal theory "cannot succeed without knowing what the standards of justice are (and perhaps what justifies those standards)" ("Racial Realities and Corrective Justice," p. 156). However, Shelby is primarily concerned with offering an adequate and complete theory of "how to respond to social injustice." He may well be right that a comprehensive strategy for addressing injustice requires a defensible ideal theory. But Anderson's more limited point and our acceptance of the claim that one doesn't have to do ideal theory to do nonideal theory doesn't require addressing all injustices at one time or in a systematic fashion.

[34] Simmons raises some concerns with such a "piecemeal" approach to addressing injustices, including the worry that moves to address *particular* injustices may leave society *less* just overall ("Ideal and Nonideal Theory," p. 21). And while we don't disagree with Simmons that certain piecemeal "fixes" could lead to greater injustice overall, we do think that in some local contexts piecemeal interventions can improve the local context in terms of justice. Slavery is a prime example here. We don't need a full theory of ideal justice to know that freeing persons from slavery and its accompanying horrors will remove an injustice. While, of course, it doesn't follow that we are closer to full justice, it is hard to imagine any plausible argument that freeing persons from slavery may leave society "less just overall."

free and equal citizenship is a sufficient basis from which to identify, condemn, and correct various forms of inequality, does require some methodological commitment to ideal theory.

It is crucial to differentiate between ideal theory (distinguished by its concern with a well-ordered society under favorable conditions) and the various other idealizations Rawls adopts in defending justice as fairness. To determine just principles for a well-ordered society, Rawls says we should design a hypothetical initial choice situation that is fair. Rawls's proposal for a fair hypothetical initial choice situation—the original position—includes numerous idealizations that are independent of the defining aspects of his account of ideal theory and, so, can be criticized or endorsed on independent grounds. Of course, the assumptions of ideal theory shape the problem the representatives in the original position are trying to solve—that is, they are choosing principles of justice for a well-ordered society characterized by strict compliance.[35] However, one may think that some of the assumptions of ideal theory are worth preserving and reject the specific methodology of the original position or other various idealizations that are part of it, such as, for example, the veil of ignorance or the claim that citizens must be understood as fully cooperating members of society over the course of a complete life.

This is an especially important point to keep in mind when considering some feminist criticisms of Rawls's work. For example, some feminists object to Rawls's characterization of citizens as those who can be "normal and fully cooperating members of society over a complete life"[36] because this assumption prevents us from considering matters of justice for those with temporary or permanent illnesses or impairments as well as those who care for some dependents.[37] Arguably, matters of justice for those with illness or impairments as well as those who care for dependents should be part of justice theorizing from the start; such matters are not a problem of extension, as Rawls says.[38] Illnesses, impairments, and caregiving are

---

[35] This is true only at the first stage of the original position. At the second stage, the parties consider whether compliance would be rational for citizens over time (given their respective conceptions of the good and/or comprehensive doctrines). Here strict compliance is not assumed but must be demonstrated as feasible (JF, pp. 88–89, 180–188). Thanks to Blain Neufeld for this point.

[36] PL, p. 20.

[37] See, e.g., Kittay, *Love's Labor*; Nussbaum, *Frontiers of Justice*.

[38] PL, p. 20.

basic aspects of human life. To address these features of human life, it may be that important assumptions or claims that are part of the methodology of justice as fairness need to be altered or jettisoned, or it may be that we need a new methodology altogether for constructing principles of justice. However, the issue of the usefulness or necessity of a methodological commitment to ideal theory may be considered entirely independent of these specific idealizations (the original position, citizens as normal and fully cooperating members of society, and so forth).

Thus far we have not questioned Rawls's initial formulation of a well-ordered society as one in which "everyone accepts and knows that the others accept the same principles of justice"[39] and in which "the basic social institutions generally satisfy and are generally known to satisfy these principles."[40] However, this specification of the well-ordered society is inconsistent with the full scope of the fact of reasonable pluralism. Rawls explicitly acknowledges that there is no single political conception of justice that we can expect all citizens to endorse as the most reasonable. Rather, there is a family of liberal conceptions of political justice, specified by various limiting features. In other words, even political conceptions of justice are subject to reasonable pluralism. It is crucial to underscore, here, that such pluralism about political conceptions of justice is reasonable in a very specific sense. All reasonable political conceptions of justice will be premised on a commitment to the criterion of reciprocity, which requires citizens to offer reasons to others that they sincerely believe others will accept as reasonable and as consistent with their equal standing as free and equal citizens. As such, all reasonable political conceptions of justice include a commitment to securing equal liberties and opportunities for all, including a list of such basic rights, assigning such rights priority over "claims of the general good and perfectionist values," and "measures ensuring for all citizens adequate all-purpose means to make effective use of their freedoms."[41] However, given that a politically liberal society will include a family of reasonable political conceptions of justice, Rawls's original account of the well-ordered society must be revised.

Blain Neufeld and Lori Watson argue for a reformulation of the idea of a well-ordered society within political liberalism (PL WOS) as follows:

---

[39] TJ, p. 4.

[40] TJ, p. 4.

[41] IPPR, p. 582.

With the idea of a family of reasonable political conceptions of justice in hand, we can formulate the PL WOS—a society regulated by a public conception of justice—as a society with the following features:

1. All citizens (as reasonable persons) endorse *a* reasonable political conception of justice (one member of the family of reasonable political conceptions of justice).
2. The basic structure is organized in compliance with (at least) one member of the family of reasonable political conceptions of justice.
3. All citizens (reasonable persons) know (1) and (2) (that is, the "publicity condition" is satisfied).
4. A public political culture obtains as characterized by a reasonable overlapping consensus and a shared commitment (among reasonable citizens) to public reason.[42]

This account of the politically liberal well-ordered society eliminates the erroneous view that citizens will all accept the very same political conception of justice and yet retains the essential feature of the idea of a well-ordered society that gives rise to the motivating questions of political liberalism and its aim to probe the limits of the practically possible.

IV. Criticisms of Ideal Theory

In Rawls's approach to nonideal theory, nonideal theory is secondary to ideal theory. It can be contrasted with approaches to nonideal theory in which theorists start from considerations of the challenges faced by persons in current societies and theorize about how the lives of individuals in those societies can be improved without reference to some theorized perfectly just society as an ideal. We call this *nonderivative nonideal theory*.[43] Some of those who press certain objections to Rawls's ideal theory claim that political theorists should embrace nonderivative nonideal theory.

Consider first the strict compliance objection.[44] In justice as fairness, representatives in the original position choose principles for the basic structure of a well-ordered society in which they are to imagine there is

---

[42] Neufeld and Watson, "The Tyranny."

[43] This is our term, but we are describing an idea found in Anderson, *The Imperative of Integration*, p. 3.

[44] See, e.g., Sen, *The Idea of Justice*, pp. 90, 79–81; Schmidtz, "Nonideal Theory."

strict compliance by members of society with the principles of justice.[45] Some say this assumption makes Rawls's theory entirely unhelpful when thinking about how to structure actual societies, as such compliance is utterly unrealistic.[46] Nonderivative nonideal theorists who focus on strict compliance claim that part of theorizing about justice requires starting with noncompliance and considering how to address it.

Gerald Gaus offers another line of criticism. He says that Rawls's commitment to ideal theory serves as a kind of "tyranny" over political philosophers' thinking about justice.[47] Gaus is particularly focused on the Rawlsian commitment of justification to reasonable persons (normalized perspectives, in Gaus's terminology).[48] He argues that diverse perspectives about justice itself are required for correctly identifying any ideal of justice, and Rawlsians exclude this kind of deep diversity of perspective through their commitment to a particular kind of ideal theorizing. Gaus concludes that ideal theorizing in the Rawlsian sense is not only futile but will actually impede our progress to a more just society.

Other critics focus on the injustices suffered by persons who are members of socially subordinated groups; they say the idealizations relied upon within political liberalism make the resulting account of justice insensitive to injustices that subordinated groups experience.[49] Those with this concern object to Rawls's strict compliance assumption, but they have much broader methodological worries about his view. These theorists cast their worries as objections to ideal theory, but their notion of ideal theory is, strictly speaking, much broader than Rawls's. For example, Charles Mills claims that ideal theory is problematic not because of its use of ideals per se but because of the way in which it "either tacitly represents the actual as a simple deviation from the ideal, not worth theorizing in its own right, or claims that starting from the ideal is at least the best way of realizing

---

[45] TJ, pp. 308–309.

[46] However, see Simmons's defense of Rawlsian ideal theory in his "Ideal and Nonideal Theory." And see Neufeld's "Why Public Reasoning Involves Ideal Theorizing."

[47] Gaus, *The Tyranny of the Ideal.*

[48] Very roughly, Gaus defines "normalized perspectives" as theoretical devices that impute some shared beliefs, norms, values, and interests, and so on to idealized persons for purposes of identifying principles of justice (*The Tyranny of the Ideal*, p. 107).

[49] See, e.g., Mills, " 'Ideal Theory' as Ideology" and "Schwartzman vs. Okin"; Schwartzman, *Challenging Liberalism* and "Non-Ideal Theorizing"; Anderson, "Toward a Non-Ideal, Relational Methodology" and *The Imperative of Integration*, pp. 5–7.

it."[50] He identifies the following types of idealizations as problematic: an idealized social ontology (e.g., abstract individuals as rights bearers with some set of shared fundamental interests), idealized capacities (e.g., reasoning skills beyond those that actual people tend to exercise), silence on historical forms of oppression, idealized social institutions (e.g., families treated in ideal terms, as nurturing centers of affection and childrearing rather than as historical institutions of patriarchy or abuse), an idealized cognitive sphere (e.g., persons will not be understood to be shaped by their social positions so that the influence of their social position on cognition will be ignored), and strict compliance.[51]

We are primarily concerned with the kind of objection expressed by Mills and others; indeed, it motivates our project to defend a version of political liberalism against the charge that it is inadequate to theorize and address forms of social subordination that women, racial minorities, and other marginalized groups continue to face, even in liberal democracies. Thus, we devote most of our attention to responding to this particular line of criticism. However, we briefly address the first two charges.

As to whether the assumption of strict compliance among citizens in a politically liberal well-ordered society damns the view to irrelevance, Neufeld's recent work on ideal theory is instructive. He argues that, if we try to imagine persons in nonideal conditions engaging in public justification in accordance with the criterion of reciprocity, then ideal theorizing is required to the extent that citizens must evaluate proposals in light of the assumption that others will comply with them. That is, insofar as offering a public reason to another citizen involves sincerely thinking it is reasonable for him or her to accept the justification, offering the reason entails believing other citizens will accept, ceteris paribus, and comply with the proposal.[52] Moreover, such local ideal theorizing "generates pressure on public reasoners to engage in full ideal theorizing" by considering "what their society would look like if *all* the main political proposals they think are required by justice were implemented and complied with by their fellow citizens."[53] As such, the assumption of strict compliance is central to public reasoning, as part of what we are doing in public justification is

---

[50] Mills, "Ideal Theory as Ideology," p. 168.

[51] Mills, "Ideal Theory as Ideology," pp. 168–169.

[52] Neufeld, "Why Public Reasoning Involves Ideal Theorizing."

[53] Neufeld, "Why Public Reasoning Involves Ideal Theorizing," p. 74.

offering reasons for principles and laws we think others will reasonably accept and, consequently (in virtue of that acceptance), follow.

Gaus's criticism of ideal theory is more difficult to address briefly. Indeed, his criticism of Rawlsian ideal theory is masterfully crafted over an entire book,[54] and an adequate response is beyond the scope of what we can do here. For now, though, it is worth highlighting a dominant thread of Gaus's criticism as it bears on our project. Gaus argues that the project of aiming to determine principles of justice for a well-ordered society (a central organizing assumption of Rawls's formulation of ideal theory) is itself a flawed project, for such a project rests on assumptions that actually serve to prevent us from identifying any ideal of justice.[55] Moreover, Gaus insists that the project of determining principles of justice for a well-ordered society is a "dangerous illusion" that "encourages us to turn our backs on pressing problems of justice in our own neighborhoods."[56] In this way, his criticism echoes the criticism of others, that political liberalism, through its approach to ideal theory, is especially ill-suited for addressing urgent matters of injustice, such as those of racial and gender inequality.

Here we begin our reply to those who charge that through its methodological commitment to ideal theory, political liberalism is particularly ill-suited for recognizing and correcting injustices that stem from nonideal conditions, especially conditions of social domination and subordination. Mills's criticism deserves special attention. Despite his concerns about ideal theory, Mills does not reject liberalism. He argues that if we jettison certain idealizations and engage in nonderivative nonideal theory, we can rehabilitate social contract theory. In particular, he proposes revising the hypothetical choice situation for principles of justice.

Mills is not concerned with principles for a well-ordered society. Rather, he describes a hypothetical choice situation in which individuals have full knowledge of the history of their society, including the social history of domination and subordination, and in which individuals are concerned with choosing principles for rectificatory racial justice for a society given historical facts and current conditions. He adopts Rawls's veil

---

[54] Neufeld and Watson attempt to provide such a reply in "The Tyranny."

[55] Again, the full argument for this claim is quite complex and difficult to summarize in a tidy fashion. The key claim is that diverse perspectives, rather than "idealized" perspectives, are necessary for identifying any ideals of justice.

[56] Gaus, *The Tyranny of the Ideal*, p. 246.

of ignorance as part of his methodology, and he asks that we imagine what principles those in a hypothetical choice situation with full knowledge of history would choose if they didn't know whether or not they would be a member of a historically oppressed racial group in that society.[57] Mills says his view is nonideal theory because "it is taken for granted that an unjust social order already exists."[58] Mills recognizes that both ideal theory and nonderivative nonideal theory invoke moral ideals, but he sees the distinction as follows: "Ideal theory aims at mapping a perfectly just society, while non-ideal theory seeks to adjudicate what corrective or rectificatory justice would require in societies that are unjust."[59]

Simply put, Mills and Rawls have entirely different projects. Mills's project, in the tradition of critical theory, aims in its first stage at understanding the historical processes of group-based oppression and inequality and at exposing the ideological supports of such oppression. Mills tries to explain how is it possible for systematic group-based oppression to be perpetuated and sustained alongside emerging and evolving expressions of moral egalitarianism. In short, he considers how we depart so radically from our (expressed) ideal of equality. This part of his view is a largely descriptive project. However, in consideration of the problems faced by individuals as members of a socially subordinated group, he develops a substantive notion of what equality requires and rectificatory principles of justice. Hence, in Mills's nonderivative nonideal theory, sensitivity to injustice prompts investigation of the conditions of individuals' lives and how those conditions are maintained and perpetuated. Moreover, Mills thinks that questions of corrective or redistributive justice are central to any theorizing about justice, and insofar as Rawls or Rawlsians put these questions on the back burner their approach to political theory is misguided.

Mills stresses that in ideal societies, the subject of ideal theorizing, certain matters don't even arise as problems of justice, such as how to correct for systemic injustice on the basis of race or gender. (We will address this concern below.) He further queries if ideal theory is supposed to help us solve the problems we face in nonideal conditions and provide a guide for nonideal theorizing, then why has so little of this work been done by

---

[57] Mills, "The Domination Contract," pp. 79–105, 95–100.

[58] Mills, "Ideal Theory as Ideology," p. 167.

[59] Mills, "The Domination Contract," p. 94n2.

Rawls or his followers?[60] We can certainly agree with Mills that more of this work needs to be done, and we think our work makes such a contribution. However, insofar as some might infer that those who do ideal theory simply assume that the conclusions of what justice demands in a well-ordered society apply mutatis mutandis in nonideal circumstances, they are mistaken. While some people may hold this view, it would be erroneous to draw this conclusion, and Rawls never says this. The circumstances of a well-ordered society are certainly different from the conditions of any actual liberal democratic state. Those who use ideal theory as a guide for nonideal theorizing should carefully account for how the circumstances in an actual society differ from a well-ordered society and theorize principles for nonideal circumstances with that in mind. We stress this point throughout this book.

Mills's reconstructive project is about constructing principles of justice for a nonideal world. He is offering a revised theory of justice. His criticism of Rawls is primarily addressed to the role that ideal theory plays in constructing principles of justice. Our interest in and defense of ideal theory is about how it is necessary to ground political egalitarianism and how it is the context within which the project of political liberalism arises. We understand the project of political liberalism as centrally about demonstrating that it is possible for citizens to engage in public, political deliberation with co-citizens in a way that respects the status of each as an equal citizen despite the fact that citizens will have deep yet reasonable differences about the nature of the good life. We don't offer a particular political conception of justice, and we don't take a position on the best way to construct a reasonable political conception of justice, since we expect our account to be compatible with all reasonable political conceptions.

In the next section, we argue that political liberalism does not flounder when it comes to diagnosing and addressing certain injustices faced by members of socially subordinated groups. In the remainder of this section, we highlight more aspects of Rawls's commitment to ideal theory as it informs the arguments in support of political liberalism.

It is with respect to the idealized conditions of a (politically liberal) well-ordered society that the questions of stability and legitimacy arise, for it is these conditions that give rise to the fact of reasonable pluralism.[61]

---

[60] Pateman and Mills, *Contract and Domination*, p. 114.

[61] Samuel Freeman claims that political liberalism is a nonideal *partial compliance* theory because he thinks that the principle of legitimacy is "designed to apply mainly under less

Again, the assumptions and idealizations that are peculiar to justice as fairness are not part of political liberalism as such.[62] While Rawls recasts justice as fairness as a political conception of justice and considers it the "most reasonable" political conception of justice, he recognizes that in a well-ordered society characterized by reasonable pluralism citizens will embrace a family of reasonable political conceptions of justice. Hence, one can be a political liberal and reject justice as fairness—its methodology, its various assumptions and idealizations, and its principles—as the most reasonable political conception of justice.

The fact of reasonable pluralism and political liberal's normative commitment to the criterion of reciprocity structures the view of public justification and public reason that follows. The criterion of reciprocity provides the framework for a particular kind of political egalitarianism. The criterion of reciprocity specifies that, when citizens offer terms of social cooperation to others, they should "think it at least reasonable for others to accept them, as free and equal citizens, and not as dominated or manipulated, or under the pressure of an inferior political or social position."[63] This criterion, Rawls says, grounds the liberal principle of legitimacy, according to which the exercise of political power is justifiable only if it stems from political principles that are, in principle, reasonably justifiable to those to whom they apply.[64]

Given the internal conception of political liberalism we hold, those to whom political principles must be justifiable are an idealized set of persons. These idealized "reasonable" persons are persons with shared commitments. They are persons who "are ready to propose principles and

---

than ideal conditions." Reading political liberalism as a nonideal theory is hard to square with Rawls's texts. On Freeman's reading of ideal theory, as requiring that all endorse a political conception of justice for its own sake and to promote their own moral autonomy, Rawls's aim to be "realistically utopian" is undermined, as Rawls regards the fact of reasonable pluralism is an inevitable outcome of free, democratic institutions. He thinks it is not a regrettable fact, but a fact to be embraced. On Freeman's reading, strict compliance requires something that Rawls argues is impossible: general agreement on a comprehensive conception of justice, where justice is regulative for all as an intrinsic good. This can't be Rawls's view. Despite Freeman's astuteness as a Rawls interpreter, we think the best reading of Rawls's political liberalism is that it is an ideal theory. Freeman, *Rawls*, p. 397.

[62] While Rawls regards justice as fairness as the most reasonable political conception of justice in *Political Liberalism* (p. xlvi), in "The Idea of Public Reason Revisited" he emphasizes that justice as fairness "is but one" reasonable political conception of justice (p. 581).

[63] IPRR, p. 578.

[64] IPRR, p. 578.

standards as fair terms of cooperation" as well as "abide by them willingly, given the assurance that others will likewise do so" *and* have "the willingness to recognize the burdens of judgment and accept their consequences for the use of public reason."[65] The burdens of judgment are the "sources" of reasonable disagreement.[66] Those to whom justification is owed are those who are free and equal in a normative sense; they have a certain moral status, standing, and authority. Of course, it doesn't follow from the fact that persons have a certain moral status, are entitled to certain treatment by others, and are owed a certain kind of justification for certain principles and laws that their material conditions in an existing society are such that they can effectively enjoy their status, standing, and authority, as we highlight and address in later chapters.

V. Ideal Theory and Justice for Members of Socially Subordinated Groups

So, given a commitment to ideal theory, what can political liberals say about the ability of political liberalism to redress the inequalities that women and racial and other minorities continue to experience in liberal democracies or may experience even in well-ordered societies? We outline two considerations here, which we develop and defend throughout the book. First, even in a well-ordered, politically liberal society in which all members of society have certain entitlements, conditions in the background culture may be such that there are social groups distinguished on the basis of gender and race. However, if persons are subordinated on the basis of social group membership as a result of the way race and gender operate in the background culture, then equal citizenship is undermined, and political liberals must redress this inequality.[67] Indeed, the criterion of reciprocity demands it, as we discuss below and more fully explain in

---

[65] PL, pp. 49, 54.

[66] Rawls introduces the concept of "the burdens of judgment" to explain how reasonable disagreement emerges among reasonable people. The sources of such disagreement include the fact that evidence is often difficult to assess, reasonable people may place different weight on relevant considerations, moral and political values can be "vague" to some extent and thus open to competing interpretations, persons' life experiences differ and shape their judgments, among other things. See PL, pp. 56–57.

[67] Abbey agrees. She says that "because the individual is the moral centre of liberalism, anything that threatens equal respect for persons must be of concern," and so, if those engaged in nonideal theory offer theories of social subordination on the basis of race, gender, and

chapter 6. Thus, inequalities in the background culture that undermine the enjoyment of substantive equality must be corrected by the state. Second, political liberalism provides a substantive ideal of equal citizenship for nonideal circumstances that can be used to diagnose social subordination that threatens equal citizenship and that should be used as a guide to remedy injustice in nonideal conditions.

Consider Elizabeth Anderson's variation of the claim that Rawlsian ideal theory cannot recognize and address the injustices faced by members of socially subordinated groups because of the way the theory assumes equality. Concerning racial injustices she says:

> Social contract theory assumes that the operative principles of society must be justifiable to all its members. A society counts as ideally just so long as the occupants of every representative social position *in that society* would approve of it in the way it operates, and prefer it to the alternatives. . . . Since no racial positions exist in the ideal society, they do not define a standpoint from which to assess racially unjust societies.[68]

A number of factors are important to consider when thinking about this objection. First, Rawls says that, even in a well-ordered society, inequalities can occur due to the separate and discreet transactions of individuals, which, if left uncorrected, can lead to injustice. And so, "even within a well-ordered society, adjustments in the basic structure are always necessary."[69] However, he thinks that "any modern society, even a well-ordered one, must rely on some inequalities to be well-designed and effectively organized" and that the issue is "what kinds of inequalities a well-ordered society would allow or be particularly concerned to avoid."[70] Conceptions of justice will be assessed, in part, with respect to the sort of inequalities they permit.

---

so on, then Rawlsian political liberals can be responsive (*The Return of Feminist Liberalism*, p. 221).

[68] Anderson, *The Imperative of Integration*, p. 5, citing Mills, *The Racial Contract*, pp. 17–19, 92–95, and Schwartzman, *Challenging Liberalism*.

[69] PL, p. 284.

[70] JF, p. 55.

However, Rawls suggests that, while there could be inequalities in income and wealth in a society well-ordered by justice as fairness, race and gender will not be relevant social positions.[71] In other words, Rawls suggests that race and gender will not be social categories that confer status or ground hierarchical relations in a well-ordered society, as all persons will enjoy basic rights and liberties and opportunities as specified by justice as fairness. Again, Rawls explicitly claims that distinctions based on race and gender are not included as the kind of "contingencies" that create inequalities in a citizen's life prospects in a well-ordered society. Thus, one might conclude that theorizing about racial or gender inequality is not required within ideal theory. This interpretation of Rawls, and his commitment to a particular understanding of ideal theory, is what gives rise to the kind of criticism expressed by Anderson and others.

However, in a following passage, Rawls weakens the claim that race and gender, for example, will not be a basis for inequalities in a well-ordered society by recognizing that such categories, even in a well-ordered society, may be used to assign unequal rights (though this would be unjust). Rawls argues that if "certain fixed natural characteristics are used as grounds for assigning unequal basic rights, or allowing some persons lesser opportunities; then such inequalities will single out relevant positions."[72] And furthermore, under such conditions, "the positions they specify are points of view from which the basic structure must be judged."[73] So Rawls does not deny that racial (or gendered) positions might exist even in a well-ordered society, and if they do, they, indeed, provide a standpoint from which to assess the justness of the basic structure.

Although Rawls may have thought that in a well-ordered society social positions (hierarchies) on the basis of racial or gender group membership are highly unlikely, we think that, in a well-ordered, politically liberal society, there are reasons to think that racial and gender categories may well persist and may serve as a basis for social hierarchies. Reasonable doctrines must affirm that all persons are free and equal citizens, which entails that all persons are viewed as having a certain status, standing, and authority as citizens and as having certain entitlements (including certain rights, liberties, and opportunities). But comprehensive doctrines are not

---

[71] JF, p. 66.

[72] JF, p. 65.

[73] JF, p. 65.

unreasonable merely because they contain gender norms and roles, even ones that lead to hierarchical social positions, in certain institutions, such as the family, private associations, or within religious institutions.

The same is true for race. Indeed, in the background culture of a well-ordered society, gender and race may shape the lives of persons in profound ways. However, if there are social positions on the basis of gender or race or social identities that work to threaten or undermine persons' ability to function as free and equal citizens, then political liberals must redress this. We develop and defend this argument in chapter 6 and apply this position to the gendered division of labor in chapter 8. We argue that the criterion of reciprocity, which is the normative core of political liberalism, demands conditions for reasonable democratic deliberation among persons as free and equal citizens. In other words, in the background culture of a politically liberal, well-ordered society, practices and institutions may emerge that threaten equal citizenship by creating social hierarchies; the state must make adjustments to the basic structure—through law and policy—to thwart such social hierarchies. So, for example, if systematic stereotypes about persons on the basis of their social group membership function to exclude them from certain opportunities or the enjoyment of the basic rights of citizens, the state must develop policies to combat such stereotypes. If certain systemic beliefs about women undermine women's testimony in rape trials, the state can adopt policies to mitigate, combat, or eradicate such systemic biases from impacting judicial outcomes. Hence, even in ideal theory, racial, gender, or other group-based hierarchies remain a threat given the way that comprehensive doctrines function in the background culture. Remediating such inequalities or the threat of them is necessary for securing substantive equality for those potentially subject to them.

It is important to stress that the criterion of reciprocity demands that, when engaged in public reason, persons must address proposals related to matters of basic justice or constitutional essentials to persons in their capacity as free and equal citizens, as possessing the accompanying normative status. This is crucial. When thinking about matters of basic justice, we need to know what is justifiable to persons who have a certain normative status. But, again, what is proposed and the justification for the proposal may address social inequalities that make the material conditions of persons' lives fall short of what they should expect given their normative status. Certainly, conditions of social subordination that undermine or threaten a person's normative status as an equal citizen are not justifiable, but there are important questions about how best to rectify such conditions, given all relevant political values. Public reason requires ideal theory in this sense: we need to know what those committed to certain ideals accept in order to know what genuine equal citizenship requires.

To clarify our response to Anderson, while it is true that political liberals do hold that the principles of justice must be justified to all persons conceived of as free and equal citizens and that their primary account of public justification aims at considering what is justifiable in a well-ordered society, these features of the view do not exclude race or gender as relevant social positions from which to assess principles of justice. Given the way that comprehensive doctrines structure persons' lives in the background culture, race and gender may well be relevant social positions. We think it is especially clear in political liberalism that, even in a well-ordered society, race and gender may persist as a basis by which person are categorized and experience social exclusion, marginalization, or subordination outside the political sphere, since comprehensive doctrines structure many aspects of the social world. As just expressed, this might sound like a strong reason for rejecting political liberalism altogether. However, note that political liberals argue precisely that inequalities that bear on equal citizenship are the sorts of inequalities we must redress through our conception of justice. Put another way, Rawls readily sees that inequalities due to income and wealth will persist even in a well-ordered society due to the transactions of individuals. Furthermore, he argues that insofar as these sorts of inequalities threaten or undermine the freedom and equality of persons as citizens, we must modify the basic structure to correct for such inequalities. We are simply making a parallel argument with distinctions based on race and gender.

Hence, if gender and race threaten equal citizenship in a politically liberal, well-ordered society, the state must address it. This answers only one part of Anderson's objection, namely, that ideal theory removes race (and gender) as relevant social positions from which to assess the justness of the basic structure. The other important objection her concern gives rise to is that ideal theories will not provide effective resources, or will not provide effective guides, regarding how to correct for injustice in nonideal circumstances.

As we stated in the introduction to this book, liberal theory as such does not provide a theory of gender or race. Rather, feminists and critical race theorists and others have focused on the material conditions of women and other social groups to develop theories of oppression on the basis of gender and race (and other social categories such as sexuality, ethnicity, and so on). Of course, at the heart of liberal theory is the idea of equal freedom, and this idea has been fundamental to egalitarian movements for justice. As Amy Baehr remarks, "Liberalism is one of the most important historical roots of feminism."[74] John Stuart Mill's *Subjection of Women* offers a powerful indictment of gender inequality from liberal principles. Similarly, many liberal feminists deploy liberal values to identify unjust and oppressive gender relations.[75] Political liberalism, similarly, offers, among other things, an interpretation of equal citizenship that can serve as the basis for a powerful indictment of oppressive and unjust gender hierarchies. In nonideal conditions, theories of gender or race particular to the social context can reveal the ways in which some persons fail to enjoy equal citizenship. And political liberalism's ideal of equal citizenship grounds the substantive entitlements that all persons as equal citizens should enjoy and provides a basis for identifying some ways in which the material conditions of persons could be unjust, as well as a basis for demanding rectificatory principles.[76] From the demands of equal citizenship in a well-ordered politically liberal society, principles for nonideal conditions can be determined together with consideration of the relevant material conditions of the society.

---

[74] Baehr, Introduction to *Varieties of Feminist Liberalism*, p. 1.

[75] See, e.g., Nussbaum, *Sex and Social Justice*; Okin, *Justice, Gender and the Family*.

[76] For a similar view of the relationship between ideal and nonideal theory, see Abbey, *The Return of Feminism Liberalism*, pp. 222–223: "Ideal theory needs information about relations of domination in any given society just as critics of such relations need ideal theory. . . . Without some engagement with ideal theory it is hard to reveal sexism, racism and other sources of dominations, let alone find terms with which to criticize them."

The Moral Foundation of Public Justification and Public Reason

The idea of public reason specifies at the deepest level the basic moral and political values that are to determine a constitutional democratic government's relation to its citizens and their relation to one another. In short, it concerns how the political relation is to be understood.

—JOHN RAWLS, *"The Idea of Public Reason Revisited"*

I. Introduction

In this chapter and the following three, we develop and defend an account of public reason for political liberalism. Our view is more restrictive of the kinds of reasons that can be permissibly introduced into public reason than are other liberal views, even other politically liberal ones. In brief, we argue that public reasons are reasons that reasonable persons as free and equal citizens, drawing on their favored reasonable political conception of justice as well as general rules of inquiry and reasoning, sincerely believe other reasonable citizens will share as reasons from the point of view of free and equal citizenship.[1] Thus, we defend a principle of exclusion,[2] according to which reasons that are not shared

---

[1] Bonham and Richardson argue that political liberals, and others, who rely on the idea that public reasons are those reasons that all reasonable persons *could* accept rather than "do" or "will" accept unnecessarily rely on the modality "could" in a way that is "otiose" once the substantive standards for reasonableness are enumerated. We agree with Bonham and Richardson on this point. See their "Liberalism, Deliberative Democracy, and 'Reasons That All Can Accept.'" Here we aim to give a description of public reasons that allows that while some citizens may accept some reasons or set of reasons as public reasons, they may ultimately endorse different public reasons as the most persuasive.

[2] We adopt Kevin Vallier's notions of a principle of exclusion and a principle of restraint. See his *Liberal Politics and Public Faith*.

by persons understood as free and equal citizens are excluded as public reasons. Furthermore, we argue that citizens have a moral duty (but not a legal duty) to follow a principle of restraint[3] for the justification of certain principles and laws. In particular, we claim that, in public, political discussion, citizens should justify matters of basic justice and constitutional essentials on the basis of reasons that are shared by persons as free and equal citizens and not on the basis of values and beliefs that draw solely from their comprehensive doctrines. Hence, we defend an "exclusive" account of public reason.

In this chapter, we focus on the principle of public justification at the heart of political liberalism and its moral foundation; in the next, we focus on norms for public deliberation. While many liberals endorse a principle of public justification, they disagree about how to interpret this principle and what it entails for an account of public reason. Part of the disagreement about public justification stems, we think, from different conceptions of liberal democracies. Here we contrast two views of liberal democracies and their particular views of public justification. We claim that political liberals view liberal democracies as a shared project among persons with the end of living on terms of mutual respect with others whom they view as free and equal citizens and whom they take to share interests with them as such. This view gives rise to the shared reasons account of public reasons as necessary to satisfy a principle of public justification. We argue in favor of this view and show its superiority to an alternative view of liberal democracies which relies on a convergence account of public justification.

II. Two Conceptions of Liberal Democracies

Compare two competing conceptions of liberal democracies. Call the first view the "mutual advantage view." On this view, liberal democracies are cooperative enterprises in which citizens aim to find mutually advantageous terms to structure their interactions with one another so they may pursue their view of the good with the assurance that the rules will be enforced by an impartial third party (the state). Liberal democracies are instrumentally valuable on this view. Persons are viewed as (naturally) free and equal. They recognize liberal democracies as the best way to protect

---

[3] IPRR, p. 577.

their freedom, and they agree to constrain their freedom in accordance with terms agreeable to everyone to maximize their ability to pursue their good. The state is the instrument that exercises coercive power to enforce the terms and may properly do this only in accordance with the terms that are justifiable to each individual member of society given his or her own values and beliefs. On the mutual advantage view, justification of political power is addressed to each individual given his or her particular values, interests, and goals. Reasons that might serve as a sufficient justification for one person may not for another, given that individuals hold diverse beliefs and values.

Call the second view "the collective enterprise view." On this view, liberal democracies are understood as the shared cooperative project of persons who value living on terms of mutual respect with others viewed as free and equal citizens and who understand themselves to have shared values and beliefs about the interests of persons as citizens. Living on terms of mutual respect with others as free and equal citizens is valued as an end in itself, and liberal democracies with constitutionally protected freedoms are viewed as partly constitutive of this way of life. Persons have their own particular interests and goals that they want to pursue, but they also see themselves as participants in a shared project in which the participants have shared interests distinct from their individual interests in securing the conditions for the exercise of their individual freedom. Importantly, among these shared interests is an interest in finding fair terms of social cooperation that secure the fundamental interests of all on an equal basis. These shared interests, among others, constrain each individuals' other pursuits, given the fundamental value they place on living on terms of mutual respect with others as free and equal citizens. Persons determine terms for social cooperation to structure their shared endeavor on the basis of their shared interests as free and equal citizens. The state uses its coercive power to enforce the terms of cooperation and properly enforces only those terms that are publicly justifiable to persons as free and equal citizens given their shared interests as such. Here, again, we arrive at an idea of public justification, but it is quite distinct from the first notion. On the collective enterprise view, public justification is addressed to persons in their role as participants in a shared project— namely, the project of living on terms of mutual respect with one another as free and equal citizens.

To better appreciate how each conception of a liberal democracy leads to a particular view of public justification, consider an analogy: The Smith family and the Rawls family are each planning a family vacation. Suppose, for the sake of simplicity, both families are composed solely of adults. The Smith family holds a family meeting to discuss where to go, with the following ground rules: family members may propose a destination of their choosing given their particular interests, but every other family member has veto power over any particular proposed destination.[4] Ultimately, if they vacation, they will go somewhere each has some particular interest in visiting and no one vetoes. There may be multiple locations that fit this description, and some decision procedure will need to be chosen for selecting among these destinations.

The Rawls family approaches vacation planning differently. Rather than beginning by each family member proposing a destination he or she would like to visit for his or her own reasons, they identify what they like to do together, and this constrains possible vacation spots. Based on their common interests they think of destinations where they can pursue their shared interests. There is a list of a few such places. At that point, each family member views any of the potential destinations as acceptable, from the point of view of the family's shared interests. There will need to be a decision procedure for choosing among the acceptable destinations. For any member of the family, a particular destination may not be his or her most preferred destination among the ones that are acceptable given the shared interests of persons as members of the family, and it may not be the destination that maximally promotes the member's other interests (his or her interests that are not Rawls family interests per se). Importantly, there are many differences between the way the Rawls family chooses a vacation destination and the way the Smith family does. One key difference is that the Rawls family has a kind of collective will that the Smith family doesn't have. This will is distinct from and not reducible to each member's will, and its resulting principles are based on the shared interests and values of individuals qua members of the family.

The Smith family and the Rawls family have different conceptions of what a family vacation is, and this leads them to different approaches to planning a family vacation and different ideas about what makes a destination an acceptable choice for a family vacation. The Smith family views a destination choice as justified when the family members converge on a location. Each family member may have different reasons for finding

---

[4] Here we mean to draw a comparison with a liberal view roughly like Vallier's in his *Liberal Politics and Public Faith*. We discuss his view below.

some location acceptable, and the family members need not endorse each other's reason(s) for endorsing a location. Amy may like a particular beach because she enjoys shell collecting there, and Brad may like it because of the country music scene, which Amy finds obnoxious and the worst part of the locale. Moreover, while the Smith family may work together to decide where to go in the sense of offering vetoes to others' suggestions or, perhaps, by trying to persuade others of the virtues of their preferred locale, they need not concern themselves with what members of the family may enjoy doing together or with what would be in the interest of the family, nor do they need to provide reasons to other family members that they think are reasonably acceptable to each qua a member of the family. Moreover, nothing in their approach to family vacation planning suggests that attempting to dominate another family member is somehow inappropriate. Each is trying to secure his or her individual interests, after all. They approach the matter of where to vacation with family members as a matter of what will fulfill their individual tastes and preferences.

In contrast, the Rawlses' understanding of a family vacation includes the idea that this endeavor and the familial relationships that make the vacation a family vacation are distinct goods that can be realized only together. The members of the Rawls family believe that they have shared interests as members of the family and that these interests are separable from (but still consistent with) their other interests given their various projects and commitments.

This example highlights two salient points for thinking about the comparative plausibility of the two models of liberal democracy sketched above. The Rawls family approaches the question of how to determine where to vacation as requiring shared deliberation. They deliberate together in their capacity as members of the Rawls family. They regard the reasons offered to one another as reasons that should be reasonably acceptable to all qua family members. This shapes in important ways how they interact. For example, domination (pressing one's individual interest against weaker members of the family) is anathema to the way they view what it means to treat other family members as equals and with respect. Moreover, their commitment to finding shared reasons emphasizes their commitment to affirming the relation of equality that holds among them as family members, each with the authority to reject or affirm reasons as fitting for their shared interests. The Smith family does not view deliberation as constitutive of any process of justification. (We will consider the role of deliberation in public justification in chapter 3.)

The second salient point of distinction is that the Smith family and the Rawls family have very different views about what mutual respect among family members requires. Imagine the disappointment and sense of disrespect a member of the Rawls family would feel upon learning that, in fact, some particular member of the family agreed to the shared destination only to advance some private interest, such as meeting a prospective business partner. In the Smith family, this would be a perfectly acceptable way to approach the family vacation. In the Rawls family it would signal that this individual member was not, in fact, invested in the same shared project and would register as a form of disrespect to the other family members. We highlight this aspect of the Rawls family's understanding of respect because we think a similar account of mutual respect is the moral foundation for public justification in political liberalism's vision of liberal democratic societies as an end in itself.

III. Political Liberalism: Liberal Democracy as a Shared Project

In this section, we articulate and defend political liberals' view that liberal democracies are a shared project of persons who value living on terms of mutual respect with others viewed as free and equal citizens, and who understand themselves to have shared values and beliefs about the interests of persons as free and equal citizens.

Political liberals locate the moral foundation of public justification in a particular ideal of democratic citizenship in which persons determine together the principles that will govern their shared political enterprise as equal citizens. This ideal is given expression in the criterion of reciprocity, which, among other things, specifies the way in which citizens relate to one another as equals. Rawls formulates the criterion of reciprocity as follows:

> When . . . terms are proposed as the most reasonable terms of fair cooperation, those proposing them must also think it at least reasonable for others to accept them, as free and equal citizens, and not as dominated or manipulated or under the pressure of an interior political or social position.[5]

---

[5] IPRR, p. 578.

This principle reflects the normative commitment that persons, as citizens, must stand in a relationship of equality with their co-citizens.[6] The criterion of reciprocity also requires a kind of collective willing, as it stipulates that those advancing certain kinds of principles must reasonably believe that others reasonably accept those principles as free and equal citizens. As the liberal principle of legitimacy on Rawls's view follows from the criterion of reciprocity, this means that the legitimacy of the state's power depends on its being arranged in accordance with principles that are, in a sense, collectively willed. Thus, in political liberalism, the particular account of public justification, emphasizing as it does a specific normative relationship between citizens, grounds the claim that public reasons must be shared reasons.

Rawls does not say very much directly to address the moral grounds of the criterion of reciprocity. Yet, just before stating the criterion in "The Idea of Public Reason Revisited," he specifies what it is for citizens to be reasonable:

> Citizens are reasonable when, viewing one another as free and equal in a system of social cooperation over generations, they are prepared to offer one another fair terms of cooperation according to what they consider the most reasonable conception of political justice; and when they agree to act on those terms, even at the cost of their own interests in particular situations, provided that other citizens also accept those terms.[7]

Reasonable persons accept the criterion of reciprocity, and elsewhere he writes that they "are not moved by the general good as such but desire for its own sake a social world in which they, as free and equal, can cooperate with others on terms all can accept,"[8] or, as we hold, on terms all accept. But, one may rightly ask at this point: Why accept the principle of reciprocity as central to realizing equal citizenship at all?

Rawls fails to adequately address the normative foundation upon which the liberal principle of legitimacy and the criterion of reciprocity ultimately

---

[6] Anderson describes the characteristics of *relational equality* in her "What's the Point of Equality?," pp. 313–314.

[7] IPRR, p. 578.

[8] PL, p. 50.

rest.[9] But this is crucial for understanding why public reasoning requires that reasons are shared in a particular sense. Charles Larmore argues that the liberal principle of legitimacy and the criterion of reciprocity rest on a principle of respect for persons.[10] He stresses that political liberals are not merely concerned with shared principles among reasonable people who have their own reasons for accepting them.[11] And, he says, "more fundamental than the political principles on which they will agree is the very commitment to organize political life along these lines, to seek principles that can be the object of reasonable agreement."[12] This statement, of course, does not explain why the *reasons* must be ones that are, in principle, shared by persons as free and equal persons, but understanding that the principles must be such that they are shared will be important to that argument. The commitment to living in accordance with principles that are the object of reasonable agreement is part of a commitment to a principle of respect for persons and a commitment to structuring one's relations with co-citizens in a particular way.

The notion of respect employed is Kantian insofar as in a constitutional democracy each person as a free and equal citizen is an end with moral authority; however, the notion is not meant to be metaphysically deep or wide such that it cannot form the basis of an overlapping consensus of reasonable comprehensive doctrines.[13] It is simply meant as an interpretation of the basic notion of citizenship in a constitutional democracy. Understanding this is critical to a proper interpretation of political liberalism as a political and not comprehensive liberalism. Concomitantly, properly valuing others as persons and also as citizens requires respecting their ability to act for reasons; this means that political principles, which structure our shared political endeavor, should be justifiable to us in some sense and should be similarly justifiable to others.[14] Insofar as we take it

---

[9] Larmore, *The Autonomy of Morality*, p. 147.

[10] Larmore thinks that respect for persons requires the justification of political power and has a coercion-centric account of public justification. We do not endorse the coercion-centric focus of his account of public justification.

[11] Larmore, *The Autonomy of Morality*, p. 143.

[12] Larmore, *The Autonomy of Morality*, p. 143.

[13] We don't think Larmore makes this clear (or clear enough). And we think Quong is too quick in his suggestion that basing public justification on respect for persons will lead to stability problems for political liberals. See Quong, "On the Idea of Public Reason," pp. 271–273.

[14] Larmore, *The Autonomy of Morality*, p. 149.

that a liberal democracy is a shared project of persons as free and equal citizens with common interests, our concern is with the justification of matters of basic justice and constitutional essentials to persons so understood.

Thus, the relevant claim is that the principle of respect for persons requires that when we understand persons as engaged in the shared project of living together with others as free and equal citizens we must be concerned with what will count as reasons for us *as free and equal citizens engaged in a cooperative enterprise.* That is, we think that, in political society, we are concerned not merely with principles that reasonable persons will accept for different reasons and not merely with a set of principles that we, as a happy matter of fact, accept for the same reasons but with principles that are based on "reasons that count for us because we can affirm [them] together"[15] and, we stress, as persons committed to a shared project. Here the basis of the authority of the principles is crucial. The basis of authority of political principles comes from the fact of agreement that certain principles are suited to govern us as those who seek to live together in a political society on terms of mutual respect.[16] Fair cooperation on terms of mutual respect for free and equal citizens is the aim of political society in a liberal democratic state. If so, what can be collectively willed for persons with that aim is not whatever principles are the object of mere consensus (or convergence, for that matter) among individuals living in the society. Rather, public justification requires that principles and laws be supported by reasons that persons viewed as free and equal citizens share. Citizens occupy various social roles and identities apart from their role and identity as citizens, of course, but what is crucial to underscore here is that it is this particular role, as citizens in a liberal democracy, that gives shape to the account of public justification. This role, this status, is what citizens share. Justification is addressed to others in their capacity as free and equal citizens engaged in a shared project of seeking fair terms of social cooperation. And, thus, reasons sufficient to justify some particular principle of cooperation must be ones that anyone, in virtue of their status as citizens, accepts as reasonable for persons so understood. Political liberals, thus, endorse a specific criterion of justification that entails a principle of

---

[15] Larmore, *The Autonomy of Morality*, p. 196.

[16] Larmore, *The Autonomy of Morality*, p. 199.

exclusion according to which any reason that is not shared by persons as free and equal citizens can't publicly justify a principle or law.

IV. Publicity and Stability: A Stability Argument for Shared Reasons

There is an important connection between political liberals' idea of public reason as requiring shared reasons (which express mutual respect) and stability in a society well ordered by a reasonable political conception of justice.[17] Rawls says that the possibility of a stable society well-ordered by a reasonable political conception of justice depends on two matters: (1) "whether people who grow up under just institutions (as the political conception defines them) acquire a normally sufficient sense of justice so that they generally comply with those institutions" and (2) "whether in view of the general facts that characterize a democracy's public political culture, and in particular the fact of reasonable pluralism, the political conception can be the focus of an overlapping consensus."[18] Each question is answered by a different component of political liberalism. The first question (whether citizens will acquire an effective sense of justice) is answered by an account of how some institutions that are part of the basic structure can be arranged such that persons develop an effective sense of justice.[19] The second question is "answered by the idea of an overlapping consensus."[20]

Political liberals try to work out an account of stability in which political power is understood as "the power of equal citizens as a collective

---

[17] Weithman develops a sophisticated argument with regard to the connection between stability and public reason; he claims that the main function of public reason is to solve the "assurance problem" with respect to compliance with the principles of justice within a well-ordered society. See his *Why Political Liberalism?* and *Rawls, Political Liberalism and Reasonable Faith*.

[18] PL, p. 141.

[19] It is important to emphasize that the account of moral development that Rawls offers in *Theory* will need substantive revision. Rawls never undertook those revisions. We don't do so here. However, we do acknowledge that it will be important to our overall account in the end to provide a satisfactory account of how citizens will acquire a sense of justice. We think the answer lies in a robust account of civic education. We gesture at such an account in Hartley and Watson, "Civic Virtue and Political Thought."

[20] PL, p. 141.

body."[21] As such, "the kind of stability required" for any reasonable political conception of justice is based on "its being a liberal political view, one that aims at being acceptable to citizens as reasonable and rational, as well as free and equal, and so as addressed to their public reason."[22] Stability for the right reasons requires this, as only such a conception can be supported by an overlapping consensus of reasonable comprehensive doctrines, under conditions of reasonable pluralism. Stability for the right reasons requires, among other things, that persons accept and act in accordance with a conception of justice not because they currently lack the power to enforce their comprehensive doctrine but because they regard a conception of justice as justified and because they have *moral* reasons to comply with the demands of justice.[23]

Thus, as Rawls emphasizes, the stability of a liberal democratic state depends on citizens being assured that others will comply with the demands of justice not simply as a matter of strategic action but because citizens genuinely accept the reasonable political conception of justice on moral grounds. And with Rawls, we take the publicity of a political conception of justice to be central to that kind of assurance. Consider Rawls's emphasis on publicity in his description of a well-ordered society:

> To say that a society is well-ordered conveys three things: first (and implied by the idea of a publicly recognized conception of justice), it is a society in which everyone accepts, and knows that everyone else accepts, the very same principles of justice, and second . . . its basic structure . . . is publicly known, or with good reason believed, to satisfy these principles. And third, its citizens have a normally effective sense of justice and so they generally comply with society's basic institutions, which they regard as just. In such a society the publicly recognized conception of justice establishes a shared point of view from which citizens' claims on society can be adjudicated.[24]

---

[21] PL, p. 143.

[22] PL, p. 143.

[23] IPRR, p. 589.

[24] PL, p. 35.

Again, as we argued in chapter 1, this statement of a well-ordered society requires revision within political liberalism, for we cannot expect that everyone accepts the very same principles of justice once we embrace the fact of reasonable pluralism. Nonetheless, this revision does not undermine the basic point here, namely, that publicity is essential to stability for the right reasons.[25]

The publicity condition strengthens the stability of the overlapping consensus, as it is a public expression of mutual respect, which deepens the strength of mutual assurance between citizens that they will honor the terms of social cooperation.[26] As Larmore emphasizes, the "public recognition" of a political conception of justice expresses a kind of mutual respect among citizens.[27] And respecting others as equal citizens requires and is partly constituted by "allegiance to principles that we affirm in the light of others having a reason, indeed the same reason, to affirm them too."[28] This is so because we are working out a political conception of justice for a specific conception of persons as free and equal citizens, and their sharing the same reasons is essential to the recognition of their shared status. Affirming that shared status through the use of public reasons is a public expression of mutual respect and, Larmore says, creates stability: "The mutual respect demonstrated by their allegiance to this common basis then is a good they can regard themselves as having achieved, and that is why the scheme of justice gains in stability."[29] This shared public framework provides the basis for a shared point of view in which citizens can make claims of justice on one another

---

[25] Recall our reasons for claiming that a revision is necessary to reconcile the account of a well-ordered society with the recognition that there will be reasonable pluralism about political conceptions of justice and not just comprehensive doctrines. For our statement of what revisions are necessary to the account of a well-ordered society, see chapter 1. This account is drawn from the work of Neufeld and Watson, "The Tyranny."

[26] See Weithman as cited in note 17 above.

[27] Larmore stresses that citizens have reason to live in accordance with a conception of justice when other citizens are publicly known to do so (*The Autonomy of Morality*, p. 201).

[28] Larmore, *The Autonomy of Morality*, p. 201. The passage from Larmore that we refer to here is one in which he explains Rawls on the connection between stability, publicity, and respect, assuming a Kantian conception of the person. Political liberals can explain that connection without assuming a substantive Kantian view, which is how we intend our discussion.

[29] Larmore, *The Autonomy of Morality*, p. 202.

and transparently observe others' response to such claims. This provides a public basis for evaluation of whether the demands of justice are being met and upheld by others. And importantly, such a public framework provides the terms for separating legitimate claims of justice from illegitimate ones; some claims of justice will be unreasonable. Given the fact of reasonable pluralism, this requires a shared point of view based on political values, and it simply must be the case that other persons as citizens find acceptable the reasons from the point of view of free and equal citizenship.[30]

Finally, how the reasonable political conception relates to different reasonable comprehensive doctrines will depend on the particular content of the reasonable comprehensive doctrines in question. Insofar as political liberals recognize the fact of reasonable pluralism, reasonable citizens may struggle to understand how someone with a different reasonable comprehensive doctrine relates a doctrine to a conception of justice. However, because reasonable persons as free and equal citizens share the point of view of free and equal citizenship (and, in principle, share reasons) and publicly recognize these reasons, reasonable citizens have reason to comply with the demands of justice that does not depend on the contingencies of the sway of social power but depends on the mutual recognition of a shared political morality. Rawls makes this point succinctly when he writes:

> The contrast [with a politically liberal society in which an overlapping consensus obtains] is a society in which when citizens are grouped by their full justifications [as provided by their comprehensive doctrines], their political conceptions are not embedded in or connected with a shared political conception. In this case, there is only a modus vivendi, and society's stability depends on a balance of forces in contingent and possibly fluctuating circumstances.[31]

---

[30] As noted in our emphasis on the need to revise the account of the well-ordered society in ways consistent with the acknowledgment of the fact of reasonable pluralism about political conceptions of justice, in "The Idea of Public Reason Revisited," Rawls recognizes a plurality of reasonable political conceptions of justice, so not all persons may endorse, strictly speaking, the same reasons, even though they, in principle, accept those reasons from the point of view of free and equal citizenship.

[31] RTH, p. 392.

V. Convergence Accounts of Public Justification

Some liberals reject the restrictive standard of public justification that is central to political liberalism's account of public reason. They reject the claims that respect for persons, a commitment to political legitimacy, or a concern with stability requires such a demanding standard. Both Gerald Gaus and Kevin Vallier reject political liberalism's account of public justification, which they emphasize is a "consensus view" and, instead, defend a "convergence view," where citizens need not share reasons in the sense we have been defending, but need only have their reasons happily converge on particular laws.

Gaus is a prominent critic of political liberalism's account of public reason and offers a well-known alternative view of public justification; his project is much broader in scope and differs from the specific aims of political liberals. His concern is with "whether the rules of our social morality are publicly justifiable to moral agents."[32] He claims that we can think of a moral or political constitution for society as a "process that is built from the ground up."[33] Individuals, using their own evaluative standards, will consider the principles they have sufficient reason to accept. The issue is not whether an individual regards certain principles as ideal, given her evaluative standards, but, rather, the question is this : "Given the pros and the cons from one's own moral conception, would some basic social charter for our social world—a certain practice of morality—be worthy of endorsement?"[34] Gaus calls a system of political rules a "tremendous good to all."[35] When individuals converge on principles that each take to be supported by sufficient reasons, the constitution has authority for each person, and that explains the authority of the constitution. Hence, Gaus says that the "authority of morality derives from conformity to the Basic Principle of Public Justification."[36]

---

[32] Gaus, *The Order of Public Reason*, p. 276.

[33] Gaus, "Moral Constitutions," p. 15.

[34] Gaus, "Moral Constitutions," p. 15.

[35] Gaus, "Public Reason Liberalism," p. 20.

[36] Gaus, *The Order of Public Reason*, p. 265. Gaus states his Basic Principle of Public Justification as follows: "A moral imperative 'φ!' in context C, based on rule L, is an authoritative requirement of social morality only if each normal moral agent has sufficient reasons to (a) internalize rule L, (b) hold that L requires φ-type acts in circumstances C and (c) moral agents generally conform to L" (p. 263).

Unlike Gaus, political liberals focus on the possibility of a just and stable liberal democratic state given that citizens view themselves as part of a particular kind of cooperative project. And while Gaus thinks the authority of the constitution stems from the fact that it is authoritative for each person, political liberals think that the authority of principles or laws for a liberal democratic society stems from the fact that they are collectively willed by persons as free and equal citizens who are together committed to a liberal, democratic society. Moreover, Gaus is concerned to provide arguments that accepting a social contract at all is preferable to rejecting any such contract, and as such he is best interpreted as engaging in a defense of an external conception of liberal theory (as we defined in chapter 1).

Vallier, too, aims to criticize consensus views of public reason, including political liberalism's, and to construct an alternative account of public reason. He shares many of Gaus's commitments and aims to defend a public reason liberalism, where public reason liberalism is understood simply as a liberalism in which the public justification of all coercive laws is required. Importantly, Vallier rejects as unnecessarily restrictive accounts of public justification in which public reasons are ones that are shared by persons as free and equal citizens and argues that such accounts are unduly burdensome for religious persons and, as a result, unfair.[37] As we will argue, Vallier's rejection of this criterion for public justification ultimately stems from his view that public justification is fundamentally about justifying the coercive power of the state and from his much less demanding standard for stability. Moreover, it is worth noting for the discussion to follow that Vallier does not endorse anything like the publicity condition that Rawls advances and that Vallier does not accept the connection between public justification and public deliberation that is central to political liberalism.

Vallier understands political liberals and all other liberals committed to public justification to affirm the following Public Justification Principle (PJP):

A coercive law L is justified only if each member I of the public P has some sufficient reasons(s) R to endorse L.[38]

---

[37] Others, too, claim that political liberalism's account of public justification unduly burdens some religious persons. We discuss these criticisms in detail in chapter 4.

[38] Vallier, *Liberal Politics and Public Faith*, p. 24.

Public reason liberals' commitment to public justification, on Vallier's view, follows from the claim that the state's coercion of our "natural" freedom requires special justification. Each person (citizen) must be able to see the reasons for the curtailment of her freedom as sufficient *for her,* otherwise she is unjustifiably coerced. Vallier, though, never defines or gives an account of coercion.[39] He separates public reason liberals into those who advance the convergence view of public justification and those who that advance the consensus view (where he locates some political liberals). Those who endorse the convergence view hold that "the set of justificatory reasons includes all reasons that citizens can see as justified for some member of the public according to her own evaluative standards, even if other members of the public do not accept those evaluative standards."[40] A law has a sufficient justification if and only if members of the public (or relevant body of the public or officials) converge on a law for reasons that can be seen as justified for each member of the public given her own evaluative standards. Reasons need only be mutually intelligible to an agent's co-citizens as reasons *for the agent* endorsing such reasons as sufficient. While the criterion of intelligibility does exclude some reasons as public reasons, the standard is minimal. Those who endorse the consensus model hold that justificatory reasons include either all the reasons that are shared or are shared by persons as free and equal citizens or all the reasons that are accessible to members of society given a common evaluative standard.[41]

Again, given intelligibility as the criterion for a public reason, few reasons fail to count as a public reason. So, for example, Vallier thinks reasons grounded in natural theology and even religious revelation count as intelligible and so can be public reasons. And on a convergence view

---

[39] It is not clear whether Vallier thinks of coercion as force backed by a threat or as something broader, say, as certain forms of power that shape our lives in profound ways whether or not there is a specific threat attached to the use of such power. However, given his emphasis on the restriction of freedom as requiring justification, it seems plausible that he thinks of coercion as force backed by a threat. If this is right, then it is not clear what Vallier's view is with respect to public justification and laws that are power conferring such as marriage and contract laws.

[40] Vallier, *Liberal Politics and Public Faith,* p. 29.

[41] Vallier, *Liberal Politics and Public Faith,* p. 28. A principle or law has a sufficient justification either if it is justified in accordance with a reason that persons share as free and equal citizens or if it is justified in accordance with a reason that is accessible to members of society, given a common evaluative standard. We will not discuss accessibility as a criterion of justification here.

of public justification, "pluralistic reasoning is the very basis of justification," and, its defenders claim, "appealing to a law justified in this manner respects each person as free and equal, without any insistence that we reason in the same way."[42] However, given that convergence is required for public justification, the set of laws that are publicly justified are just the set of laws that each citizen has his or her own reasons for accepting as sufficient to justify each individual member of the set. If citizen A rejects law L as an intelligible reason, citizen A will have a defeater reason for law L, and, hence, such a law will not enjoy public justification.

VI. Against Mutual Intelligibility

Convergence public reason liberals and political liberals disagree about the foundation for public justification, and, as a result, they offer very different accounts of public reason. Here we offer some considerations for why we think political liberals have a superior view. First, Vallier begins with a common but we think unsatisfactory characterization of the basis and need for public justification in a liberal democratic state. Again, he focuses primarily on the claim that the state's restriction of our natural freedom, through its coercive power, requires justification. This view fails to capture what is distinctive about the modern idea of liberal democracies, which is that such states are a shared project of citizens who engage in democratic discussion to find shared terms of social cooperation in order to live on terms of mutual respect with their co-citizens. As Anderson stresses in her defense of relational equality, if you consider the history of egalitarian political movements, activists worked against social hierarchies based on an alleged unequal moral worth among human beings, and they sought democratic societies in which persons stand in relations of equality.[43] Equal citizenship and the recognition of the collective project of an egalitarian democracy are fundamental to a dominant vision of liberal democracies. Shared terms of social cooperation for persons as free and equal citizens protect and interpret persons' understanding of citizenship and the aims of their political society. On Vallier's view, suppose that for some proposed law each person in a society has sufficient reason to accept it. There is a set of individuals who each endorse a particular law,

---

[42] Gaus and Vallier, "The Roles of Religious Conviction," pp. 58–59.

[43] Anderson, "What's the Point of Equality?," pp. 313–314.

but there is no shared will in this society. There are simply discrete, individual wills. Members of society as such don't have a common project or shared aims. They are legitimately subject to the state's power just when, as a fortunate (?) matter of fact, it happens that each person has sufficient reason to follow the same proposal.

Furthermore, the sufficient reasons of individuals need not recognize, respect, or be consistent with the recognition of the person's own or others' standing as an equal citizen in a democratic society. For example, it is one thing to support the legalization of polygamy on the grounds that, if the state is going to recognize legal marriage, it should not discriminate against those who would like to exchange legal marital rights and obligations with more than one partner, and it is quite another to support polygamy on the grounds that women, by God's law or nature's, are inferior to men and, thereby, meant to service men's needs and care for their children and that some men may need multiple wives.[44]

In addition, on Vallier's view, there will be serious problems with determining what a law requires and how it is to be interpreted. Courts must do this all the time and often consider the underlying reasons or rationale for a law when it was enacted. Consider, for example, the U.S. Supreme Court's deliberation over the scope of the Equal Protection Clause of the 14th Amendment. Immediately after its passage, the Court had to consider whether the protections within the Amendment were specific to African Americans who were former slaves and, so, whether the purpose of the Amendment was to protect against racial inequality, specifically black racial inequality.[45] Moreover, the Court had to decide if the Equal Protection Clause was aimed only at facial distinctions in the law or whether a disparate impact could violate equal protection.[46] In both of these kinds of cases, the Court had to determine the meaning of the underlying value of equality, and so the rationale for including such protection in the U.S. Constitution as well as its "fit" with other Amendments that guarantee basic rights. The mere observation of a kind of convergence on the Amendment was insufficient to settle these substantive matters of interpretation. Whether one supports or rejects the decisions that ultimately came to expand the scope and meaning of the Equal Protection

---

[44] This example is from Hartley's book review of Vallier's *Liberal Politics and Public Faith*.

[45] The *Slaughter-House Cases*, 83 U.S. 36 (1872).

[46] *Yick Wo v. Hopkins*, 118 U.S. 356 (1886).

Clause, arguing for one interpretation over another requires enumeration of the underlying reasons for a particular interpretation as well as substantive rationales about how such interpretations fit with other fundamental rights. Moreover, justifying any particular decision or reading requires offering substantive reasons for the position that extends well beyond appealing to mere convergence upon the Amendment itself.

Interestingly, Vallier claims that, for purposes of public justification, while "citizens can act on whatever reasons they like . . . officials should restrain themselves."[47] For Vallier, this means that legislators are subject to "proposal restraint" and "not reason restraint," as he thinks that legislators can vote for a proposal on whatever grounds they think justify it as long as they "justifiably believe that the law they support is publicly justified."[48] Judges, on Vallier's view, are "responsible for interpreting passed legislation and policies in accord with broader legal standards, such as constitutional constraints," and must be sensitive to consistency with "previous rulings." He claims that as judicial reasoning bears on future judicial decisions and, hence, reason, restraint in the form of "something like a consensus requirement" is needed. It is because of the particular role of legislators and judges that some form of restraint is appropriate for them. But we think that it is precisely that persons in their role as citizen are engaged in a shared enterprise that they must use restraint in public reason when it comes to those matters that determine the fundamental nature of the liberal democratic state.

Vallier's limited recognition of a consensus standard of reasoning in the case of judges, and with it a commitment to a principle of restraint, is revealing. He appears to hold that those with authority and power in constitutional democracies have a duty to act in ways consistent with the democratic ideal we have been defending thus far. And we think it is precisely this democratic ideal that confers such authority on citizens. Vallier stops short of endorsing a shareability standard for public reasons and a corollary principle of restraint for citizens, in part, because he thinks that citizens are not efficacious when it comes to arguing for, or voting for, laws.[49] We think this is a dim view of citizenship.

---

[47] Vallier, *Liberal Politics and Public Faith*, p. 193.

[48] Vallier, *Liberal Politics and Public Faith*, p. 193.

[49] Vallier, *Liberal Politics and Public Faith*, pp. 187–188.

A convergence view of public reason also lacks an important kind of *normative* stability.[50] Recall that part of the project of political liberalism is to show that stability for the right reasons is possible and doing so is a part of public justification.

> The reason [this is important to demonstrate] is that when citizens affirm reasonable though different comprehensive doctrines, seeing whether an overlapping consensus on the political conception is possible is a way of checking whether there are sufficient reasons for proposing justice as fairness (or some other reasonable doctrine) which can be sincerely defended before others without criticizing or rejecting their deepest religious and philosophical commitments.[51]

Rawls thinks demonstrating this possibility is an essential element of demonstrating that the conditions of democratic legitimacy are possible. One way of understanding the convergence model of public reason is to read it as insisting on a kind of overlapping consensus for each particular law and not for a shared political conception of justice. So it appears an overlapping "convergence" on this law and that law, and so on, is a happy coincidence. But the basis for social unity, and continued commitment to seeking fair terms of social cooperation, is absent on this account. The contingencies of convergence—due to the "possibly fluctuating circumstances" connected with revisions of persons' views and, as a result, the laws that can be supported and the balance of power within a society—provide no deep assurance to a sustained commitment, by anyone, to laws that happen to find convergence at a given time.

Here is another way of putting the point: On a convergence account, each citizen has his or her own particular reasons for endorsing a law that enjoys convergence. Those reasons may or may not be stable. Consider someone who can't settle her view on some particular law, say, mandated waiting periods for gun purchase. Today, she rejects any waiting period, persuaded by the NRA. Tomorrow, in the aftermath of another public shooting, she thinks mandated waiting periods are warranted. The next

---

[50] Vallier raises various empirical objections to political liberalism's account of stability. We do not address those here.

[51] RTH, p. 390.

day, she reads an editorial denouncing such mandates for waiting periods as an unreasonable infringement on liberty. Any law on this question, whether for or against mandated waiting periods, oscillates between enjoying public justification and lacking it (supposing there is convergence among others). Moreover, she need not publicly deliberate with others about which policy is most justified, nor does she need to consider what would be justifiable from the point of view of citizens; she need only consult her own values (fluctuating though they may be).

Thus, this account misses the way in which public justification is addressed to other co-citizens. The project of public justification is not solely concerned with making sure adequate reasons are endorsed by each individual separately considered, but rather it is concerned with citizens engaging together in the project of public justification to find principles and laws that are mutually acceptable to reasonable persons given reasons that they share as citizens.

And, so, in a politically liberal society, where public reason applies, laws and policies having to do with matters of basic justice must be such that they are justified to persons as free and equal citizens. And a political conception of justice must be the object of an overlapping consensus of reasonable comprehensive doctrines. Changes in a particular person's view of the good or worldview will not affect whether a law is justified from the point of view of a free and equal citizen and will not affect whether a particular political conception is the subject of an overlapping consensus. Political liberals, then, provide an account of public reason that is superior to convergence accounts because it offers normative stability not available to convergence theorists.[52]

VII. Justifying Coercion

Given Gaus's and Vallier's more limited interpretation of the ideal of liberal democracy, as reflected in a "mutual advantage" conception, their account focuses on state coercion as the object of public justification. Political liberals, too, are concerned with the justification of the state's coercive

---

[52] Weithman argues for a similar claim with reference to citizens' political *autonomy*. Roughly, the Rawlsian view makes possible political autonomy through its ideal of public reason; the convergence view does not. And the ideal of public reason and political autonomy is fundamental to "the inherent stability of just institutions." See Weithman, "Convergence and Political Autonomy" and *Rawls, Political Liberalism and Reasonable Faith*, chapter 8. Thanks to Blain Neufeld for calling our attention to this.

power, but to appreciate their concern with public justification one has to understand how they view society. Rawls focuses on the set of institutions within the basic structure, which together profoundly shape and structure citizens' choices, opportunities, and ways of living. Describing the basic structure as the subject of justification relies on a much broader understanding of coercion than the one employed by Gaus and Vallier.

On this view, while all political power may not be directly coercive in the strict sense of an order backed by a threat, the basic structure as one system profoundly affects our lives, as it constructs options, opportunities, relationships, and ways of relating to others, and it constrains our pursuits. And, moreover, various kinds of power-conferring laws are ultimately enforceable by the state through the judiciary or executive function of the state, which are parts of the basic structure. In short, the basic structure is coercive in the sense that it structures and defines our life possibilities so profoundly it exerts a "force" over who or what we may become. It is coercive in another sense insofar as the apparatus of the state functions to enforce all legally recognized rights, including power-conferring laws.

Emphasizing the coercive function of the basic structure in terms of its profound effect over citizens' lives highlights the emphasis on the collective and cooperative features of liberal democracies as captured by the second view—the cooperative enterprise view. Here public justification is primarily concerned with how we, collectively, live together under a set of institutions designed to secure justice for us. The account of public justification concerns justifying the rules of those institutions to each other as citizens in terms that respect one another as equal members of a cooperative enterprise in which we hold power together. Political liberalism's account of public justification concerns the set of institutions we create together to secure basic justice and fundamental rights, and, thus, two points of departure between political liberals and other public reason liberals concerns the scope and content of public reason. We turn to these matters in the following chapter.

Exclusive Public Reason

The definitive idea for deliberative democracy is the idea of deliberation itself. When citizens deliberate, they exchange views and debate their supporting reasons concerning public political questions. They suppose that their political opinions may be revised by discussion with other citizens; and therefore these opinions are not simply a fixed outcome of their existing private or nonpolitical interests.

—JOHN RAWLS, *"The Idea of Public Reason Revisited"*

I. Introduction

In the previous chapter, we developed and defended an account of the moral foundation of public justification for political liberalism; we argued that political liberals are committed to a collective enterprise view of liberal democracy in which the demand for public justification is grounded in a particular account of mutual respect. This account of mutual respect entails a commitment to a shared reasons standard for public justification. Thus, public reasons must be shared reasons. However, political liberals disagree about the scope of public reason, that is, the principles, laws, and policies to which the idea of public reason applies. Also, they disagree about the norms for public deliberation within the idea of public reason when it comes to citizens appealing to their comprehensive doctrines.

Any account of public reason must address these issues and explain the connection between them as well as how they relate to the appropriate standard of public justification. With respect to scope, one might claim that the idea of public reason should apply to all laws and policies. We reject this view and argue here that the moral foundation for political liberalism delimits a narrow scope for the idea of public reason, such that public reasons are required only for matters of basic justice and constitutional essentials. With respect to norms for public discussion within the scope of public reason, some political liberals permit persons to draw upon their comprehensive doctrines in the context of discussing laws and policies—not to justify laws or policies but for other purposes, such as strengthening the stability of an overlapping consensus of reasonable comprehensive doctrines or, even, strengthening the ideal of public reason itself. We argue that arguments for these claims are not convincing. We defend the view that appealing to one's comprehensive doctrine where the idea of public reason applies is contrary to the kind of respect owed to persons as free and equal citizens. Hence, the most defensible idea of public reason is an exclusive view, according to which citizens have a moral duty to never appeal to their comprehensive doctrines when the idea of public reason applies.

Chapter 2 was primarily concerned with the connection between the requirement of public justification and the *kinds* of reasons that count as public reasons. This chapter primarily concerns public deliberation in the context of public reason. In chapter 2, we argued for a principle of exclusion with respect to the justification of (certain) principles and laws; in particular, we claimed that certain principles and laws must be justified on the basis of reasons that are shared by persons *as* free and equal citizens. In this chapter, we argue for a principle of restraint for public deliberation that pairs with the principle of exclusion we defended earlier. Principles of restraint are normative constraints that govern the public, political deliberation of citizens where public reason applies.[1] Normative constraints that entail that citizens exercise restraint in public reasoning are often referred to as "the duty of civility."[2] Our defense of exclusive public reason entails that citizens have a moral duty of civility to exercise restraint in public, political deliberation by excluding appeals to their comprehensive doctrines where the norms of public reason apply. It is crucial to emphasize, as we previously noted, that this is a moral and not a legal duty,[3] and so it in no way threatens the right to freedom of expression in a liberal, democratic polity.[4] Thus, while people are certainly free to express

---

[1] We adopt Vallier's notion of a principle of exclusion and a principle of restraint. See his *Liberal Politics and Public Faith.*

[2] As Rawls says, "The ideal of citizenship imposes a moral, not a legal, duty—the duty of civility—to be able to explain to one another on those fundamental questions how the principles and policies they advocate and vote for can be supported by the political values of public reason" (PL, p. 217).

[3] IPRR, pp. 576–577.

[4] Kevin Vallier makes the argument that a principle of restraint infringes upon liberty in his "Public Justification versus Public Deliberation," p. 146. He says that a principle of restraint "encourages citizens to morally sanction those who rely on private reasons in their political

whatever views they want, even on matters that ought to be reserved for public reason arguments, without fear of legal reprisal, they are nonetheless proper subjects of moral criticism and rebuke for violating the norms of civility.

II. The Scope of Public Reason

Before we discuss the scope of public reason, we stress that political liberals take the idea of public reason only to concern the "public political forum." Not all discussions of political matters fall within the public political forum.[5] Rawls specifies that the public political forum consists of the discourse of judges, of government officials, and of political candidates. When persons in their role as judges, government officials, and political candidates follow the norms of the idea of public reason, they satisfy the *duty of civility*. Citizens, too, should follow the norms of the idea of public reason when voting and view themselves as legislators engaged in public, political debate. Moreover, when citizens have a "public, political platform" in which they aim to persuade other persons as citizens about the most reasonable interpretation of constitutional essentials or advocate for laws or policies that are matters of basic justice, they should follow the norms of public reason. On such a platform persons engage others in their role as citizens. It is crucial to emphasize that the *duty of civility* is for persons as citizens in certain contexts. It is not a duty for the whole of life, even public life. Again, the duty of civility is a moral duty, not a legal one. Thus, it is, we argue, a principle for treating one's co-citizens with the proper respect in the context of a constitutional, democratic polity regarding their shared exercise of political power. Central to the plausibility of our argument is the limited scope of this duty, to which we now turn.

Political liberals as well as other public reason liberals disagree about the scope of public reason. Rawls endorses the view that the scope of public reason is limited to matters of basic justice and constitutional

---

lives" and, as a result, is an unacceptable infringement of liberty. We claim that insofar as the principle applies only in a certain public, political context and applies to persons in their role as citizens engaged in the collective enterprise of determining the principles that structure society, a principle of restraint is not an unjustified infringement on liberty. Moreover, people are, in fact, free to appeal to whatever reasons they like.

[5] IPRR, p. 575.

essentials.[6] Quong calls this "the narrow view" and contrasts it to his own view, "the broad view," in which, insofar as possible, persons should always give public reasons for laws and policies.[7] Rawls says surprisingly little about why he supports the narrow view. The reasons he offers often seem more of a practical nature rather than rooted in the values and ideas that inform and shape his account of public justification. For example, Rawls says that "to find a complete political conception we need to identify a class of fundamental questions for which the conception's political values yield reasonable answers," and he claims that political values can determine matters of basic justice and constitutional essentials.[8] Here he emphasizes the need for completeness with respect to public reason. He adds that "there is the greatest urgency for citizens to reach practical agreement in judgment about constitutional essentials."[9] Beyond matters of basic justice and constitutional essentials, he claims that "it is often more reasonable to go beyond the political conception and the values its principles express, and to invoke nonpolitical values that such a view does not include" and that agreement on matters of basic justice and constitutional essentials is typically enough to sustain "fair" and "willing" cooperation among free and equal citizens.[10] Furthermore, he says that when matters of basic justice and constitutional essentials are not at issue, then public reasons are not "attainable nor desirable."[11] Rawls's remarks supply some reason to prefer the narrow view to the broad view, or, perhaps, they simply gesture at some such reasons. However, a decisive reason to prefer the narrow view to the broad view is far from clear in Rawls's work.

Of course, one implication of the narrow view is that in public political debate, when constitutional essentials and matters of basic justice are not at issue, it is consistent with the duty of civility for citizens to appeal to any of their values and beliefs. This picture seems to fit well with the basic notion of a liberal constitutional democracy in which once everyone's basic entitlements as equal citizens are protected, including, of course, certain fundamental rights through the constitution and supporting laws,

---

[6] IPRR, p. 575; Quong, *Liberalism without Perfectionism*, p. 274.

[7] Quong, *Liberalism without Perfectionism*, p. 274.

[8] PL, p. 227.

[9] PL, p. 227.

[10] PL, p. 230.

[11] JF, p. 91n13.

then other political matters are decided based on the preferences of the majority and through representative government. We will show that not only does the narrow view fit well with the familiar picture of a constitutional democracy but, also, that the narrow view follows from properly appreciating political liberalism's view of the need for public justification.

First, consider the case for Quong's broad view, which, recall, is the view that "the idea of public reason ought to apply, whenever possible, to all decisions where citizens exercise political power over one another."[12] The motivation for this view is the thought that all exercises of political power ought to be justifiable to those subject to them. Quong thinks that even in discussions of laws and policies that do not concern matters of basic justice or constitutional essentials, public reasons are often available.[13] For example, he asks us to imagine city residents debating whether to spend public funds on a new football stadium or a new art museum. There may be good public reasons, Quong claims, for preferring one to the other. A principle of fairness may favor a football stadium if there is already an art museum, or a principle of economic gain may favor a football stadium if it promises to be more profitable.[14] (Of course, not all economic gains for a community are public goods in the sense of serving the interests of most members of the community.) If it is permissible to give nonpublic reasons for certain laws and policies when public reasons are available, then Quong is concerned that there will be laws and policies that are not publicly justifiable to some citizens, for such policies will be based on reasons some citizens may reasonably reject.[15] On the basis of this claim, Quong holds that public reasons should always trump nonpublic reasons when such reasons are available. He claims it would be inconsistent with the idea of public reason to allow nonpublic reasons to determine outcomes in cases where public reasons are available.[16]

---

[12] Quong, *Liberalism without Perfectionism*, p. 274.

[13] While Quong appears to share our understanding of public reasons as what citizens share from the point of view of free and equal citizenship, he sometimes refers to "public considerations" in the context of discussing public reasons (see, for example, p. 256 of *Liberalism without Perfectionism*). The idea of "public considerations" is a broader and looser notion, which in the various contexts in which Quong uses it seems to be an appeal to something like a notion of public goods, where that means goods or resources enjoyed by members of the public.

[14] Quong, *Liberalism without Perfectionism*, p. 280.

[15] Quong, *Liberalism without Perfectionism*, p. 275.

[16] Quong, *Liberalism without Perfectionism*, p. 281.

Absent a good argument for limiting the scope of public reason, we should, Quong argues, accept the broad view. The conclusion seems drawn too quickly. For it is certainly possible, and consistent with democratic values, to argue that, on some types of issues, a proper procedure can confer public justification. If citizens endorse the procedure and accept that the procedure itself is legitimate, then public justification is conferred. Simple majority voting is one example of such a procedure. Of course there are contexts in which such a procedure itself would be inconsistent with equal respect and concern for all citizens, such as, for example, voting on basic civil rights because civil rights are essential to securing the conditions of free and equal citizenship. However, the point is that outside the scope of public reason, public justification can be conferred via democratic procedures. Thus, Quong's concern that failing to appeal to public reasons in all contexts entails that some laws won't enjoy public justification is overstated.

We think that the idea of public reason has a limited scope, and the reason for this stems from the moral foundation of political liberalism. On our interpretation of political liberalism, the moral foundation of public reason is a principle of respect for persons as free and equal citizens in a constitutional democracy. This conception of the person includes the idea that persons, as such, are ends with moral authority. As citizens, persons have the authority to make claims of justice upon their fellow citizens. Political liberals ask how persons, so understood, can live together as free and equal citizens and establish fair terms of social cooperation for a constitutional democracy. The social relationship of persons as free and equal citizens is fundamental, and it is through public reason that the substantive content of this relationship—the relationship of free and equal citizenship—takes shape. Hence, Rawls says, "The idea of public reason specifies at the deepest level the basic moral and political values that are to determine a constitutional democratic government's relation to its citizens and their relation to one another."[17] Certain laws and policies in a liberal democratic society fundamentally determine the relationship of free and equal citizenship, and others, simply put, do not. It is because matters of basic justice and constitutional essentials shape and secure this relationship—a relation where citizens stand as free and equal—that they

---

[17] IPRR, p. 574.

are the subject of public reasoning. Other principles and laws do not have this function.

The criterion of reciprocity, discussed in chapter 2, is an interpretation of a principle for equal respect for free and equal citizens in a liberal democratic state. Again, according to the criterion of reciprocity persons must propose terms "as the most reasonable terms of fair cooperation" and hold that it is "reasonable for others to accept them, as free and equal citizens, and not as dominated or manipulated or under the pressure of an inferior social position."[18] This criterion concerns how persons viewed in a particular way can find principles that will secure and inform a certain relationship among citizens so that, among other things, persons as citizens can enjoy a certain *standing* relative to each other. Public reason is the reason of persons as citizens who aim to secure and interpret this relationship through public deliberation. Indeed, Rawls says, "To make more explicit the role of the criterion of reciprocity as expressed in public reason, note that its role is to specify the nature of the political relation in a constitutional democratic regime as one of civic friendship."[19] The scope of public reason applies to just those issues in which the nature of the political relationship of citizens in a constitutional democratic regime is at stake, and it does not apply to other issues. The interests that are persons' interests as free and equal citizens are limited.

Of course, certain moral considerations such as fairness can be appealed to when discussing issues of free and equal citizenship or other matters (such as how to spend money for public goods in a community). For example, if policy concerning the fair value of political liberties is being discussed (which we take to be, unquestionably, within the scope of public reason), and I appeal to fair access to public, political offices to justify a policy and claim that such fair access is central to equal standing among free and equal citizens, then the value of fairness is being used as part of a public reason. However, suppose my community is debating using tax revenue to construct a hall for concerts or build a sports complex, and I claim that there is already a sports complex in town and fairness requires a music hall. Here I'm concerned with fairness in balancing the personal interests of citizens (or, actually, given the interests of persons in the community that will enjoy the good) and not the interests and needs of persons as free

---

[18] IPRR, p. 578.

[19] IPRR, p. 579.

and equal citizens as such. In other words, appeals to fairness are not always appeals to a political value (or grounded in public reason). In short, appeals to fairness that concern the fundamental interests and needs of citizens are, of course, grounded in public reasons. But appeals to fairness in securing the opportunities for citizens to enjoy recreation, given their private and particular interests in specific forms of recreation, are not.

The content of public reason derives from a reasonable political conception of justice in conjunction with a particular notion of free and equal citizenship. That is why political liberals hold that public reasons must be shared from the point of view of free and equal citizenship. Moreover, they must be shared in a very specific sense. They must be shared as the reasons of *citizens*, drawing upon a reasonable political conception of justice. As we have emphasized, the mere fact that some reasons or set of reasons are shared does not make them *public* reasons. Quong's appeal to fairness suggests that some specification of "fairness" is a reason citizens will or can share, as opposed to a direct appeal to the value of the arts or some other value. But the fact that some rough notion of fairness may be shared across comprehensive doctrines doesn't by itself make an appeal to fairness a public reason. Rather, the content of public reasons requires an appeal to what citizens' needs and interests are *as citizens*. It is hard to imagine any argument for or against football stadiums or art museums that do that.

Of course, the issues to which public reason applies can be blurry. There are paradigmatic cases at each end of the continuum. Freedoms of thought, expression, and association are central to basic justice and constitutional essentials, and these freedoms clearly shape the fundamental relations among citizens. On the other end of the continuum, for example, are routine and mundane matters such as policies for sanitation and traffic coordination.[20] We simply see no compelling reason to think that public reasons are morally required to decide the latter kinds of cases. Yet, again, there will be hard cases in which a group of citizens think a matter pertains to basic justice, while others disagree. Perhaps some kinds of environmental issues are examples. We think that hard cases—cases in

---

[20] In conversation, Amy Baehr asks us, "If some group doesn't have their waste removed, or is poisoned due to lack of adequate sanitation—isn't that a matter of basic justice because it bears on the relationship of equal citizenship?" We think that, yes, if some set of laws or policies are shown to undermine the equal standing of some citizens, then they become a matter of basic justice.

which people disagree about whether an issue is a matter of basic justice or a constitutional essential—require public discussion about whether the norms for public reason should apply. This is not a threat to public reason, but, rather, it is simply recognition that the nature and essentials of a constitutional democracy and the social relationship of free and equal citizenship is itself determined through an ongoing process of public deliberation. This is not to say that everything is up for debate. Rather, what must be shown is that some issue in question relates to the fundamental relationship of persons as free and equal citizens and/or their interests as such, which includes the social conditions necessary for reciprocity among such citizens, as discussed in chapter 6.

Our argument is not merely a variation of the basic interests argument for the narrow view of public reason. On this view, as developed by Peter de Marneffe, the idea of public reason concerns a fair distribution of the goods that are the basic interests of citizens as well as a determination of "fair procedures" for conflicts between nonbasic interests. Basic interests are interests in the goods needed by persons as free and equal citizens, such as the social primary goods, and it is principles for the fair distribution of basic interests that are the proper subject of the idea of public reason.[21]

We think the basic interests view is mistaken because it takes the fundamental point of the idea of public reason to be determining the distribution of certain goods among citizens rather than securing the relationship of persons as free and equal citizens, which, we claim, the idea of public reason interprets and which citizens shape through public deliberation and the determination of certain fundamental principles and laws. These principles and laws secure the standing of persons as free and equal citizens and give them access to the goods needed to interact with others on a basis of equality. Hence, we understand political liberalism as a theory of relational equality like Anderson's democratic equality in which the relationship of citizens is fundamental and the distribution of goods is secondary to that (even if that relationship requires a certain distribution of goods to be realized).[22]

We need to address a concern raised by Quong according to which the basic interests view "proposes to leave *everything* that does not concern

---

[21] de Marneffe, "Liberalism, Liberty and Neutrality," pp. 258–260.

[22] Anderson, "What's the Point of Equality?," pp. 313–314.

essentials to the mercy of voting or some other fair procedural mechanism unconstrained by the norms of public reason."[23] This is a problem, he thinks, because there are public reasons that are relevant in other cases, and such reasons should trump other considerations. For example, consider, again, the case of city residents deciding how to spend public funds; even if the majority of residents prefer football to art, if there are no art museums, fairness may trump the preference of the majority. Given our earlier claims, it is our view that public spending for public goods that have to do with entertainment or cultural or aesthetic values is outside the scope of public reason (excepting special circumstances in which a proposed public good—e.g., racist statues in the public square—is contrary to status of persons as free and equal citizens).[24] Such goods are in the interests of members of a community, but they do not have to do with securing the status of all persons as free and equal citizens. Certainly, when communities decide how to spend money for public goods, persons may appeal to fairness, but, again, this appeal to fairness is not fairness in the distribution of the goods central to equal citizenship. Rather, it is fairness for public spending among those who live in a localized community and have particular interests. While public goods such as art museums and football stadiums do make it easier for some people to pursue their view of the good, and so they relate to one of the two moral powers,[25] such goods are not central to citizenship. That is, they are not central to how citizens understand what is needed to structure the main institutions of society so that free and equal citizenship can be realized. Hence, against Quong, we simply don't think that there are public reasons in this case.

As we have stressed, the idea of public reason applies only to principles and laws that concern the fundamental relationship between persons as free and equal citizens, and these principles and laws are those that concern matters of basic justice and constitutional essentials. The constitution will specify a decision-making procedure for other laws and principles that is justifiable from the point of view of persons as free and equal

---

[23] Of course, many of these "procedural mechanisms" are themselves justified via public reason (at least insofar as they are part of the basic structure, e.g., legislatures). Thanks to Blain Neufeld for emphasizing this point. Quote at Quong, *Liberalism without Perfectionism*, p. 281.

[24] Thanks to Amy Baehr for asking us to clarify our view with respect to this type of case.

[25] Rawls understands the two moral powers as the capacity to form, revise, and pursue a rational conception of the good and the capacity for a sense of justice (PL, p. 19).

citizens. With respect to laws and policies that are not matters of basic justice or constitutional essentials, persons can appeal to values and beliefs that are part of their comprehensive doctrines. The principles of exclusion and restraint fundamental to the idea of public reason do not apply because persons' status as free and equal citizens is not at issue. Consider, again, that the principle of respect that grounds political liberalism takes citizens as persons as ends with moral authority. Political liberals view such persons as committed to the democratic ideal of standing in a relationship of equal citizenship with others where each pursues his or her own view of the good, consistent with equal freedom for others. The role of public reason is to interpret that idea and secure that relationship among citizens. When the terms of that fundamental relationship are not at stake and when a person's status as a free and equal citizen is secure, there is no justification for restricting persons' reasoning about law and policy.

III. Public Deliberation: Exclusive, Inclusive, and Wide Accounts of Public Reason's Duty of Civility

Any plausible interpretation of political liberalism holds that the public justification of certain principles and laws requires that those laws be justified on the basis of reasons that are shared by persons as free and equal citizens. These reasons stem from reasonable political conceptions of justice, which are based on the values that persons as free and equal citizens share. As such, we can describe public reasoning as reasoning from the point of view of a person as a free and equal citizen.

Political liberals vary with respect to whether and for what reason it is morally permissible for persons to appeal to their comprehensive doctrines in the context of public reasoning. In this regard, political liberals offer different interpretations of the duty of civility, which constrains those engaged in public, political deliberation where the norms of public reasoning apply. However, despite different interpretations of the duty of civility, all political liberals endorse a stronger requirement of restraint for judges, legislators, public officials, and candidates for political office than for citizens. To fulfill the moral duty of civility public officials are restricted from ever appealing to their comprehensive doctrines when deliberating about the principles and laws to which the idea of public reason applies. A clear case of violating such a duty by legislators or judges would involve invoking beliefs from comprehensive doctrines (such as a view about God's law or Kantian autonomy) as the basis for legislation or a judicial decision.

Hence, when it comes to the duty of civility, the disagreement among political liberals really concerns what is required of *citizens*. Rawls explicitly states that citizens fulfill the ideal of public reason when they "think of themselves as if they were legislators and ask themselves what statutes, supported by what reasons satisfying the criterion of reciprocity, they would think it most reasonable to enact."[26] Rawls, though, and some other political liberals do not think that, when the idea of public reason applies, the duty of civility precludes citizens from ever appealing to claims that are part of their comprehensive doctrine.

Rawls admits he was originally drawn to an *exclusive view of public reason*, according to which "comprehensive doctrines are never to be introduced into public reason."[27] Then Rawls adopted, for some time, what he called an *inclusive view of public reason*, even though he eventually adopts an even more permissive view, which we discuss below. According to the inclusive view, citizens can refer to their comprehensive doctrines "in certain situations" where public reasoning applies, "provided they do this in ways that strengthen the idea of public reason itself."[28] One example he offers of an appropriate situation is of a "nearly well-ordered society" in which there is disagreement about what fair equality of opportunity requires when it comes to public funding and education. Some citizens think that there should be public education funding only for public schools; others support public funding for parochial schools, too. Perhaps, in such a case, persons "may come to doubt the sincerity of one another's allegiance to fundamental political values," and it may bolster "mutual trust and public confidence" if persons can explain how their comprehensive doctrines support certain values such as fair equality of opportunity.[29] Here the role of appealing to one's comprehensive doctrine is instrumental—it is in the service of furthering public trust and confidence and demonstrating one's sincere commitment to a reasonable political conception of justice.

---

[26] IPPR, p. 577.

[27] PL, p. 247.

[28] PL, p. 247.

[29] PL, pp. 248–249.

Rawls also discusses the case of abolitionists and the case of Dr. Martin Luther King Jr.'s work for civil rights as examples that suggest that an inclusive view is superior to an exclusive one. In both of these cases, advocates for racial equality appealed to Christian views to argue for reform to ensure substantive equal citizenship for racial minorities.[30] An important and frequently ignored point in these cases is that abolitionists and King also gave public reasons.[31] Yet, for Rawls, what is important is that persons' appeals to their comprehensive doctrines helped to make unjust circumstances more just. Hence, in accordance with the inclusive view, persons do not violate the duty of civility if they appeal to their comprehensive doctrine in public reasoning to strengthen the ideal of public reason itself.

Later, Rawls rejects the inclusive view in favor of the even more permissive *wide view*, in which "reasonable comprehensive doctrines . . . may be introduced in public political discussion at any time, provided that in due course proper political reasons—and not reasons given solely by comprehensive doctrines—are presented that are sufficient to support whatever the comprehensive doctrines introduced are said to support."[32] The demand for the eventual provision of public reasons is Rawls's *proviso*. With the proviso, Rawls drops the requirement that distinguished the inclusive view—namely, that appealing to comprehensive doctrines in public reason was acceptable only as means to strengthen the idea of public reason itself. In his later work, Rawls sees no reason for restricting appeals to comprehensive doctrines as long as public reasons are provided *at some point*. That is, Rawls holds the fairly odd position that citizens fulfill the duty of civility when public reasons are provided "in due course" for the principles and laws that that citizen endorses. So a citizen does not actually have to provide the public reasons herself; it just must be the case that such reasons are provided by someone in due course.[33] As an initial matter, it is surely odd to suggest that whether one fulfills a moral duty is dependent on what *some other person* may do at some future time.

---

[30] Certainly not all abolitionists advocated for racial equality; indeed, some maintained a commitment to white supremacy but rejected slavery. Others, of course, advocated for not just the abolition of slavery but reforms that would ensure the full enjoyment of citizenship rights to all (even women).

[31] Thanks to Micah Schwartzman for emphasizing this point.

[32] IPRR, p. 591.

[33] PL, pp. xlix–l.

Furthermore, Rawls sees the wide view of public reason, as reflected in the proviso, as an improvement over the inclusive view, because "it has the further advantage of showing to other citizens the roots in our comprehensive doctrines of our allegiance to the political conception, which strengthens the stability in the presence of a reasonable overlapping consensus."[34] This amounts to the view that because our comprehensive doctrines contain supporting reasons (though perfectionist ones or nonpublic ones) that coincide with public reasons (though, again, at the time of reason-giving this may or may not be known), our co-citizens are given greater assurance of our commitment to a reasonable conception of justice governing the terms of social cooperation.

In our earlier work, we criticized both the inclusive view of public reason and the wide view of public reason.[35] We argued that claims from comprehensive doctrines can never play a justificatory role in public reason. We defended an exclusive view of public reason on the basis that in public political debate justification is always addressed *to others*, and, as such, nonshared reasons simply cannot play the role of offering a justification *to others*. This is how we read the demands of the reciprocity condition.[36] However, as it stands, our earlier view needs to be made more precise and developed, which is what we aim to do here.

Some commentators think the differences among the wide, inclusive, and exclusive views of public reason have to do, in part, with whether claims from reasonable comprehensive doctrines can justify principles and laws within public reason.[37] We read the distinction similarly in our previous work. We now think that reading isn't correct. In our "Shared Reasons" article, we used the distinctions among the wide, inclusive, and exclusive views of public reason to describe accounts of public reason across a range of views not all of which can be described as politically

---

[34] PL, p. l.

[35] Hartley and Watson, "Feminism, Religion, and Shared Reasons."

[36] For a defense of a more inclusive account of public reason than ours that also emphasizes the importance of reciprocity, see Laden, *Reasonably Radical*.

[37] See, e.g., Solum, "Inclusive Public Reason." David Reidy argues that the wide view of public reason is not wide enough, as nonpublic reasons will have to play a justificatory role to address some issues. He claims, "Even in well-developed liberal democracies public reason will prove just too thin for many citizens to resolve many fundamental political issues in a reasoned way without a resolution-determinative appeal to non-public reasons" ("Rawls's Wide View," p. 52).

liberal. That is, not all of the views we considered in that article are, in fact, committed to the core features of political liberalism.

As we use the distinctions here, we are considering a debate among political liberals all of whom hold that only public reasons can provide sufficient *justification* for principles and laws within the scope of the idea of public reason; in other words, no one described as a political liberal can hold that nonpublic reasons (reasons from full or partially comprehensive doctrines) play a justificatory role in matters determined to be within the scope of public reason. This follows from the claim that public reasons must be shared reasons; to enjoy public justification (public) reasons must be shared from the point of view of free and equal citizens. Thus, what political liberals disagree about is whether appealing to comprehensive doctrines concerning matters where the scope of public reason applies is compatible with the duty of civility.

We think that three issues are important to examine when considering whether appealing to comprehensive doctrines is ever morally permissible where public reason applies: (1) Are such appeals consistent with showing respect for one's co-citizens? (2) If so, could an appeal to reasons specific to one's reasonable comprehensive doctrine help to strengthen the idea of public reason itself? (3) Could such an appeal, as Rawls says, strengthen stability in the presence of a reasonable overlapping consensus?

IV. A Defense of Exclusive Public Reason

We defend an exclusive view of public reason. We argue that even if we suppose that appealing to one's reasonable comprehensive doctrine within public reason is compatible with showing respect for one's fellow citizens, it is not at all clear that permitting this would strengthen the stability of an overlapping consensus on a reasonable political conception of justice. And we argue that it is not at all clear how appealing to one's reasonable comprehensive doctrine could help to strengthen the idea of public reason itself. Finally, we show that it is simply not compatible with showing proper respect for co-citizens to appeal to one's comprehensive doctrine within public reason.

First, suppose it is consistent with showing respect to co-citizens to appeal to one's comprehensive doctrine within public reason so long as public reasons are provided as justifications for relevant principles and laws *in due course*. Why should we think this would strengthen the stability of an overlapping consensus of reasonable comprehensive doctrines?

Note that political liberals hold that the possibility of a just and stable liberal democratic regime among free and equal citizens given the fact of reasonable pluralism depends, inter alia, on an overlapping consensus of reasonable comprehensive doctrines on a reasonable political conception of justice. Those who accept a reasonable comprehensive doctrine reconcile their view with a reasonable political conception of justice, a conception of justice that can be formulated independently of any comprehensive doctrine and solely in terms of public, political values.[38] Rawls says, "Citizens' mutual knowledge of one another's religious and nonreligious doctrines expressed in the wide view of public political culture recognizes that the roots of democratic citizens' allegiance to their political conceptions lie in their respective comprehensive doctrines, both religious and nonreligious."[39] And, he continues, "we may think of the reasonable comprehensive doctrines that support society's reasonable political conceptions as those conceptions' vital social basis, giving them enduring strength and vigor."[40] Yet, Rawls also emphasizes that even with the wide view of public reason, where it is permissible to introduce one's reasonable comprehensive doctrine into public reasoning, this "does not change the nature and content of justification in public reason itself."[41] So the issue is simply whether appealing to one's comprehensive doctrine to show how one's doctrine *supports* political values can make an overlapping consensus more stable.[42]

---

[38] Rawls recognizes a family of reasonable political conceptions of justice will be part of any politically liberal society, but when there is an overlapping consensus on one such political conception, citizens accept it as appropriate to order the basic structure of a liberal democratic regime in light of that particular conception.

[39] IPRR, p. 592.

[40] IPRR, p. 592.

[41] IPPR, p. 592.

[42] Weithman argues in favor of the wide view of public reason over the exclusive view we defend on the grounds that the wide view is better able to solve the assurance (stability) problem that motivates the turn to political liberalism. See his *Rawls, Political Liberalism*, chapter 7, pp. 150–167. As we argue in the text that follows, predictions about the likelihood of assurance are largely empirical and cannot easily be made outside a particular context. Aside from the empirical predictions, we think that the exclusive view best manifests the value of mutual respect.

This is doubtful. First, consider that public reason is meant to direct our actions in the present; in particular, it is used to determine what principles and laws should be adopted. The proviso simply requires that public reasons be given in due course. Whether the proviso is satisfied and whether appeals to one's comprehensive doctrine serve to make an overlapping consensus more stable must be determined later. But, again, the point of public deliberation is to settle fundamental political questions in the present. So, in any particular case, one can't know that one's introduction of one's comprehensive doctrine in public reasoning will have this effect. And, once again, whether it will have the intended effect in the future is a complex matter about which actors in the present simply can't have adequate knowledge to make a sound prediction.

Consider, too, the particular cases Rawls uses to support the proviso's plausibility: the abolitionists and activists in the civil rights movement. In each of these cases the introduction of comprehensive values aimed at providing a particular interpretation of certain political values and justifying those values. As it turns out, in the cases of the abolitionists and activists in the civil rights movement, their visions for greater civil equality helped move views about justice in a reasonable direction. We know this retrospectively, although in both cases proper public reason arguments were also given. Nonetheless, in any particular case the introduction of comprehensive values, when the political conception of justice is unsettled, may be divisive.

Moreover, where the political conception of justice is settled, why should we think that introduction of comprehensive values into public reasoning will help support, by making more stable, an overlapping consensus on a reasonable political conception of justice? A reasonable person accepts that other reasonable persons have reasonable comprehensive doctrines. Yet, she does not think doctrines other than hers are justified, and she may deny the basis for their justification. How does it show her others' commitment to the political conception to see how others support political values given their comprehensive doctrines?

Arguably, what shows the reasonable person others' commitment to the political conception is not knowing how others' relate their comprehensive doctrine to political values (which citizens are free to do outside the context of public reason) but, rather, is seeing others' commitment to public justification by their offering justifications they believe are shared from the point of view of free and equal citizenship. Indeed, Rawls carefully uses the phrase "introduction" of comprehensive doctrine rather than "invocation" or some similar word to elide the fact that when they are introduced in public reasoning it is, more often than not, as justifications. Offering reasons internal to a particular comprehensive doctrine to show support for a reasonable political conception of justice may be divisive and undermine a commitment to shared reasons. Claiming that a wide view of public reason is likely to increase stability is an empirical prediction, the plausibility of which is hard to assess outside of a particular context. We think the plausibility of this prediction depends on a range of variables, including how often such appeals are made, and by whom (e.g., how much social power and privilege do such persons wield in the society?), and as to what issues?

Consider Rawls's example about public support for parochial schools. Those who support public funding for parochial schools are often religious persons with a personal interest in such schools as sites for education in a religious context and often with religious content. Would a citizen's appeal to her religious comprehensive doctrine in public reasoning really assure others of her commitment to her political conception? Or would it make others unsure that the laws and policies she favors are supported by public reasons as opposed to values and beliefs distinctive of her comprehensive doctrine? And, furthermore, in some cases, would it not make others doubt her commitment to providing public reasons and result in instability? These questions can't be settled outside of a particular politically liberal well-ordered society. If the nonideal conditions of public, political debates in modern Western democracies provide any guidance on this issue, then it may be quite divisive.

Consider now whether appealing to one's reasonable comprehensive doctrine in public reasoning could help to strengthen the idea of public reason itself. One might see this issue merely as a restatement of the previous one. Indeed, Rawls, at times, does. In his defense of the inclusive view in his early work, he posited that appealing to one's comprehensive doctrine could further public trust and confidence. But Rawls also says in his discussion of the abolitionists and Martin Luther King that persons' appealing to their comprehensive doctrines could be a way to help make unjust circumstances more just and closer to the ideal of public reason. However, here the distinction between ideal and nonideal theory is important.

It is one matter to ask about the appropriate norms for the idea of public reasoning in a society that is manifestly unjust—this was the circumstances of both the abolitionists and King—and another to ask about the norms of public reasoning in a well-ordered society or even a nearly just society when all citizens enjoy equal basic rights and liberties. Yet, even so, it is hard to see the case that appealing to one's reasonable comprehensive doctrine could help to strengthen the ideal of public reasoning itself. At the core of this ideal is the criterion of reciprocity. Reciprocity requires a commitment to propose terms of cooperation to others that one thinks are reasonable for them to accept as free and equal citizens. Given the fact of reasonable pluralism and the aims of public justification, it is only reasonable for persons to propose terms for cooperation that are supported on the basis of public reasons. And public reasons are reasons that persons share from the point of view of free and equal citizenship. Even if under nonideal conditions, appeals to nonpublic reasons could help in the realization of more just conditions, it is not correct to say that this helps to strength the ideal of public reason itself. So, while such appeals may move an unjust state to a more just one, as in the case of King, this is a separate point from the idea that such appeals strengthen the ideal of public reason itself. And in any case, as we noted above, whether such strengthening occurs can be known only after the fact, often well after the fact. Ultimately, these are empirical questions; however, we think there are normative reasons for preferring the exclusive view.

Now consider whether it is compatible with showing proper respect for fellow citizens to appeal to one's comprehensive doctrine within public reasoning. We think it is not. Reasonable persons are committed to the criterion of reciprocity. This involves acceptance of a particular view of public justification, and Rawls says in his description of the idea of public reasoning that "public justification is not simply valid reasoning, but argument addressed to others."[43] We would stress it is argument addressed to persons as free and equal citizens because such persons have a certain status and authority and share a commitment to a common endeavor. Indeed, as we stressed in chapter 2, the criterion of reciprocity is an interpretation of respect for persons as free and equal citizens in a liberal democratic state. Where the idea of public reason applies, when persons appeal to their comprehensive doctrines in discussion of principles and policies they do not engage others as free and equal citizens. That is, they do not engage in discourse about the fundamental structure of their democratic state from the point of view of free and equal citizenship. And,

---

[43] IPRR, p. 594.

so, they fail to engage them in the way they are owed as free and equal citizens. Moreover, they most certainly will appeal to reasons (grounded in comprehensive doctrines) that other citizens reasonably reject, even if they are used as support for why they accept political values.

Now consider a second argument for rejecting the wide view in favor of the exclusive view, which we call "the argument from political autonomy." An "autonomous political doctrine" is

> one that represents, or displays, the political principles of justice—the fair terms of social cooperation—as reached by using the principles of practical reason in union with the appropriate conception of persons as free and equal and of society as a fair system of cooperation over time. . . . Autonomy is a matter of how the view presents the political values as ordered.[44]

Rawls calls this "doctrinal autonomy." And doctrinal autonomy, for a reasonable political conception of justice, is achieved if that conception is freestanding, that is, it does not draw upon nor does it rely upon nonpolitical values. An autonomous doctrine orders the political values internally and does not seek deeper justification from comprehensive values.[45] Citizens are politically autonomous when they affirm the political doctrine as a whole. Political autonomy demands that citizens "act upon laws fairly and legitimately enacted on the basis of public reason under conditions of equal political power."[46]

Political autonomy requires at least that citizens employ shared reasons—the reasons drawn from a freestanding political conception of justice—in public reasoning.[47] As an initial matter, we note that the use of nonpublic reasons for matters concerning basic justice and constitutional essentials undermines political autonomy, for such reasons may be reasonably rejected by citizens who do not regard such reasons as authoritative. To allow nonpublic reasons to play a role in determining how to interpret

---

[44] PL, p. 98.

[45] PL, pp. 98–99.

[46] Freeman, *Rawls*, p. 401.

[47] Weithman defends the wide view of public reason, including the proviso, as consistent with the political autonomy of a politically liberal society, though, importantly, he emphasizes that political autonomy is a matter of degree. See his *Rawls, Political Liberalism*, especially chapters 7 and 8.

constitutional essentials and matters of basic justice undermines citizens' political autonomy, too. Such reasons do not address all reasonable citizens as such and do not form part of a shared political conception of justice; hence, introducing them in public, political debate when fundamental matters are at stake is inconsistent with the political autonomy both of the political conception of justice and of citizens. Where public reason applies, to allow nonpublic reasons to play other roles (show one's support for a political conception from one's comprehensive doctrine) threatens to undermine political autonomy by introducing into the very context that persons occupy in their role as citizens reasons that are not shared by persons as citizens.

V. Does Shared Reasoning Require Identical Reasoning?

We now turn to consider two additional objections some might make to our view. Gaus and Vallier claim "consensus" accounts of public justification are inconsistent with "members of the public reasoning on pluralistic standards."[48] In short, they worry that if public justification requires that reasons be shared, all citizens must reason in exactly the same way. Public reasoning becomes the reasoning of one, and, thus, the problem of pluralism is not taken seriously.[49] Gaus and Vallier attach this criticism to the reasoners in Rawls's original position; however, the original position is a methodology specific to a particular political conception of justice. All reasonable political conceptions of justice need not embrace it or some version of it. Yet, one might think that insofar as we claim that where the

---

[48] Gaus and Vallier, "The Roles of Religious Conviction," p. 58.

[49] In the passage criticizing shareability as the appropriate standard for public reasons, Gaus and Vallier write, "Consequently although the original position begins by posing a problem of choice among people who disagree, the problem is reduced to a choice by one person" ("The Roles of Religious Conviction," p. 58). However, the original position and the veil of ignorance are devices of representation aimed at modeling what representatives for members of a well-ordered society would select as principles of justice. "Justice as Fairness" is Rawls's particular account and defense of a reasonable political conception of justice. The account of political justification and the role of public reasons in democratic legitimacy are separable from Rawls's defense of justice as fairness. In the context of public reason, citizens draw from the political conception of justice they think most reasonable, which may not be justice as fairness. So one can accept political liberalism, the criterion of reciprocity, and the idea/ideal of public reason and, at the same time, reject justice as fairness as the most reasonable political conception of justice (as well as reject the original position).

idea of public reason applies, persons should reason from the point of view of free and equal citizens, the criticism extends to our view.

Does an account of public reasons as shared reasons assume all citizens "reason identically?"[50] To the contrary, political liberals recognize that there will be a family of *reasonable* political conceptions of justice. All of these conceptions must be derived or formulated from political values or values that persons as free and equal citizens share. However, persons will order and interpret these values in different ways. They will claim that different principles or laws are required to respect them. Now, Rawls does claim that all reasonable political conceptions of justice will share certain features. However, this does not mean that all persons reason identically as free and equal citizens. Rawls says, "Citizens will of course differ as to which conception of political justice they think the most reasonable, but they will agree that all are reasonable, even if barely so."[51]

For political liberals, the justification of political authority requires that those who are subject to such authority be able to accept the terms of that authority (the fundamental principles and terms of basic justice) as consistent with their standing as free and equal citizens. Public reasons are reasons about how to structure the political relationship of citizens as such and how citizens empower the state to secure a relationship of equality among citizens. Mutual recognition of the equal standing of all citizens qua citizens requires that if X is a reason for me, it is a reason for you in the sense that it is a reason that is supported from the point of view of free and equal citizenship. It doesn't follow from this that citizens must reason in an identical fashion or that genuinely pluralistic reasoning is excluded.

That identical reasoning is not required by a shared reasons account is shown by reflecting on the more recent debate over how to respond to historical exclusion of gays and lesbians from the legal institution of marriage. A range of public reason arguments were made. Some persons argued for extension of civil unions that parallel all the legal benefits of marriage while reserving the word "marriage" for heterosexual couples. Other persons argued for the full extension of marriage rights and entitlements to gays and lesbians, rights and entitlements that are identical to the rights now enjoyed by dyadic heterosexual relationships. Others argued for the

---

[50] Gaus and Vallier ask this ("The Roles of Religious Conviction," p. 58).

[51] IPRR, p. 578.

abolishment of legal marriage. Some argued that the state should not offer civil unions or marriage rights and entitlements to gays and lesbians. Sometimes the reasons for exclusion took the *form* of public reasons (e.g., concern for child welfare and a stable family life), even though they lacked an empirical basis.

Putting aside the last sort of position to make a narrow point here, each of the other three public reason positions described above were offered sincerely as policy for how to deal with the exclusion of gays and lesbians from the goods of legally recognized marital relationships. The conclusions of these positions (and we have presented only the conclusions) were offered as being consistent with the recognition of the equal standing of gay and lesbian citizens, although this is not to say that, on reflection, all three positions were. The reasoning that led to the different conclusions presumably rested upon different evaluations of the political goods or rights at stake. Those in favor of full extension of marriage rights presumably viewed marriage as not a mere collection of rights and benefits but also as a social status, which has accompanying implications. Those in favor of civil unions for gays and lesbians may have reduced the importance of legal marriage to rights and benefits, such that a "separate but equal" approach was not an infringement of civil rights. Those in favor of abolishment of legal marriage may have placed greater emphasis on the importance of freedom from state regulation of personal relationships. Appealing to public reasons is compatible with different orderings and weightings of the political goods or rights in any particular case. The demand that the reasons be shared implies that when offering public reasons the proponent of the view sincerely believes that he or she is relying on political values, which are those values accepted by free and equal citizens, and that he or she is ordering those values reasonably. When public reason arguments are made, persons as free and equal citizens determine which argument is most reasonable. Public reasoning is an active, deliberative endeavor; persons in their role as free and equal citizens are open to discussion and debate and reflect on the best or most appropriate ordering of political values in light of public, political discussion. Moreover, it may be that the argument one finds most persuasive doesn't win the day, and by one's lights it is a less optimal policy. In such cases, the principle or policy will, nonetheless, be legitimate provided it rests on a reasonable political conception of justice.

Consider the structure of one type of judicial reasoning, which is analogous to public reasoning in some ways. A number of justices may agree on a holding, but they may have different rationales for that holding that depend, for example, on different constitutional principles or interpretations of the law. Even in some landmark decisions the best the Supreme Court of the United States can do is garner a plurality opinion, such that the justices settle on a holding but a majority does not accept a single rationale. Nonetheless, each rationale is developed in terms of public, political values and offers public reasons as to what the author regards as the most reasonable ordering of such values.

VI. The Completeness of Public Reason

Some have challenged the ideal of public reason on the grounds that the idea of public reason is incomplete.[52] The *idea* of public reason concerns the "basic moral and political values" that structure a liberal democratic state and the norms for public justification and deliberation, and the *ideal* of public reason concerns the satisfaction of the idea by those to whom public reason applies.[53] Critics claim that the content of public reason is insufficient to give determinate answers to controversial matters, even of constitutional essentials and matters of basic justice.[54] For example, the intractability of the abortion debate in American politics is often cited to suggest public reason's insufficiency. Those critics claim that if public reason cannot settle an issue, citizens will inevitability draw on nonpublic reasons, reasons from their comprehensive doctrines, for resolution. Indeed, Quong notes that some favor the narrow view of the scope of public reason on the grounds that adopting a narrow scope will solve the incompleteness challenge.[55] Although we do not defend the narrow view because of concerns about incompleteness, we think the concern about incompleteness needs to be addressed. Here we can only highlight the direction we think political liberals should take.

---

[52] See, e.g., Greenawalt, *Religious Convictions*.

[53] IPRR, pp. 574–577.

[54] Sam Freeman argues that "far from being incomplete . . . public reason is overdetermined insofar as it provides more than one politically reasonable answer to many questions" (*Justice and the Social Contract*, p. 244). So long as citizens accept as politically reasonable the range of answers, the conditions of public justification are satisfied, even if individuals' most preferred (most reasonable from their point of view) policy is not adopted.

[55] Quong, *Liberalism without Perfectionism*, pp. 281–287.

Micah Schwartzman stresses that there are two ways to understand the charge of incompleteness.[56] One might claim that public reason is *inconclusive*: "citizens have competing but *inconclusive* public justifications for a given political decision." Or one might claim that public reason is *indeterminate*: "citizens do not have sufficient public reason to decide between mutually exclusive political outcomes."[57] With respect to the worry about inconclusiveness, the problem is that the existence of competing but reasonable public reasons prevents citizens from coalescing on a unique answer to some set of fundamental political questions. This is supposed to undermine public reason's ability to solve political controversies. With respect to the worry about indeterminacy, the problem is that public reason can't resolve some matters because it doesn't have the sufficient resources to generate any outcome at all.

We do not think the inconclusiveness charge provides a good reason to reject the ideal of public reason. For political liberals, neither public justification nor legitimacy requires that all reasonable persons accept the same public reason for a given law or policy, nor does either require that all reasonable citizens accept the same law or policy as most reasonable. Rawls and other political liberals recognize that a family of reasonable political conceptions of justice exist, and there is no reason to think citizens will all endorse precisely the same one. Citizens will offer public reasons from the set of the family of reasonable political conceptions of justice, and, in some instances, there will be a set of reasonable answers to some fundamental question or constitutional essential. This is determinate content. Some other mechanism—depending on the context (e.g., referendum or judicial decision-making)—will select among the reasonable laws and reasonable grounds, all of which are justified to persons as free and equal citizens in the relevant sense.

The charge of indeterminacy is more serious. Here, political liberals should be more worried. If the charge sticks, then there will be some subset of (fundamental) political matters that public reason does not settle. Abortion is a favored example to support this charge. Critics claim that some citizens will give considerable, if not ultimate, weight to the value of human life, while others will give greater weight to equality for women. Faced with the conflict between these two values, public reason,

---

[56] Schwartzman, "The Completeness of Public Reason," p. 193.

[57] Schwartzman, "The Completeness of Public Reason," p. 193.

it is thought, will not settle which value warrants greater weight, and citizens must resort to their comprehensive doctrines.

We think the worry about indeterminacy can be addressed, but we can't fully address it here. However, consider the case of abortion again. First, as Schwartzman claims, the constraints of public reason simply preclude some political positions, such as, arguably, a complete ban on abortion in the case of rape or incest pregnancy that endangers a woman's health.[58] And, with some positions off the table, we think that public reason has the resources to deliver reasonable solutions. For example, Freeman, interpreting Rawls, argues that prohibiting abortion altogether and, thus, denying women a right to choose throughout pregnancy would demand a plausible case for the "constitutional personality of the fetus," and this, he says, "has not been made" and "it is not clear how it could be" within public reason.[59] This is a particular interpretation about how the political values of a reasonable political conception can answer one seemingly problematic case for political liberalism. And, with respect to the matter of abortion in particular, instead of presenting political liberals with a case of problematic indeterminacy, we think it actually raises a different question: Is it reasonable to hope that persons, for purposes of settling fundamental questions of justice as citizens, will regard political values as overriding? We think that this depends on whether the argument we outlined for the moral foundation of public reason in chapter 2 is compelling. Our sympathizers and our critics alike may worry that in defending such an exclusive account our view is vulnerable to serious objections concerning the ability of some religious persons to participate in public reasoning without thwarting their integrity. Critics may claim that the demands of public reason will result in laws that unfairly disadvantage some religious persons in their religious practices. We address these concerns in the next two chapters.

---

[58] Schwartzman, "The Completeness of Public Reason," p. 203.

[59] Freeman, *Justice and the Social Contract*, p. 246.

4

Integrity and the Case for Restraint

Referring to citizens holding such a religious doctrine as citizens of faith, we ask: How is it possible for citizens of faith to be wholehearted members of a democratic society when they endorse an institutional structure satisfying a liberal political conception of justice with its own intrinsic political ideals and values, and when they are not simply going along with it in view of the balance of political and social forces?

—JOHN RAWLS, *Political Liberalism*

I. Introduction

Thus far, we have defended an exclusive account of the idea of public reason. We argue that public reasons are reasons that reasonable persons as free and equal citizens, drawing on their favored reasonable political conception of justice as well as general rules of inquiry and reasoning, sincerely believe other reasonable citizens will share from the point of view of free and equal citizenship. Hence, for the justification of matters of basic justice and constitutional essentials, we endorse a principle of exclusion according to which values and beliefs peculiar to comprehensive doctrines cannot justify principles, laws, and policies.[1] And, for public, political deliberation about matters of basic justice and constitutional essentials, we endorse a principle of restraint such that citizens have a duty of civility to refrain from appealing to their comprehensive doctrines. Some may think our view privileges secular worldviews and raises concerns about the ability of some religious persons to participate in public, political debate as equals or on fair terms. They may think

---

[1] We adopt Kevin Vallier's terminology for public reason of "principle of exclusion" and "principle of restraint" (*Liberal Politics and Public Faith*, pp. 49–52).

that our account is just too demanding for some religiously oriented citizens and threatens or undermines their integrity. In this chapter, we examine and address this and similar worries as they apply to our account of public reason.

II. Religious Citizens and Integrity

Consider two ways in which some persons of faith may object that political liberalism's idea of public reason threatens or undermines their integrity. First, some persons may think insofar as the demands of public reasoning preclude citizens from appealing to their comprehensive doctrines in public, political discussions of matters of basic justice or constitutional essentials, citizens' integrity will be frustrated or thwarted. Persons are prohibited from appealing to values and beliefs that are not shared but that may, for some persons, explain life's meaning and what is sacred or required by their ultimate values. Such values and beliefs may be central to a person's identity and self-understanding. For example, as the issue of abortion raises a fundamental constitutional matter, those who hold certain religious worldviews—such as the beliefs that fetuses are ensouled at conception and, thus, have full moral standing—may believe that the requirements of public reason hinder them from supporting principles on the basis of beliefs that are central to their identity and their fundamental values.

Second, some persons may think that, given the demands of public reason, the kinds of principles and laws that are justifiable will have the result of unfairly disadvantaging or burdening particular religious obligations, commitments, rituals, and practices that are a matter of integrity for some religious persons. In the United States, the constitutional right to the free exercise of religion together with legislation such as religious freedom and restoration acts provide a basis for exemptions for persons of faith from generally applicable laws. The justification of such acts is sometimes framed in terms of protecting the integrity of persons of faith to act in accordance with their conscience. Both kinds of concerns about the integrity of persons of faith have been pressed as criticisms against political liberalism's account of public reason. In this chapter, we consider the first sort of objection; in chapter 5 we consider the case for religious exemptions from generally applicable laws.

III. Alienation and Integrity

With respect to integrity and the demands of public reason, some critics argue that any principle of restraint as such unduly burdens religious citizens in their participation in public reason; they extend this criticism to accounts even more inclusive than ours.[2] This criticism has been expressed in terms of the alienation of believers and concern for the integrity of persons of faith. While these objections share a common concern, they aren't identical; each emphasizes a different component of the supposed burden on religiously oriented citizens.

Consider alienation. Some religious critics worry that political liberalism's idea of public reason unduly burdens citizens of faith because, rather than creating conditions for religious citizens to participate in political discourse without being alienated from their deeply held convictions, the idea of public reason's principles of exclusion and restraint result in precisely such alienation.[3] Kevin Vallier, drawing on Michael Perry's version of the objection, states the concern in terms of the integrity of believers. The concern is that public reason requires the "privatization" of religious beliefs (and also other beliefs grounded in comprehensive values), and such privatization "is said to require citizens of faith to repress their fundamental commitments when participating in politics, thereby forcing them to violate their integrity."[4] Vallier correctly notes that this objection, if correct, would apply to all persons who hold comprehensive doctrines. So, presumably, anyone in a politically liberal state could have integrity concerns; believers are simply a subset. However, in the literature, political liberalism is claimed to be especially burdensome for and, thereby, unfair to persons of faith, but, again, if such persons are so burdened it is as persons who wish to introduce values and beliefs from their comprehensive doctrines into public reason and not as persons of faith per se.

The alienation objection and the integrity objection are grounded in a similar concern, namely, fair participation of people of faith in a politically liberal state, but, again, these objections are not the same.

---

[2] In this chapter we put aside one peculiar type of integrity challenge to political liberalism. Micah Schwartzman considers the possibility that the demands of public reason pressure citizens to be insincere in public deliberation. If so, one might claim that public reason violates a person's integrity. See Schwartzman's "The Sincerity of Public Reason."

[3] See, e.g., Quinn, "Political Liberalism."

[4] Vallier, "Liberalism, Religion and Integrity," p. 149.

Alienation involves estrangement or detachment. To be alien is literally to be foreign. The focus of the alienation objection is that believers, as a paradigmatic example, can participate in public, political discourse only if they detach or estrange themselves from their fundamental values and beliefs and limit their discourse to public reasons. In other words, the focus of this objection is that citizens of faith (or all citizens) will have to distance themselves from their faith (or their comprehensive worldview) to comply with the demands of public reason. This distancing is claimed to be a kind of problematic alienation, as the demands of public reason preclude persons from justifying laws on the basis of the whole truth as they see it. It is thought that the restraint required to engage in public reason induces a kind of psychic strain in persons in which they must treat their most deeply held convictions as "foreign" in some way.

This objection goes to the heart of political liberalism, for if it is successful *either* (1) it means that a commitment to public reason cannot be adequately grounded in some or all reasonable persons' reasonable comprehensive doctrines (what Rawls calls "full justification" is not possible)[5] *or* (2) it means that such an embedding of the political conception of justice within some or all reasonable persons' reasonable comprehensive doctrines will involve a kind of psychic strain to the point of inducing feelings of estrangement. Note, though, that even if there is alienation or psychic strain, its mere presence may not be unacceptable. Those who wish to push this line of criticism must show that alienation or such psychic strain is unjustifiable. To the extent that the argument focuses on such psychic strain for religious persons, in particular, the suggestion seems to be that nonbelievers don't have similar burdens, and so there is a fundamental unfairness at stake. Believers are asked to carry a burden nonbelievers are not, so a principle of restraint "unduly" or "substantially"

---

[5] Rawls defines full justification as follows: "Full justification is carried out by an individual citizen as a member of civil society. (We assume that each citizen affirms both a political conception and a comprehensive doctrine.) In this case, the citizen accepts a political conception and fills out its justification by embedding it in some way into the citizen's comprehensive doctrine as either true or reasonable, depending upon what the doctrine allows. Some may consider the political conception of justice even though it is not accepted by other people. Whether our view is endorsed by them is not given sufficient weight to suspect its full justification in our own eyes." He goes on to say, and this is important, "Thus it is left to each citizen, individually or in association with others, to say how the claims of political justice are to be ordered, or weighed, against nonpolitical values. The political conception gives no guidance in such questions, since it does not say how nonpolitical values are to be counted" (PL, pp. 386–387).

burdens believers. The hypothesized reason that religious believers face a more significant burden in public reason seems to be the claim that the values religious believers hold are held more strongly, for they are attached to beliefs about the fundamental meaning of life (or an afterlife). Certainly, it is an empirical question as to whether religious believers, individually, hold their beliefs and comprehensive values more strongly than those who are not religious. But even if they do, whether that has any normative weight is a separate matter.

We might understand the worry that psychic strain can result from trying to reconcile a political conception of justice with one's comprehensive doctrine as the worry that attempting such reconciliation may, in fact, preclude what Frankfurt calls "wholeheartedness." Indeed, consider the quote at the beginning of this chapter, in which Rawls asks how persons of faith can be wholehearted members of a liberal democratic society. Wholeheartedness, for Frankfurt, includes, inter alia, the elimination for agents of "inconsistent second-order desires" and of ambivalence with respect to whether "to identify with a particular desire"; wholeheartedness requires a unified self.[6] Framed in terms of wholeheartedness, the concern can be expressed as follows: insofar as believers face greater obstacles to achieving a "unified self" under the demands of a principle of restraint, such a principle unduly burdens believers and, again, as such is unfair.

Those concerned with integrity and not simply alienation may also focus on wholeheartedness, too. Wholeheartedness is central to one of three dominant conceptions of integrity that Cheshire Calhoun helpfully distinguishes in her work; indeed, we take her to have identified the important conceptions of integrity for our purpose of analyzing concerns about integrity and public reason. Calhoun says that wholeheartedness as related to integrity means "integrating competing desires into a single ordering as well as separating some desires from the self and relegating them to 'outlaw' status."[7] Recall that inconsistency of desires and ambivalence spoil wholeheartedness on this view. An individual who is "of two minds" doesn't have integrity.[8] Calhoun calls this the integrated-self view of integrity. Here we might understand the integrity objection as the worry that the demands of public reason create circumstances that lead to

---

[6] Calhoun, "Standing for Something," p. 237.

[7] Calhoun, "Standing for Something," p. 237.

[8] Calhoun, "Standing for Something," p. 238.

persons of faith being placed in a position of having "two minds": on the one hand, they may want to honor the terms of public reason, and, on the other hand, they may want to appeal to their worldviews to ground laws. Insofar as integrity demands "self-integration" and the norms of public reason prevent individuals from appealing to their worldviews, public reason's principle of restraint could be thought to violate the integrity of persons of faith.

Putting aside whether consistency with respect to one's desires and nonambivalence really are central to integrity,[9] does the integrity objection based on this conception of integrity pose a challenge for an exclusive idea of public reason as we have defended it? We think it doesn't. The notion of integrity upon which it is based can't exclude those persons who endorse the oppression and intolerance of others from making similar integrity-based objections. As Calhoun says, central to this understanding of integrity is that "any person whose actions are fully determined by her own endorsements has integrity."[10] It can't be the case that an idea of public reason must be such that all persons (reasonable and unreasonable alike) must be able to maintain integrity in the integrated-self sense.

An account of public reason for a liberal democratic state does not have to structure political discourse to respect a type of integrity in which persons may not view others as free and equal citizens or persons may aim to use the power of the state to dominate and oppress. Irrespective of the issue of how robust a principle of restraint is warranted in public reason, all public reason liberals should acknowledge that persons who would use the power of the state to dominate other citizens do not require accommodation for the sake of integrity.

Hence, the integrity objection, to be successful, must distinguish between the kind of integrity the state must respect and the kind it is not bound to respect. Put differently, on the self-integration view of integrity, anyone, even those who are unreasonable and who have no desire to cooperate with others on fair terms, can claim their integrity is undermined by norms of public reason that require restraint. However, all political liberals should find it acceptable to exclude from public reason worldviews that are inherently intolerant or find domination acceptable. Therefore,

---

[9] Calhoun argues that neither is needed for integrity.

[10] Calhoun, "Standing for Something," p. 238.

the kind of integrity concerns that animate the integrity objection cannot be adequately grounded in such an integrated-self conception of integrity.

Consider another conception of integrity, which Calhoun calls the identity view and locates in the work of Bernard Williams. On this view, integrity is a matter of "fidelity to those projects and principles which are constitutive of one's core identity."[11] This is distinguishable from the integrated-self view insofar as it homes in on constitutive commitments rather than all commitments. Central to this view is an idea of an individual's character that consists of a person's foundational commitments and projects that give meaning and value to her life; a person with integrity lives in accordance with the commitments that she takes to define who she is. Integrity, so understood, entails that an agent acts in concert with her most deeply held convictions. To the extent that any agent fails to maintain fidelity to her foundational commitments, she lacks integrity in that respect. Expressed as a concern over the integrity of believers in a politically liberal state with a norm of restraint, the claim would be that failing to express one's foundational commitments in public reason undermines one's integrity to the extent that it blocks agents from publicly expressing fidelity to their foundational commitments. Even more, insofar as the demands of public reason may require a kind of privileging of the norms and values of public reason and this results in laws that seem in tension with a person's foundational commitments, it may be claimed that the idea of public reason substantially burdens some persons' integrity.

Importantly, both the integrated-self view of integrity and the identity view of integrity are formal in the sense that there are no substantive constraints on the content of either the desires *or* the commitments and projects one has relative to assessing integrity. On either account, both a human rights activist working to help all people have basic rights and a mobster who kills his wife when he learns she is secretly a loyal member of another group may be viewed as having integrity, provided these actions either reflect their considered endorsements or cohere with their fundamental values. So, ultimately, objections to the exclusive account of public reason, and its principle of restraint, based on the identity view of integrity fail for the same reason that objections based on the integrated-self view fail: the inability of persons who have no

---

[11] Calhoun, "Standing for Something," p. 235.

desire or commitment to engage on fair terms of social cooperation with others and to respect the freedom and equality of others as citizens does not, and should not, trouble public reason liberals and the identity view does not distinguish between the integrity of reasonable and unreasonable persons. This means that political liberals need not be concerned with developing an account of public reason that is consistent with this sort of integrity.

Consider yet another dominant conception of integrity, which Calhoun calls the clean-hands view. According to this view, integrity involves "endorsing and, should the occasion arise, standing on some bottom-line principles that define what the agent is willing to have done through her agency and thus the limits beyond which she will not cooperate with evil."[12] Integrity is fundamentally about the "importance of principle" and the "purity" of agency; those with integrity regard some actions as morally wrong independent of their results, and they refuse to be complicit in the violation of their "bottom-line" principles.[13]

This way of understanding integrity resonates well with the kind of problem persons of faith are alleged to face when subject to the demands of an exclusive idea of public reason. For example, given the exclusive idea of public reason's principle of restraint, persons of faith can be subjected to moral criticism for introducing as justifications for laws or accommodations their religiously grounded reasons in public, political debate. Yet this understanding of integrity, too, is a formal account; the bottom-line principles of an agent are a matter of the ones that she decides are her bottom line. And if this is the operative notion of integrity, then while one person's bottom-line principle may involve a refusal to harm living things if there is any way to avoid it, another person's may involve standing up for a worldview in which women are viewed as by nature properly subservient to men.

Public reason liberals, broadly, and political liberals specifically are not committed to tolerating, or accommodating, the intolerant in the law, although the intolerant, of course, have free speech. Hence, any rendering of the integrity objection must be sensitive to the fact that some persons' objections to the demands of public reason are unwarranted, and their framing of such concerns in terms of integrity does not in and of itself

---

[12] Calhoun, "Standing for Something," p. 246.

[13] Calhoun, "Standing for Something," p. 247.

imply that accommodation is necessary. Political liberals, specifically, should reject a formal account of integrity insofar as it potentially raises integrity concerns for the unreasonable and the intolerant, and those are not persons whom political liberals need countenance in crafting their account of public reason. It is reasonable persons with whom political liberalism is concerned.

However, surely there is some way of better stating concerns about alienation and integrity. We might start by putting the issue as follows: the demands of public reason—insofar as they entail a principle of restraint in public deliberation—prevent (some subset of) *reasonable* persons from acting with integrity when participating in public reason, and this is an unacceptable burden. But how can we precisely state this worry when we build in the substantive requirement of reasonableness? Rawls says that reasonable persons have two characteristics. First, he says that reasonable persons "are ready to propose principles and standards as fair terms of cooperation and to abide by them willingly, given the assurance that others will likewise do so."[14] Second, he claims that reasonable persons have a "willingness to recognize the burdens of judgment and to accept their consequences for the use of public reason in directing the legitimate exercise of political power in a constitutional regime."[15] To restate the integrity objection, one might claim that the demands of public reason infringe upon the integrity of reasonable persons of faith and prevent their participation in public, political debate as equals. We still need a notion of integrity to ground these concerns. We will return to the clean-hands picture to see if it fares any better when this qualification is added.

If principles or laws (e.g., legal abortion) that can be publicly justified given the exclusive view of public reason conflict with the moral tenets of a reasonable person's faith or conflict with how she understands her faith to best be practiced, then it might be argued that the exclusive view of public reason precludes reasonable persons from purity of agency or "forces" them to cooperate with evil. What is worse, perhaps, is that insofar as laws are viewed as collectively willed (and that is the ground of their authority, too), the law is *in their name qua citizen*. To maintain integrity, it might be argued that reasonable persons of faith must take a stand and assert their fundamental principles in public deliberation; however, by taking a stand

---

[14] PL, p. 49.

[15] PL, p. 54.

with respect to their so-called bottom-line principles, reasonable persons of faith would violate the demands of public reason. Persons of faith, then, can either maintain integrity or respect the demands of public reason, but not both.

This way of stating the objection is a bit misguided. Importantly, political liberalism's idea of public reason starts with the idea that "insistence on the whole truth in politics" is "incompatible with democratic citizenship and the idea of legitimate law."[16] Reasonable persons think that principles of basic justice and constitutional essentials must be ones that reasonable persons viewed as free and equal citizens accept as reasonable. Furthermore, agreeing to respect the outcome of public reason does not mean that one thinks the results of public reason reflect the truth in any sense but, again, only that from the point of view of a free and equal citizen, the outcome is reasonable to accept. In other words, the outcome is justified from the political point of view. Consider Rawls's discussion about disagreement over the legal right to abortion:

> Some may, of course, reject a decision, as Catholics may reject a decision to grant a right to abortion. They may present an argument in public reason for denying it and fail to win a majority. But they need not exercise the right of abortion in their own case. They can recognize the right as belonging to legitimate law and therefore do not resist it with force. To do that would be unreasonable; it would mean their attempting to impose their own comprehensive doctrine, which a majority of other citizens who follow public reason do not accept.[17]

Hence, reasonable persons of faith can't reasonably be thought of as being made to do, or collaborating with, evil. They accept a certain procedure and norms for the determination of legitimate law, and the outcome of this procedure is regarded as reasonable to accept from the point of view of a person as a free and equal citizen. Insisting on the whole truth as one sees it from within one's comprehensive doctrine as the basis for constitutional essentials and matters of basic justice that govern others who reasonably reject such comprehensive values is to simply reject the

---

[16] IPRR, p. 579.

[17] PL, pp. liv–lv.

foundational assumptions of political liberalism and, perhaps, public reason liberalism altogether. If one accepts the fact of *reasonable* pluralism and desires to find terms of social cooperation that are reasonably acceptable to those who are subject to them, then one is at least committed to the claim that insisting upon one's own comprehensive doctrines as the basis for legitimate law for all persons, even those who reject such doctrines, is simply unreasonable. With regard to the controversial issue of abortion, it is important to remember that persons of faith need not regard abortions as morally permissible. Rather, they must simply recognize the right as a matter of legitimate law.

But, perhaps, when the issue is a religious exemption from a generally applicable law as opposed to justification for a law, concerns about the integrity of persons of faith will fare better. There may seem to be a difference between wanting to use one's worldview to ground a law for everyone when one knows that reasonable people disagree about how the world is and what is of value and wanting to use one's worldview to justify an exemption from a generally applicable law that one takes to burden one's practice of one's faith. We will address this in chapter 5. Still, though, we need something other than the merely formal accounts of integrity we have considered thus far, for we need some way of distinguishing between reasonable claims for exemption and unreasonable ones, and a formal account of integrity can't do that work.

Calhoun claims that on each of the views of integrity we have discussed—the integrated-self view, the identity view, and the clean-hands view—integrity is understood as a personal virtue, and she claims that integrity is, in fact, a social virtue. Understanding integrity as a social virtue may allow us to get more purchase from integrity worries about the idea of public reason. According to Calhoun, personal virtues involve "having the proper relation to oneself," whereas social virtues involve "having the proper relation to others."[18] Integrity as a social virtue concerns "standing for principles and values that, in one's own best judgment, are worthy of defense because they concern how *we*, as beings interested in living justly and well, can do so."[19] She understands integrity as standing for something in the context of "viewing oneself as a member of an evaluating

---

[18] Calhoun, "Standing for Something," p. 252.

[19] Calhoun, "Standing for Something," p. 254.

community" and "caring about what that community endorses."[20] She claims that an agent with integrity both *regards* her judgments as valuable because it is from her point of view that "what is worth doing" is determined and *treats her* judgments as valuable to co-deliberators also committed to "what is worth doing."[21]

On this view of integrity as standing for something, having one's integrity challenged or undermined is about facing unjust pressure to forgo one's best judgment before others. So we can develop the concern about the integrity of persons of faith, on this account, as follows: public reason, with its principle of restraint, leaves persons of faith open to moral criticism for violating the duty of civility if they advocate for what they truly stand for before others. Some have claimed that such a norm of restraint requires the privatization of religious beliefs. Stating the concern in terms of privatization, however, is a mischaracterization of political liberalism. Privatization suggests that norms for all public deliberation require refraining from all appeals to religious beliefs in public discussion. Political liberals don't claim this. The public is much broader than the political. It includes some of the institutions in the "background culture" of civil society; civil society includes, among other things, the media, universities, churches, various associations—scientific groups, clubs, teams, and so on.[22] Open and free discussion, unfettered by any principles of restraint, is the norm in any public domain of life within a liberal democracy (e.g., the media and public square). Pointing this out doesn't dismiss the objection altogether, of course.

Our main response to this formulation of the integrity objection when it comes to justifying generally applicable laws on the basis of one's worldview has to do with the important difference between standing for what one fundamentally endorses before others (as one might do by penning an editorial, joining a social activist group, or organizing a protest) and claiming what one stands for can justify the use of state power to enforce such laws upon those others. When one understands oneself to be engaged in a cooperative project with them, when one understands the authority of laws to stem from their ability to be collectively willed, and when one acknowledges reasonable disagreement among reasonable persons the demands one can reasonably make on others is limited.

---

[20] Calhoun, "Standing for Something," p. 254.

[21] Calhoun, "Standing for Something," p. 258.

[22] PL, pp. 14, 215.

Advocating for political principles, policies, or legislation isn't simply about sharing with fellow co-deliberators what one thinks matters or is of value. Justifications must be addressed to others as engaged in a particular kind of project—namely, determining shared terms of social cooperation that respect each person as a free and equal citizen.

To give the integrity objection force, one would have to argue that the conditions of the use of public reason generate an unfair distribution of the benefits and burdens of social cooperation to some subset of reasonable citizens, and we address this below. Otherwise either persons of faith (or others strongly committed to the strength of their comprehensive values) are committed to finding fair terms of cooperation for persons viewed as free and equal citizens or they are not. If they are not interested in finding fair terms of cooperation, so described, then the political liberal does not aim to convince such persons to accept liberal values. Political liberals, in working out whether political liberalism is internally consistent, do not aim to convince skeptics of liberalism, in whatever form, to embrace liberal ideals.[23] Rather, political liberals ask: Given the fact of reason pluralism, is a just and stable society among persons viewed as free and equal citizens possible? Respecting the integrity of reasonable persons can't mean that the outcomes of public, political deliberation will track a person's deliberative judgments about what matters independent of considering how political principles can be legitimate. So, too, respecting the integrity of reasonable persons does not mean that norms for public, political deliberation must be such that persons can appeal to their deliberative judgment about what matters if there are good reasons for restricting such appeals, and political liberals think that there are.

IV. Integrity and Realizing Citizenship

Paul Weithman advances a different version of the integrity objection, and we would be remiss not to address it here. He claims that an account of public reason that excludes reasons grounded in religious beliefs from the justificatory domain and that restrains person from offering such reasons as justifications in public reason will unduly burden believers

---

[23] Of course, we do think there are things to be said and arguments to be made to such skeptics. We are just emphasizing here that the project of political liberalism is not conceived of as justifying the liberal project to nonliberals; rather it is, as we argued in chapter 1, best understood as aiming to show that liberalism is internally consistent.

in the "realization of citizenship."[24] He stresses that in the United States churches helped some persons realize their citizenship by encouraging and supporting their political participation, for example, African Americans during the civil rights era. And, for example, churches have organized political discussions and provided political education and skills. These services help persons (especially minorities and the poor) develop "a sense of self-worth," which enables participatory citizenship. An account of public reason that includes a principle of exclusion and restraint hinders this mechanism for the development of citizenship.

Of course, as Vallier points out, "no public reason liberal argues that citizens should not discuss their religious reasons or organize politically in church." And, as he continues, "they merely require that, when voting or arguing in the public sphere, citizens should rely primarily on nonreligious considerations."[25] Nonetheless, Vallier thinks that in a society in which numerous principles of restraint restrict public deliberation, persons of faith may feel alienated from their faith due to norms of restraint.[26] Vallier stresses the role that religiously grounded arguments played in the political activism of Desmond Tutu; one could make similar claims about Dr. Martin Luther King Jr.'s work. Such arguments certainly helped to persuade persons to work toward more just societies. Speaking of Tutu's work for justice, Vallier says, "If the principles of restraint advocated by public reason liberals had been widely acknowledged within South African society, Tutu's witness would have been substantially muted."[27]

We think that this integrity objection fails to undermine an exclusive account of public reason. First, political liberals certainly would not oppose religious institutions organizing political discussions, encouraging citizens' political participation, and educating citizens on matters of politics and civic virtue. Political liberals should, indeed, welcome this. Second, with respect to political liberalism's principle of restraint and the role that religious considerations have often played in creating more just societies, we, again, think that it is important to distinguish between norms for public deliberation in a well-ordered society and in a society that is manifestly unjust and plagued with gross civil rights violations.

---

[24] Weithman, *Religion and the Obligations of Citizenship*, p. 22.

[25] Vallier, "Liberalism, Religion and Integrity," p. 158.

[26] Vallier, "Liberalism, Religion and Integrity," p. 159.

[27] Vallier, "Liberalism, Religion and Integrity," p. 150.

Different norms in these societies may be justifiable. However, in the case of both Tutu and King, public reason arguments were available and made by them. Absent manifest injustice, we think that the norms we defend as part of an exclusive account of public reason are appropriate because these norms express proper respect for persons as free and equal citizens and they allow citizens to define and understand their relationship from a shared standpoint. As we argued above, this is consistent with respecting the integrity of persons who accept the values constitutive of a liberal democratic society.

We have suggested that concerns about integrity do not challenge an exclusive account of public reason, in part, because persons as free and equal citizens adopt a particular point of view for public, political deliberation. When persons adopt a particular point of view as citizens, they regard it as appropriate to respect a principle of restraint. This is similar to how persons in various professional roles put aside their particular worldviews for a certain purpose when acting in a particular domain. Consider that lawyers recognize and are bound to certain professional duties. In their professional sphere, they act in accordance with the norms of the profession, but they may not recognize these norms as appropriate for other spheres of life, associations, and relationships. Pharmacists, too, recognize certain professional norms, and in their role as pharmacists act in accordance with professional norms such as dispensing medications with a valid prescription even if their personal beliefs and values are such that they do not think that persons should use certain medications. The point is that persons who have certain professional roles must be guided by the norms of their profession, and not their particular beliefs and values, when they act in their professional role. This is not generally thought to undermine integrity. Of course, should the exercise of professional duties be judged to be too onerous or in deep conflict with one's broader value scheme, any individual may choose to leave a profession. This is where the analogy between persons in professional roles and persons deliberating as free and equal citizens is weakest—leaving political society is not a realistic option for many. But, importantly, there is a similarity between persons in their professional roles who must not treat their comprehensive values as definitive in executing their professional duties but, rather, must give primacy to their defined professional ethics, *and* persons in the role of a free and equal citizen. Citizens, similarly, must not treat their comprehensive values as definitive and hence primary when the idea of public reason applies, for citizenship entails taking up a particular point of view that acknowledges both the role of coercive law for all citizens and the ideal of democratic citizenship as a relation among equals, including those with whom one has reasonable disagreement.

V. Stability

The concerns that animate the various versions of the integrity objection raise questions that threaten to show that political liberalism is not possible. Political liberals, again, are concerned with the possibility of a just and stable liberal democratic state, where stability is not a mere modus vivendi but "stability for the right reasons." It must be the case that some reasonable political conception of justice can structure the main institutions of society viewed as a system, and such a reasonable political conception of justice can have the support of an overlapping consensus of reasonable comprehensive doctrines. A central condition for such stability is that citizens will come to judge that political values "normally outweigh" their comprehensive values, should the two come into conflict.[28] Even more, stability requires that citizens endorse the political conception of justice for moral reasons, not merely as a strategic arrangement or the best they can do under the circumstances. This is "stability for the right reasons." Thinking of concerns about integrity in terms of stability leads to important questions: (1) Are the defenders of the integrity objection denying that a basic structure organized in accordance with a reasonable political conception of justice could help to engender the moral motivation (a sense of justice) needed so that believers will "normally" judge that political values outweigh their comprehensive values when the two conflict? (2) Or are they denying that a political conception of justice can be a module, or find full justification, within some reasonable comprehensive doctrines? In other words, are they denying the possibility that reasonable religious or nonreligious comprehensive doctrines have the internal resources to justify, on moral grounds, some reasonable political conception of justice? Defenders of integrity challenges could have both worries in mind.

The first question is, ultimately, an empirical question that we won't try to address here. The second question can be addressed by showing that some reasonable comprehensive doctrines have the resources to support the central tenets of any reasonable political conception of justice. Rawls

---

[28] PL, p. 157.

aims to do this when he offers three examples of reasonable comprehensive doctrines that he thinks can support a reasonable political conception of justice. He considers a religious doctrine (with an account of free faith), a comprehensive liberal doctrine (such as found in Kant and Mill), and a pluralist view that is only partially comprehensive.[29] In each case, he aims to establish that the fundamental ideas ("society as a fair system of cooperation and of citizens as reasonable and rational, free and equal") can find support, and be endorsed, as a part of those doctrines. These illustrations are useful; however, the key to the argument lies in the claim that any reasonable comprehensive doctrine must come to recognize that cooperation with others on fair terms is possible only under a reasonable constitutional democracy. In addressing the question, Rawls writes:

> How is it possible—or is it—for those of faith, as well as the nonreligious (secular), to endorse a constitutional regime even when their comprehensive doctrines may not prosper under it, and indeed may decline? Here the answer lies in the religious or nonreligious doctrine's understanding and accepting that, except by endorsing a reasonable constitutional democracy, there is no other way fairly to ensure the liberty of its adherents consistent with the equal liberties of other reasonable free and equal citizens.[30]

Philosophers, aiming to establish the plausibility of political liberalism, can make arguments from conjecture as to how some reasonable comprehensive doctrine can support a political conception of justice. Rawls engages in such "reasoning from conjecture" in aiming to show how various comprehensive doctrines can support a political conception of justice and become part of a reasonable overlapping consensus. Moreover, he thinks such reasoning from conjecture has an important role to play within political society, among citizens. "In this case we reason from what we believe, or conjecture, may be other people's basic doctrines, religious or philosophical, and seek to show them that despite what they may think, they can still endorse a reasonable political conception of justice."[31] Beyond such illustrations and arguments from conjecture, we cannot know in

---

[29] PL, p. 145.

[30] IPRR, p. 590.

[31] IPRR, p. 591.

advance whether a reasonable overlapping consensus will emerge. At this point, the best we can do is offer arguments that it is a plausible hope, a realistic hope. Part of establishing that such a hope is reasonable, and not delusional, of course, is showing that the demands of justice and the use of public reason are not too much, too much psychic strain or too much of a burden or, even, an unfair burden. This is what the integrity objection, in some of its versions, denies. We do not think this objection is ultimately successful, as we have tried to show here.

5

Religious Exemptions

In the question of liberty of conscience, which has for some years been so much bandied amongst us, one thing that hath chiefly perplexed the question, kept up the dispute, and increased the animosity, hath been, I conceive, this, that both parties have, with equal zeal and mistake, too much enlarged their pretensions, whilst one side preach up absolute obedience, and the other claim universal liberty in matters of conscience, without assigning what those things are which have a title to liberty, or showing the boundaries of imposition and obedience.

—JOHN LOCKE, *"An Essay Concerning Toleration"*

I. Introduction

In the United States, the Religious Clauses of the U.S. Constitution together with federal and state religious freedom and restoration acts treat religion as special.[1] The Establishment Clause precludes the state from instituting a state religion. Furthermore, as interpreted in constitutional law doctrine, it forbids laws that are motivated solely by religious purposes.[2] As such, religious purposes appear to be singled out for exclusion in justifying laws, and so are special in that regard.[3] The Free Exercise Clause protects the

---

[1] For a very informative discussion of U.S. constitutional doctrine, as well as useful taxonomy of the ways in which one might treat religion as "special", see Schwartzman, "What If Religion Is Not Special?"

[2] Schwartzman, "What If Religion Is Not Special?," p. 356.

[3] In *Lemon v. Kurtzman*, 403 U.S. 602 (1971), the U.S. Supreme Court articulated a three-part test for Establishment Clause analysis. *Lemon*'s holding articulated a strong test for constitutional permissibility. According to *Lemon*, first, the Court must ask whether the law has a secular purpose; if it does not, it violates the Establishment Clause. Second, the Court must ask whether the primary effect of the law is to inhibit or advance religion; if so, it violates the Establishment Clause. Third, the Court must assess whether there is excessive government entanglement with religion; if so, the law violates the Establishment Clause. However, multiple rulings since *Lemon* have weakened the requirement of "a secular purpose." Current constitutional doctrine defines as impermissible laws that are solely

practice of religion, and the federal and state religious freedom and restoration acts provide conditions under which persons can claim exemptions from generally applicable laws if a law substantially burdens a person's religious practice.[4] Hence, religion is special in this way, too. The ability to live in accordance with other commitments, including secular moral obligations, is not given such special treatment in the law, though, occasionally, exemptions have been granted on secular grounds.[5]

As a matter of political morality, the special treatment of religion in the law raises important questions. In this chapter, we consider if political liberals can recognize religion as special and, as a result, recognize exemptions from generally applicable laws on religious grounds. Hence, we advance the discussion of religion and integrity in the previous chapter insofar as some persons may claim that absent a basis for religious exemptions from some generally applicable laws, the demands of public reason will result in laws that unfairly disadvantage or burden religious persons.

Political liberalism must imply a principle substantively like the U.S. Constitution's Establishment Clause. Central to political liberalism is the recognition of the fact of reasonable pluralism.[6] The state does not make official comparisons or assessments of the value of different *reasonable* comprehensive doctrines (although not all comprehensive doctrines are viewed as reasonable), and the state's establishment of religion would threaten this commitment. Moreover, with respect to matters related to principles of basic justice and constitutional essentials, political liberals require that only reasons shared by persons as free and equal citizens (in their capacity as citizens) can serve as sufficient justifications for certain

---

"motivated by an impermissible purpose" (religion) or when "it can be said that the law's preeminent purpose is religious." For further discussion, see Esbeck, "The Lemon Test."

[4] For an overview of Free Exercise exemptions and related issues, see Duncan, "Free Exercise under Current Doctrine."

[5] In *United States v. Seeger*, 380 U.S. 163 (1965), the Court held that conscientious objector status could not be restricted solely to religious beliefs. Considering the section of the relevant statute's reference to a Supreme Being, the Court says, the relevant test of belief "in relation to a Supreme Being" is "whether a given belief that is sincere and meaningful occupies a place in the life of its possessor parallel to that filled by the orthodox belief in God of one who clearly qualifies for the exemption" (p. 67). Other examples of exemptions on moral grounds (as well as religious) include participation in executions (18 U.S.C. § 3579(b) (1994)) and participation in sterilization or abortion (42 U.S.C.§ 300a-7(b)(1) (2000)).

[6] PL, p. xx.

principles and laws.[7] Insofar as principles and laws are reasonable for all persons to accept as free and equal citizens, state establishment of religion is a nonstarter.

Furthermore, political liberals' basic commitments suggest that we should be skeptical that religious accommodations or exemptions from laws are appropriate. If certain principles and laws are viewed as reasonably justified to reasonable persons as free and equal citizens, on what grounds could an exemption be claimed? In other words, if certain principles and laws must be justifiable to all reasonable persons as reasonable from the point of view of free and equal citizens, then the idea of an exemption from those principles and laws that are reasonably justified seems peculiar. One requesting an exemption would be saying something like "Yes, that principle or law is reasonably justifiable to *me* as a citizen, and yet, given my particular worldview, I should be exempted from compliance." Of course, political liberals need not claim that the idea of public reason applies to all laws and policies; Rawls limits the idea of public reason to matters of basic justice and constitutional essentials.[8] And we defended this scope of public reason in chapter 3. The idea of exemptions from generally applicable laws might have some traction in cases in which the idea of public reason does not apply. Further complicating matters for political liberals, however, is the centrality of equal liberty of conscience to the view, which is regarded as a constitutional essential and as a motivating feature of the project. Indeed, Rawls makes it quite clear that protecting liberty of conscience is a central motivation for persons to seek terms of cooperation in political society and that sacrificing such liberty is rational only in very limited circumstances. Thus, perhaps, religious or conscience-based exemptions would be recognized as warranted in some cases within a politically liberal society.

We argue that despite these initial grounds for skepticism, political liberals can recognize religious accommodations or exemptions in some limited cases. However, we claim that political liberals cannot single out religion, in particular, for special treatment; when other commitments

---

[7] See, e.g., PL, IPRR, and Quong, *Liberalism without Perfectionism*. Some argue that political liberalism's core commitments are consistent with either an account of shared reasons or accessible reasons as public reasons. See Vallier, *Liberal Politics and Public Faith*.

[8] Compare with Quong, though, who argues the scope of public reason includes all laws and policies for which a public justification is possible (*Liberalism without Perfectionism*, pp. 273–287). We discuss and critique Quong's view in chapter 3.

function in the same way as religiously based commitments, those commitments should enjoy the same status as grounds for exemptions. Political liberals cannot recognize exemptions or accommodations on any basis from a law that is needed to secure and protect the equal standing of all persons as free and equal citizens. Of course, some cases are complex, as our discussion will show. We close by considering the objection that our view is not administrable and, hence, is practically unworkable. We offer reasons for thinking this worry is unwarranted.

II. Rawls on Equal Liberty of Conscience and Conscientious Refusal

Rawls never explicitly addresses the issue of religious exemptions from generally applicable laws. However, he does discuss both equal liberty of conscience and conscientious refusal. We examine his views on these topics, together with our interpretation of the key commitments of political liberalism, to develop our view. In *Theory*, he says, "The parties [in the original position] must assume that they may have moral, religious, or philosophical interests which they cannot put in jeopardy unless there is no alternative. One might say that they regard themselves as having moral or religious obligations which they must keep themselves free to honor."[9] He continues that since the parties in the original position are behind the veil of ignorance and do not know their own values and beliefs, they will choose a principle of equal liberty, including equal liberty of conscience: "They cannot take chances with their liberty by permitting the dominant religious or moral doctrine to persecute or to suppress others if they wish."[10] Constitutional principles are, then, determined in accordance with the principle of equal liberty and equal liberty of conscience, which Rawls claims will result in a regime "guaranteeing moral liberty and freedom of thought and belief, and of religious practice."[11] Rawls does not single out religion in his discussions of equal liberty; rather he treats religiously grounded claims of conscience as a type of broader moral conscience. While such principles respecting forms of conscience are central values in liberal democracies, they do admit of limitation in

---

[9] TJ, pp. 180–181.

[10] TJ, p. 180.

[11] TJ, p. 186.

some cases; he recognizes "public order and security" as appropriate for justifying limits on liberty of conscience.[12] Rawls says this is reflected in the reasoning of those in the original position. He adds: "disruption of these conditions is a danger for the liberty of all" and "the maintenance of public order is understood as a necessary condition for everyone's achieving his ends whatever they are (provided they live within certain limits) and for his fulfilling his interpretation of his moral and religious obligations."[13]

While Rawls never explicitly addresses the question of the justifiability of religious exemptions, he has a lengthy discussion of the justification of conscientious refusal. This discussion is instructive. Rawls understands conscientious refusal as the refusal to obey a legal injunction or an administrative order grounded in an appeal to values that reflect one's "conscience."[14] Although a person may claim to conscientiously refuse to obey an order or injunction by appealing to political principles, a person may do so on religious or moral grounds as well;[15] a pacifist's refusal to join the army is a paradigm case. Consider Rawls's analysis of conscientious refusal on religious grounds:

> It is a difficult matter to find the right course when some men appeal to religious principles in refusing to do actions which, it seems, are required by principles of political justice. Does the pacifist possess an immunity from military service in a just war, assuming that there are such wars? Or is the state permitted to impose hardships for noncompliance? There is a temptation to say that the law must always respect the dictates of conscience, but this cannot be right. . . . A theory of justice must work out from its own point of view how to treat those who dissent from it. . . . If a religion is denied its full expression, it is presumably because it is in violation of the equal liberties of others. In general, the degree of tolerance accorded opposing moral conceptions depends upon the

---

[12] TJ, p. 186.

[13] TJ, p. 187.

[14] TJ, pp. 323–324.

[15] TJ, p. 324.

extent to which they can be allowed an equal place within a just system of liberty.[16]

From his discussion of equal liberty of conscience and conscientious refusal, we should note that Rawls clearly distinguishes the category of conscientious concerns—moral or religious—from other commitments or projects as potentially grounding claims for exemptions (or at least justifiable excuses, even if not formal legal exemptions). Yet, Rawls does not discuss exemptions from generally applicable laws apart from his discussion of pacifism. One reason Rawls may not offer such a discussion is that he may have thought that under the conditions of ideal theory claims for exemptions from generally applicable laws would not arise.[17] After all, if fundamental laws and principles are justified by shared reasons to all *reasonable* people, on what grounds could an individual claim an entitlement to an exemption? What is clear from the quote above is that a principle of equal liberty is a limiting principle for considering any claims for exemptions. The principle of equal liberty may not be violated, and so any consideration of whether and when exemptions may be permitted must respect this boundary.

III. Political Liberalism, Freedom of Religion, and Freedom of Conscience

Political liberals recognize a plurality of reasonable and conflicting comprehensive doctrines, and, as noted, the state does not judge the value of or make comparisons about the worth of them. This is not to say that political liberals aim for neutrality of effect when it comes to how laws affect comprehensive doctrines.[18] That is not possible, and what matters

---

[16] TJ, p. 325.

[17] In *Political Liberalism*, Rawls does say, though, that "justice as fairness honors, as far as it can, the claims of those who wish to withdraw from the modern world in accordance with the injunctions of their religion, provided only that they acknowledge the principles of the political conception of justice and appreciate its political ideals of person and society" (p. 200).

[18] Rawls distinguishes "neutrality of aim" from "neutrality of effect" in specifying the kind of "neutrality" with which political liberalism is concerned. Political liberalism does not aim for neutrality of effect—where all comprehensive doctrines are equally impacted, as it were, by the principles of justice. Rather, it tries to be neutral in its aim: "Institutions and policies

for those laws under the scope of public reason is that they are publicly justified. We will return to this below. Here the point is just that *if* political liberals should recognize some religious exemptions on the basis of respecting conscientious concerns, then there seems to be a prima facie reason for them to recognize some exemptions having to do with secular, moral beliefs that concern moral conscience. Religious conscience and moral conscience should be treated the same in this regard.[19]

Yet some argue that if exemptions or accommodations are warranted in certain circumstances, there aren't good reasons to privilege moral or religiously grounded claims of conscience over other deeply held commitments or projects that are neither moral nor religious. Indeed, Simon May argues that "there is nothing special about moral conscience that would justify granting an exemption . . . that is not also shared by a variety of non-moral desires, motivations, concerns or projects."[20] He claims that the primary ways one might try to distinguish conscience from nonmoral projects apply to some nonmoral projects. For example, agents can understand projects that do not concern moral commitments to impose categorical demands, to concern life's ultimate meaning, to be the object of intense desires, and to be central to their identities.[21] Consider May's "Chester," who, like some of his friends, seeks an exemption from military service. His friends have objections to military service on the basis of religious or moral grounds; he, however, bases his claim on his project of being a chess grandmaster. He understands his project to place "categorical demands on his life," as do moral demands. In addition, he thinks that chess exemplifies "the awesome beauty of the mathematical universe," and so he understands the pursuit of greatness in chess to be a part of pursuing ultimate meaning. Being a chess player is a fundamental aspect of Chester's identity and rests on value claims that function in the same way as moral or religious claims do for some people. Assuming one

---

are neutral in the sense that they can be endorsed by citizens generally as within the scope of a public political conception" (PL, pp. 192–194).

[19] Perry argues that moral freedom is equivalent to religious freedom and so can similarly ground claims to accommodations or exemptions. See Perry, "From Religious Freedom to Moral Freedom."

[20] May, "Exemptions for Conscience," p. 191. This leads May to question the justifiability of any exemptions or accommodations. See also Arneson, "Against Freedom of Conscience," arguing that privileging conscience (and religious liberty) is "wrongful discrimination."

[21] May, "Exemptions for Conscience," pp. 197–198

finds May's Chester a compelling case for thinking nonmoral pursuits are not principally distinguishable from moral or religious pursuits, at least as concerns claims for exemptions, it raises the question as to whether political liberals should distinguish considerations of conscience from other categorical demands or life-defining commitments that are not moral in character when it comes to considering potential grounds for exemptions from generally applicable laws.

There are two issues here. One is whether there is a principled moral reason for political liberals to treat matters of conscience (religious or moral) differently from other projects that persons take to impose categorical demands or life-defining commitments when it comes to accommodations or exemptions. The other issue is, even if there is no principled reason for distinguishing between matters of conscience and other categorical or life-defining commitments, there may be practical reasons for doing so (e.g., administrative feasibility).

We do not see any principled grounds on which political liberals could treat matters of conscience differently from other projects that persons take to impose categorical demands or life-defining commitments. When describing the idea of a person's conception of the good Rawls stresses that persons are viewed as free to revise and change over the course of a life, and he says that persons should be thought of as having a determinate conception of the good that is broadly understood to include what is of value in human life. This is not limited to moral or religious concerns. In most cases, Rawls says that such a conception of the good includes "a more or less determinate scheme of final ends, that is, ends we want to realize for their own sake, as well as attachments to other persons and loyalties to various groups and associations," and that we relate to our view of the good "our relation to the world—religious, philosophical, and moral—by reference to which the value and significance of our ends and attachments are understood."[22] That some individuals will give nonmoral projects or commitments the same fundamental place that others give religion or morality in their lives is certainly possible and is not for that reason either irrational or unreasonable (as political liberals use these terms). However, it is hard to think of very many cases in which nonmoral

---

[22] PL, pp. 19–20.

projects or commitments function in the same way as religion and morality do for many people.[23] Yet, it is possible.

Imagine a vegetarian who is not a vegetarian on moral grounds but who embraces a vegetarian lifestyle as part of commitment to living in harmony with nature, which she regards as an aesthetic value. Such a person will see vegetarianism as central to her identity, as giving expression to fundamental meaning in the natural world. However, even in a case such as this, it is hard to imagine how generally applicable *laws* would interfere with the expression and practice of this worldview. To find conflict between expression and practice of this worldview or Chester's (in May's case) and generally applicable laws, we must look to extreme cases like conscription. Part of the explanation of why such conflicts are rare is surely that there are few cases of persons with such deep nonmoral commitments, but an additional part of the explanation, we conjecture, may simply be that many such projects and commitments don't tend to raise conflicts with laws insofar as persons with such commitments choose life plans with respect to employment or education that reflect their deeper values.

Religious and moral worldviews, however, may give rise to more conflicts with generally applicable laws because we don't have to go to extreme examples to find such principles ordering persons' lives, and some religious and moral views more often relate to or present tensions with aspects of mainstream social institutions. We will not consider nonmoral cases in any further detail here. We simply note that *if* political liberals should permit the recognition of exemptions or accommodations in certain circumstances, then they have no principled reason for privileging matters of conscience (religious or moral) over nonmoral commitments that are part of a person's view of the good. The principles we develop below, then, apply mutatis mutandis to nonmoral cases.

---

[23] Consider Nussbaum's alternative view in *Liberty of Conscience*. She favors special treatment for religion but relates it to conscience. She appeals to the work of Roger Williams, who emphasizes conscience. She claims that conscience is "the faculty with which each person searches for the ultimate meaning of life" and claims it has intrinsic worth and value (p. 168). Then she claims that "we ought to respect the space required by any activity that has the general shape of searching for the ultimate meaning of life except where that search violates the rights of others or comes up against some compelling state interest" (p. 169). She claims we can understand why religion gets special treatment if we understand it as tied to conscience so viewed, and she suggests that we can ease claims of unfairness by those who are not religious by "extending the account of religion as far as we can" (p. 173). In short, Nussbaum endorses singling out religion because she doesn't think a broader notion of conscience is workable in the law.

So far we have suggested that claims of moral conscience and claims grounded in religious belief should be treated as substantively similar, however it is they should be treated. Yet, Andrew Koppelman claims that the free exercise of religion should be distinguished from freedom of conscience, and he stresses that in many cases in which religious exemptions or accommodations in the United States are recognized and widely supported, they are not based on claims of conscience.[24] As he notes, religious practices are much broader than the category of religious conscience. He cites the use of peyote as part of ceremonies in the Native American Church as an example. It is often not duty that motivates persons to seek a religious exemption or accommodation but, rather, Koppelman says, factors such as habit, custom, coping with misfortune, or a desire to feel close to God. So, does this suggest that if political liberals should recognize accommodations or exemptions in certain cases, that categorical demands or life-defining commitments should not serve as the focus of the basis of accommodations or exemptions? We don't think so.

If exemptions or accommodations should be recognized at all, then there must be a compelling case, which only fundamental commitments may be able to justify. Otherwise accommodations or exemptions are simply unfair. However, if exemptions or accommodations should be recognized in some cases, then when practices or customs are central to a fundamental commitment, perhaps the case can be made to provide exemptions. In the peyote case, while the use of peyote isn't required by religious principles, it is believed to facilitate spirituality as central to the religious principles. In other kinds of cases, such as seeking exemptions from zoning laws, the claim to expand one's religious institution seems prima facie less compelling, for such a claim doesn't rest on the centrality of pursuing that claim as a part of one's religious practice, although we can imagine cases in which such centrality might be grounded (seeing a specific piece of land as sacred, for example). Our aim here is not to settle the various kinds of considerations relevant to granting or refusing to grant such an exemption, but simply to further explore more generally if and when political liberals may recognize accommodations or exemptions. And here we have argued that if political liberals should permit exemptions in some cases, there are no principled reasons for restricting the grounds of such claims to those grounded in moral or religious conscience.

---

[24] Koppelman, *Defending American Religious Neutrality*, p. 134.

IV. Equal Citizenship, Accommodations, and Exemptions

As we have argued, the idea of public reason "specifies at the deepest level the basic moral and political values that are to determine a constitutional democratic government's relation to its citizens and their relation to one another."[25] The moral foundation of the idea of public reason is the criterion of reciprocity. It requires that where public reason applies "when . . . terms are proposed as the most reasonable terms of fair cooperation, those proposing them must also think it at least reasonable for others to accept them, as free and equal citizens, and not as dominated or manipulated, or under the pressure of an inferior political or social position."[26] The very possibility of public reason requires the elimination of social conditions of domination and subordination relevant to reasonable democratic deliberation among equal citizens and the social conditions necessary for equal respect among persons as free and equal citizens.[27]

As previously argued, the scope of the idea of public reason is limited to matters of basic justice and constitutional essentials. Matters of basic justice and constitutional essentials concern persons' fundamental entitlements as free and equal citizens or their needs as free and equal citizens. Rawls claims that there is a plurality of reasonable political conceptions of justice that supply the "content" of public reason, but any reasonable political conception of justice includes "basic rights, liberties and opportunities" and priority for these over "claims of the general good or perfectionist value" as well as some general means for persons to pursue their good.[28] Central among citizens' needs are civil rights, some of which enable and protect the standing of all persons as free and equal citizens by forbidding discrimination in certain contexts on certain grounds. Such rights enable and protect participation in the public, political sphere for all as free and equal citizens as well as protect persons as equal citizens in civil society, in the workplace, and in all places of public accommodation.

---

[25] IPRR, p. 574.

[26] IPRR, p. 578.

[27] See Hartley and Watson, "Is a Feminist Political Liberalism Possible?," and see chapter 6 here, which is a revised version of that article.

[28] IPRR, pp. 581–582.

These rights enable the enjoyment of liberties of expression and conscience and the pursuit of reasonable conceptions of the good.

Now we are in a position to see why, in certain types of cases, political liberals cannot recognize accommodations or exemptions. First, imagine a politically liberal state in which a wedding vendor refuses to provide a service for a same-sex couple's wedding ceremony. Suppose, in that state, legal marriage[29] is recognized and individuals can marry one other person regardless of their sex or the sex of the person they want to marry. Also imagine that it is recognized that in order to secure the standing of all persons as free and equal citizens, discrimination on the basis of sexual orientation in places of public accommodation is prohibited. However, the vendor believes that same-sex marriage is immoral, and same-sex marriage is contrary to her religious beliefs. And on the basis of her deeply held religious beliefs, the vendor asks for an exemption from the requirement of accommodating persons regardless of sexual orientation. She thinks she will be violating morality and her religion if she serves the couple and that, in doing so, she will be cooperating with evil.

Despite the fact that there may be several other wedding vendors in the area who could deliver the same product, political liberals cannot recognize an exemption in this sort of case.[30] Here the vendor seeks an exemption from a law whose purpose is to enable and protect a person's standing as an equal citizen. That is, the antidiscrimination law in question protects a person's ability to participate in various spheres of social life as an equal member of society and the ability of the person to pursue a view of the good like fellow citizens. In other words, allowing public discrimination on the basis of factors such as sexual orientation, sex, or race creates a kind of second-class citizenship for some members of society. Such persons don't enjoy the same access to goods, even if identical goods are available

---

[29] On political liberalism and marriage, see Brake, "Minimal Marriage"; Hartley and Watson, "Political Liberalism, Marriage and the Family"; chapter 9 of this book.

[30] For alternative analyses of such cases, though not in the framework of political liberalism, see Corvino, Anderson, and Girgis, *Debating Religious Liberty and Discrimination*. Corvino argues that wedding vendors should not be legally required to make custom items such as cakes for gay weddings (or for other persons whose "lifestyle" they reject as immoral). However, he does think that they should be required to sell noncustom items that are readily available for public purchase. He thinks that custom items involve artistic or free expression, and persons should not be required to curtail such expression when it comes to values they reject.

elsewhere.[31] And insofar as being denied the rights and liberties that other persons as citizens enjoy in places of public accommodation affects their standing in the public, political sphere, their ability to engage in public reasoning is compromised.[32] Someone might claim that the liberty of the vendor to refuse service to a same-sex couple is a matter of equal standing, too; one might say it is important to one's standing as an equal citizen to enjoy the liberty to live in accordance with beliefs and values fundamental to one's identity. But this is precisely why understanding the role of the criterion of reciprocity and political liberalism's view of public reason is so important.

Principles of basic justice and constitutional essentials must be justified to persons viewed as free and equal citizens. Persons have the two moral powers: a capacity for a rational conception of the good and a capacity for a sense of justice. Persons' objective needs as citizens are developed in consideration of the interests associated with these capacities.[33] All persons need to be able to participate in certain spheres of social life as equals for political equality and in order to pursue their view of the good. This requires that persons are to be protected from discrimination on certain bases that are irrelevant to their status as citizens—such as sex, race, and sexual orientation.

Comprehensive doctrines and particular views of the good exist and develop within larger social contexts; for political liberals, the relevant context is that of equal citizenship. Equal liberty to live in accordance with one's values and beliefs is recognized in the context of citizens as such

---

[31] Koppelman disagrees with this analysis. He argues that persons should be allowed to refuse service to gays and lesbians on religious grounds provided they are willing to publicly state their intention to discriminate as such. He argues thinking that such discrimination should be prohibited by providers of public accommodations rests on a misunderstanding of the purpose of antidiscrimination law. Antidiscrimination law aims to undo structural inequalities rather than mere personal injuries, since discrimination against gays in public accommodations is relatively rare and few will be willing to announce themselves as public discriminators, granting the accommodation is the best way to protect equal liberty for the religious. See his "Gay Rights, Religious Accommodations."

[32] We argue for this claim in Hartley and Watson, "Is A Feminist Political Liberalism Possible?" and in chapter 6.

[33] Political liberals need not, and we do not, accept Rawls's social primary goods as the proper metric of justice. Political liberals, though, should endorse an objective metric of justice, and, so, we will refer to persons' objective needs or interests as citizens. Indeed, we also think that Rawls's conception of personhood is exclusionary and unacceptable as it stands, but we can't address that here either.

having certain entitlements, including being served in places of public accommodation regardless of sex, race, or sexual orientation. In this way, we
might say that—from the public, political point of view—one's standing
as an equal citizen is prior to one's conception of the good. Claims to
accommodations or entitlements to pursue one's conception of the good
in ways that conflict with the basic recognition of the equal standing of all
citizens, as citizens, don't get uptake because they fail to understand that
pursuit of one's good requires living in accordance with the principles and
laws justified to all persons as free and equal citizens; this includes the
laws that protect the recognition of all persons as free and equal citizens.
The wedding vendor's refusal to serve same-sex couples is unacceptable
in a liberal democratic state ordered by public reason because places of
public accommodation cannot deny service to persons due to factors that
undermine, threaten, or deny their status as equal citizens. In effect, the
wedding vendor is claiming "my equal liberty" requires the denial of your
equal liberty; this is not a claim that is consistent with the norms of reciprocity that are foundational to liberal justice.

Consider another case. In a politically liberal society, access to basic
health care is a matter of justice. In recognition of this, the state provides
all citizens with access to a health care package, and this includes access to
various contraceptives for women, including emergency contraceptives.
Suppose this package is publicly justified in accordance with the interests
of persons as free and equal citizens. Now imagine a pharmacist in this
state refuses to fill a prescription for a woman who seeks an emergency
contraceptive. The pharmacist regards the use of the contraceptive in
question to be contrary to her religious doctrine and morally wrong. She
claims the state should exempt pharmacists from dispensing medications
that pharmacists understand to be contrary to their religious and/or
moral beliefs.

Should the state exempt pharmacists from having to dispense
medications to which they have a conscientious objection? Here, again,
we argue political liberals cannot recognize an exemption under these
conditions. If a particular health care package is publicly justified to all
persons as free and equal citizens, then pharmacists must dispense medication in accordance with the law or find other work. Citizens depend
on health care professionals for access to certain goods. Some will argue
that the woman who seeks an emergency contraceptive may have other
options from pharmacists who are not conscientious objectors and that,
when this is the case, exemptions should be recognized in order to respect

conscientious-objector pharmacists.[34] We disagree. Pharmacists must fill prescriptions in accordance with the law. It is their job to give those with valid prescriptions the medications to which they are legally entitled, as health care is a basic good for which they provide access. While it would be nice for a fellow pharmacist (working at the same time and location) to immediately step in and fill a prescription for another pharmacist who has an objection or concern about some medication, this is not required.

The underlying principle in both these cases is that where claims for exemptions rest on a supposed individual right to refuse to recognize or respect equal citizenship and the entitlements that flow from equal citizenship, such as the fundamental rights of others, political liberals will reject such claims. To reemphasize a point made earlier: the right to pursue one's conception of the good is conditioned upon accepting the basic framework of liberal justice and endorsement of the criterion of reciprocity. Moreover, as we emphasized earlier, reciprocity requires that when one proposes reasonable terms of fair cooperation, "those proposing them must also think it is at least reasonable for others to accept them, as free and equal citizens, and not as dominated or manipulated, or under the pressure of an inferior political or social position."[35] Religious claims to exemptions from civil rights laws are not compatible with political liberalism's view of reciprocity among citizens. The refusal to grant an exemption in cases like this does not similarly rest on a claim of *inferiority*; in fact, such refusal can be read as premised on *equality*. We require the equal recognition of all citizens as free and equal, and so treat all conceptions of the good as subject to the same restraints.

A more difficult issue arises in cases where claims to self-governance of religious institutions and doctrines conflict with fundamental liberal, democratic principles. Presently in the United States churches are permitted a "ministerial exemption" that excuses them from certain sex discrimination laws (and other discrimination laws as well).[36]

---

[34] Thanks to Kevin Vallier for urging us to address this in the text.

[35] IPPR, p. 578.

[36] The Equal Employment Opportunity Commission (EEOC) describes the ministerial exception as follows: "Courts have held, based on First Amendment constitutional considerations, that clergy members cannot bring claims under the federal employment discrimination laws, including Title VII, the Age Discrimination in Employment Act, the Equal Pay Act, and the Americans with Disabilities Act, because '[t]he relationship between an organized church and its ministers is its lifeblood.'" This "ministerial exception" comes not from the text of the statutes but from the First Amendment principle that governmental

Imagine a politically liberal state in which a church refuses to ordain women as priests because religious doctrine requires that priests be male. Suppose in the state there is also a principle of basic justice requiring fair equality of opportunity in employment and that in connection with that principle there are laws prohibiting sex discrimination in the workplace. Imagine the church in this case claims that, according to its religious doctrine, "maleness" is an essential qualification for priesthood. One might claim that religious freedom requires that members of religious institutions be able to define and interpret their own doctrine and that their doctrines may bear on qualifications for church employment. We certainly agree that members of religious institutions must be free to define and interpret their own doctrines and that religious institutions can certainly discriminate among members and nonmembers in certain cases as well as with respect to a variety of factors.

However, as Cass Sunstein asks, members of religious institutions must comply with "ordinary civil and criminal law" in their religious practices; why should they be permitted to discriminate on the basis of sex in employment even if sex or gender discrimination is part of their doctrine?[37] Sunstein suggests that there is a possible justification for treating criminal and civil law asymmetrically in cases in which the effect of a law on a religion (or religious institution) outweighs the nature and strength of a state's interest in a law. However, he thinks there is "no general barrier" (on liberal grounds) "to applying such laws to religious institutions."[38] For Sunstein, whether such asymmetry is

---

regulation of church administration, including the appointment of clergy, impedes the free exercise of religion and constitutes impermissible government entanglement with church authority. Thus, courts will not ordinarily consider whether a church's employment decision concerning one of its ministers was based on discriminatory grounds, although some courts have allowed ministers to bring sexual harassment claims.

The ministerial exception applies only to those employees who perform essentially religious functions, namely those whose primary duties consist of engaging in church governance, supervising a religious order, or conducting religious ritual, worship, or instruction. The exception is not limited to ordained clergy, and has been applied by courts to others involved in clergy-like roles who conduct services or provide pastoral counseling. However, the exception does not necessarily apply to everyone with a title typically conferred upon clergy (e.g., a minister). In short, in each case it is necessary to make a factual determination of whether the function of the position is one to which the exception applies." See EEOC, *Compliance Manual*, July 22, 2008, http://www.eeoc.gov/policy/docs/religion.html.

[37] Sunstein, "Should Sex Equality Law Apply to Religious Institutions?"

[38] Sunstein, "Should Sex Equality Law Apply to Religious Institutions?," p. 93.

justifiable in a particular case will depend on the analysis of the relative interests at stake.

More strongly, Clare Chambers argues that liberals are too quick to permit liberal values such as religious choice or freedom of association to justify religious exemptions from employment antidiscrimination laws. Chambers singles out Brian Barry for criticism, as Barry is a liberal who champions equal opportunity in employment and who, nonetheless, argues that the state should not require Catholics to ordain women because "freedom of religious worship . . . can be achieved only if people are free to attach themselves to churches with a variety of doctrines."[39] Chambers rejects this argument; she argues the choice of individuals to follow their view of a doctrine isn't violated if women are ordained since no one would require any Catholic to interact with priests who are women (e.g., receive sacraments from a woman). (But, of course, some members of the church would likely be required to act against a doctrine they accept in ordaining women.) Chambers adds that in these cases, liberals errone-ously focus on freedom of association, on adults' voluntary membership in religious institutions, and on the liberal protection of persons' freedom of exit. She claims that the liberal preoccupation with choice as the "de-terminant of justice" misses that cultural and religious norms socially construct persons' choices and options and, under certain conditions, frustrate or undermine freedom and equality. Further, she argues that we should not let choice settle questions of justice when both of the following factors are present: "the choice in question harms the chooser in relation to those who choose differently" and "there are identifiable pressures on the choosing group to make that choice."[40] When religious groups engage in sex-based employment discrimination, there are gendered outcomes that advantage men and disadvantage women, and there is incredible pressure on women to accept the circumstance, even if they prefer the situation were otherwise.

In her analysis, Chambers stresses that individuals are largely born into religious groups and that children are nonvoluntarily indoctrinated into their parents' beliefs. This influences what children believe: "that women are not equal to men in the arena of worship, that women are not fit to lead their fellow worshippers, and that the voice of women does not

---

[39] Chambers, *Sex, Culture, and Justice*, p. 141 (quoting Barry's *Culture and Equality*, p. 174).

[40] Chambers, *Sex, Culture, and Justice*, p. 120.

need to be heard when religious leaders are formulating policy."[41] Women within the group who want to take certain positions do not have the opportunity. Women's choices, Chambers adds, are surely further affected by the fact that when women are restricted from leadership positions they have less power when it comes to the group's policies on the rights of women in the group.[42] We agree with many of Chambers's claims. Some liberals are too quick to make choice the determinant of justice and do not properly attend to the ways in which social norms construct choices and options in ways that result in the subordination of some social groups to others.

However, as we argue in chapter 6 and later chapters, political liberalism's criterion of reciprocity requires the elimination of social positions that undermine persons' standing as free and equal citizens and, too, requires the state to secure the conditions of recognition respect among persons as free and equal citizens. Certainly, social norms and practices as they operate through institutions and associations may create and sustain precisely the kinds of social positions that political liberals must address as contrary to equal citizenship. A church that refuses to ordain women, unquestionably expresses the view that women are not equal to men and that women within and outside of the church are inferior in certain respects; also, women within the church suffer in terms of power and privilege and, perhaps, other goods. Does this undermine women's position as free and equal citizens in society? It depends.

If this religious doctrine is so widely held in the background culture of society that the influence of the church structures much of social life, then it may. Securing free and equal citizenship for all members of society may require that the church be prevented from sex discrimination in employment as it draws from members of the church to fill open positions. However, if the church is one of many in a pluralistic society with numerous comprehensive doctrines, then a number of factors must be taken into account, which most likely support permitting a religious exemption for sex discrimination in employment.

Imagine the religious institution whose doctrine forbids the ordination of women is one among many in a society in which some persons are religious and some are not and that among the various religious institutions

---

[41] Chambers, *Sex, Culture, and Justice*, p. 141.

[42] Chambers, *Sex, Culture, and Justice*, pp. 141–142.

in society there are varied views about sex and gender. The church's doctrine is not benign when it comes to the status of women as free and equal citizens, but its affect is blunted in the background culture by various other views. Furthermore, other factors are important: considerations such as freedom of expression and association as well as the protections and entitlements of women as free and equal citizens, including women's right to exit any private association and, too, consideration of the fact that private associations differ from public accommodations in that they are not open to the public but membership is based on common commitment to norms and practices, which are voluntarily endorsed by adults.

None of this is to deny Chambers's views about the social construction of choice, but it is meant to deny that equal citizenship for women in most modern democracies demands that women be ordained in all of society's religious institutions. Here we should stress that civil rights laws, in their particulars, are always aimed at being responsive to the actual conditions of inequality that serve to subordinate members of marginalized groups. That civil rights laws in the United States, for example, targeted education, housing, public accommodations, and the like was a response to the particular forms of inequality manifest in particular historical conditions.

To more fully make our case, consider how we would distinguish between this matter and the pharmacist case, in which we concluded no exemptions are permissible for acts of conscience that deny women access to the medications concerning their reproductive care and health. As we emphasized, pharmacies are public accommodations, under the meaning of relevant civil rights laws, and we argued that permitting individual pharmacists to refuse to dispense medication to women for which they have a prescription denies them their basic rights. But, unlike pharmacies, churches are private associations that impose conditions on membership consistent with their religious beliefs. It is not, for example, discrimination on the basis of religion for a church to refuse membership to someone who expressly rejects its core principles of religious interpretation. Nor is it discrimination on the basis of religion for a Catholic church to refuse to perform marriage ceremonies for non-Catholics. In other words, churches by the kind of associations that they are—holders and interpreters of a religious doctrine—permissibly limit access to participation and enjoyment of the services and goods they offer. Moreover, it is crucial that membership in a religious institution is fully voluntary for adults and there can be no legal penalty for exit.

As Chambers points out, persons often inherit their religion, and children raised within religious doctrines do not exercise choice about membership. However, we think that her emphasis on the fact that adult women originally inherited their religion (from their families, presumably) is overblown. In sufficiently liberal modern societies and with sufficient education, many adults reject the religion of their families of origin; thus under liberal conditions it seems unlikely that too many adult women feel trapped in their religion. Children are a separate concern, however, and again, sufficiently robust education in liberal societies is a necessary measure to ensure that adults are capable of (psychological) exit from any religious institution and of accepting or rejecting its doctrines.

So, while politically liberal states are not prevented in all cases from intervening in religious institutions with sex discriminatory practices, whether it is justified in a particular case depends. Fair equality of opportunity in employment is a matter of basic justice, and antidiscrimination laws in employment are crucial to securing such opportunity. However, a religious institution is a private association, composed of individuals who affirm, roughly, the same doctrine; it is not a business of public accommodation, it does not draw from the general public for persons suitable to fill the position in question, and it is not for profit. These are crucial differences from the kinds of cases we considered above. Of course, fair equality of opportunity is a fundamental issue of justice, as are sex and racial equality. And gender norms that are part of religious doctrines affect persons' general views about proper gender relations and social roles, and children are nonvoluntarily subjected to their parents' views and the doctrines of religious institutions. State intervention that denies practices related to the internal workings of religious doctrines for the sake of sex or racial equality in employment, through coercive laws barring such religiously based discrimination, is reasonably considered unduly intrusive in most cases. Yet, concerns about sex equality can be addressed through citizenship education and other social policy. For example, if tax exemption status for religious institutions is permissible in a politically liberal society,[43] then the state may refuse to grant it to institutions whose practices are in tension with fair equality of opportunity.[44] Thus, we think that while the state usually oversteps if it aims to coercively restructure

---

[43] But we are very skeptical of this!

[44] Consider *Bob Jones University v. United States*, 461 U.S. 574 (1983).

religious doctrine through laws, the state need not provide supports (in the form of tax exemption) to such religious institutions.

There are other cases, too, where exemptions are warranted. In a politically liberal society, entitlement to the goods of basic justice can be conditioned, for those who are able, upon the willingness to participate in the scheme of cooperation. So, for example, for those who are able to participate in the workforce or do socially necessary work such as caring for dependent members of society, access to all-purpose means to pursue a view of the good (income and wealth) can be conditioned upon the willingness to perform available work for which one is qualified.[45] Consider just the labor market for the sake of this example. In any society, employers may set the workweek for their firm in accordance with various factors, including customs and traditions some of which may stem from majority religious observances. This is not as such unjust. But imagine an individual whose employer changes the workweek and his new schedule conflicts with his weekly day of religious observance.[46] He refuses to work on that day, and his employer dismisses him for cause. Dismissal for cause makes the individual ineligible for unemployment insurance from the state. The individual seeks an exemption in this case on the grounds that the practice of his religion forbids him from working on that day, and he claims he would be denied equal citizenship if his claim is not granted. Political liberals can certainly recognize an exemption for the individual in this case on the grounds of equal citizenship. Insofar as an individual holds a reasonable comprehensive doctrine, we can say that it is a historical contingency that his religion or cultural traditions are not in the majority in the area and, thus, the customs upon which the workweek for the region is based.

Hence, when it comes to the principles and laws that protect equal citizenship, political liberals do not settle the matter of accommodations and exemptions by considering the burden of a law on a person against the interest of the state. Rather, if a law is needed to protect and secure the equal

---

[45] When describing one way in which *democratic equality* ensures individual responsibility, Elizabeth Anderson states, "In the typical case of an able-bodied adult . . . access to a decent income would be conditioned on responsible performance of one's duties in one's job, assuming a job was available" ("What's the Point of Equality?," p. 328). We think political liberals would endorse this.

[46] We have in mind circumstances similar to those described in *Sherbert v. Verner* 374 U.S. 398 (1963).

standing of all persons as free and equal citizens, then exemptions and accommodations—even if grounded in deeply held commitments—are precluded. We stress that those laws that secure free and equal citizenship for all are justified on the basis of public reasons that are shared by persons viewed as free and equal citizens. Of course, sometimes accommodations or exemptions from laws that help to secure persons' interests as free and equal citizens can be recognized if recognizing the accommodation or exemption will not undermine the persons' fundamental interests as citizens and sometimes exemptions are needed to secure equal citizenship, too.

V. Accommodations and Exemptions beyond Equal Citizenship

In many cases, requests for accommodations or exemptions do not raise issues that relate to considerations of the fundamental interests of citizens, that is, issues related to matters of basic justice or constitutional essentials. And political liberals restrict the requirements of public reason to matters relating to basic justice and constitutional essentials.[47] Outside the scope of public reason, persons as citizens or as public officials need not be concerned with offering reasons for laws and policies that they think are reasonably shared by persons as free and equal citizens. Indeed, the objective interests of citizens, arguably, do not provide a basis of reasons for all the policies and laws that could be legitimately enacted in a politically liberal state. For example, persons' fundamental interests as citizens will not settle, albeit they may contribute to, issues such as zoning laws, environmental protections, and some choices about public spending (such as whether and how to allocate funds among public libraries, the arts, and recreational areas). With this in mind, consider, again, that in a politically liberal society, the state does not assess the value of or compare the value of reasonable comprehensive doctrines. Of course, the state recognizes that generally applicable laws affect individuals differently in their pursuit of the good. However, neutrality of effect is not possible. What is important is whether a law has a sufficient justification. However, what if a law significantly burdens an individual in his or her religious practice or

---

[47] Quong, again, argues that public reason should apply to all laws and policies for which a public justification is possible (*Liberalism without Perfectionism*, pp. 273–287). Hence, his view would entail a different analysis for accommodations and exemptions.

in fulfilling a moral obligation or in living in accordance with his or her deep commitments? How should political liberals address requests for accommodations or exemptions outside of the scope of public reason?

A just society secures for individuals the conditions of freedom for all persons on a basis of mutual respect. But some legitimate laws, while important and while they serve the public good or common interest, severely infringe upon the pursuit of reasonable views of the good. In the United States, the Religious Freedom and Restoration Act of 1993 prevents the federal government from "substantially burdening" a person's religious exercise unless the government shows a "compelling state interest" and the law is the "least restrictive means" for advancing that interest.[48] We think that, outside the scope of public reason, political liberals, too, should be committed to the recognition of accommodations or exemptions from generally applicable laws when such a law imposes a severe burden on a person's pursuit of the good and when this burden is not outweighed by the state's interest in the law. Certainly, some more precise notion of a severe burden is in order as well as some way of understanding how strong a state's interest needs to be to outweigh a severe burden. We cannot address that here. Rather, we simply aim to highlight why political liberals should make some room for some accommodations or exemptions from generally applicable laws and offer an example of a compelling case.

Again, central to political liberalism is the recognition of the fact of reasonable pluralism: reasonable people will accept a plurality of different and irreconcilable yet reasonable comprehensive doctrines. In recognition of this and in recognition of the fact that generally applicable laws may serve important interests but, nonetheless, impose severe burdens on some persons' fundamental commitments, political liberals should be especially sensitive to the imposition of severe burdens on reasonable pursuits of the good without weighty justification. Of course, from the point of view of the state, persons are responsible for their ends. Rawls says:

> Citizens as free and equal are to be at liberty to take charge of their lives and each is expected by others to adapt their conception of the good to their expected fair share of primary goods. The only restriction on plans of life is their being compatible with the public

---

[48] 42 U.S. Code § 2000bb-1.

principles of justice, and claims may be advanced only for certain kinds of things (primary goods) and in ways specified by those principles.[49]

Of course, in this passage, Rawls specifically has in mind principles of basic justice and constitutional essentials. Claims of fundamental justice must concern what people are entitled to given the public political conception of justice. And where principles of fundamental justice are concerned, citizens must conform their pursuits to be compatible with those principles. Yet it is not true that "the *only* restriction on plans of life is their being compatible with the public principles of justice." In modern liberal democratic states, the state makes numerous laws to facilitate cooperative projects for the public good and common interests. These laws affect a person's pursuit of the good, and in a just, politically liberal society, there would very likely be some such laws. As a result, while citizens must be responsible for their ends, given principles of basic justice, constitutional essentials, and justifiable generally applicable laws, accommodations and exemptions can be warranted if severe burdens are imposed for the sake of common interests, for coordination, or for the public good when those interests are not sufficiently weighty.

Consider an example. Suppose that a state's drug law is such that it prohibits possession of peyote. However, use of peyote during ceremonies is part of the rituals of the Native American Church. It is a severe burden for members of the church to not be able to engage in ritualistic use of the drug during ceremonies. While the state's interest in public health and safety may justify the prohibition of possession of certain drugs, an exemption in this case for members of the church would not undermine the state's interest in prohibiting certain drugs for public health and safety considerations. Or consider laws that require persons to wear helmets when operating motorcycles, given concern for public safety and health care costs. Sikhs object that such laws burden the practice of their religion, as Sikh men and some Sikh women take wearing a turban to be central to their religious practice, and this precludes wearing a helmet. Here we think that an exemption is justifiable as an exemption for Sikhs from helmet laws would not undermine the state's interest in public safety and the cost of health care.

---

[49] PL, pp. 189–190.

VI. Practical Considerations

We conclude by addressing some of the practical considerations in granting exemptions and considering the "anarchy objection." The anarchy objection has to do with the fact that recognizing exemptions from generally applicable laws may undermine the rule of law altogether. One might think the wider the scope of possible grounds for exemptions, the greater the threat to the rule of law. After all, if exemptions are easily granted and become common in a society, then it is reasonable to worry that the authority of law will be undermined or that widespread exemptions will mean that there is no "common" law applicable to all.

As we argued above, political liberals do not have a principled moral reason for distinguishing claims of religious or moral conscience from other, similarly strongly held nonmoral claims. This raises a host of concerns. One may worry that in granting nonmoral and nonreligious claims as possible grounds for claiming an exemption to a generally applicable law, granting exemptions becomes legally unadministrable. That is, the courts are going to need methods for distinguishing sincere claims from insincere claims, and one reason for restricting the scope of exemptions to religious claims is because this category is long recognized, we know well enough what religion is, and so this category can be legally administrated with relative ease. Using religion as a proxy (and not even conscience) allows that where one can make the argument that other sorts of claims are substantively similar, and so serve a similar functional role in citizens' lives, exemptions may be extended to these kinds of claims. Hence, some argue that granting exemptions for religious concerns is the paradigm case, and recognizing this allows us to have a legally workable category.

A few considerations suggest broadening the scope of possible grounds for exemptions will not result in a legally unadministrable category. First, for political liberals, claims for exemptions are limited to certain types of cases and are impermissible where civil or equal rights are at stake. Hence, the number of cases should be decidedly fewer. Second, the state could appoint an agency, similar to the EEOC, to oversee exemption claims. Third, the burden of proof falls on the claimant to show that the beliefs in question are sincerely held. And mere possession of such a view is not enough to ground an exemption; one must also show that the law in question is a substantial burden to one's defining commitments or obligations and that the government's interest fails to be compelling enough to justify restricting one in one's practices. These are high bars to pass, and much depends, of course, on how the notion of a substantial burden is understood.

In addition to these considerations, Micah Schwartzman identifies a number of factors that effectively put the anarchy concern to rest: In the United States there is already a significant body of law that "extends protections beyond the category of religion without threatening the legitimacy of political or legal institutions";[50] given the diversity and prevalence of religions in a state like the United States, if the anarchy objection were of serious practical concern, it seems like recognizing religious exemptions alone would be sufficient to trigger the worry.[51] But the United States hasn't fallen into anarchy even recognizing the broader kinds of exemptions for religious reasons, which we argue against. Thus, as a purely empirical matter, the concern that granting exemptions would produce a "lawless" state seems groundless.

---

[50] Schwartzman, "Religion, Equality, and Anarchy."

[51] Schwartzman, "Religion, Equality, and Anarchy," p. 9.

PART TWO

Feminist Political Liberalism

Is a Feminist Political Liberalism Possible?

Rawls suggests in the introduction to *Political Liberalism* that the inequality and oppression of women can be thought about, within the framework of his theory, by appeal to the same principle of equality that Lincoln invoked in order to condemn slavery. He does not elaborate further on this intriguing suggestion. . . . The key issue is whether we read the legacy of Lincoln as entailing purely formal equality between black and white Americans or whether we read it as requiring various measures aimed at considerably more substantive equality.

—SUSAN M. OKIN, *"Political Liberalism, Justice and Gender"*

I. Introduction

In the first part of the book we developed a particular account of the idea of public reason for political liberalism and defended that account from some central objections.[1] Our concern in the rest of the book is

---

[1] An earlier version of this chapter was published in the *Journal of Ethics & Social Philosophy* 5, no. 1 (2010). Here we revise some portions of that earlier argument. For comments on earlier drafts, we thank Matt Zwolinksi, Orly Lobel, Blain Neufeld, and anonymous reviewers. Special thanks go to Peter Vallentyne for his very generous comments and suggestions. An even earlier version of this chapter was presented at Georgia State University. We thank audience participants for helpful suggestions and criticisms. Since the article was published, various criticisms of our view have been raised by scholars similarly interested in the feminist potential of political liberalism. Gina Schouten raises important worries, which we address in chapter 8. Ruth Abbey, too, raises concerns about our view; she claims that our account is too restrictive of pluralism. She notes that toleration of pluralism was a primary motivation for the shift to political liberalism; as such, she implies that our view will ultimately fail to be defensible as a political rather than partially comprehensive view. See her "Introduction: Biography of a Bibliography. Three Decades of Feminist Response to Rawls," in *Feminist Interpretations of John Rawls*, p. 20. Abbey's concern represents a serious challenge to our project. We sketch an initial answer to her worry at the end of this chapter and further develop our response in the conclusion.

to demonstrate that this understanding of political liberalism, with its account of public reason, is a feminist political liberalism.

This claim may illicit some initial skepticism, for we argued for an exclusive account of public reason, in which reasons drawn from comprehensive doctrines are not permissible in public reason, which concerns matters of basic justice and constitutional essentials. Feminist theories, in their many and varied forms, are partial or full comprehensive doctrines. Hence, one may think that in our defense of exclusive public reason, we have problematically limited feminists' ability to argue for sex equality, as feminists should not give reasons particular to their comprehensive doctrines but must offer others public reason for laws and policies.

We now aim to show that not only is political liberalism a feminist liberalism but that political liberalism has substantive resources to secure sex equality. Specifically, we aim to show that, within public reason, there are powerful resources for advancing sex equality and feminists need not worry that being precluded from appealing to their comprehensive doctrine (as required by the duty of civility) will hamper the realization of a just society.

How is a distinctly feminist political liberalism possible? Certainly the answer depends in part on what one means by feminism, as there is disagreement over what feminism is. For our purposes, all we mean by feminism is a view that is, broadly, committed to the following claims: (1) gender inequality exists and is pervasive, and (2) it should be eliminated. In this chapter, we aim to lay the groundwork to establish that political liberalism has the resources necessary to recognize and address varied forms of sex inequality relevant to free and equal citizenship. By extension, our arguments apply to other socially subordinated groups, including groups subordinated on the basis of race, sexuality, gender identity or expression, ethnicity, disability, and so forth.

To be more precise about our project in this chapter, consider that some feminists claim that political liberalism maintains its position as a *political* liberalism at the expense of securing substantive equality for women or, they argue, that the only way for liberalism to address substantive equality for women is by relying on comprehensive values.[2]

---

[2] Okin forcefully expresses the first concern in "Political Liberalism, Justice, and Gender," "Justice and Gender," and "'Forty Acres and a Mule' for Women." Abbey makes the second

Others have suggested that political liberalism can be feminist insofar as particular political conceptions of justice can have substantive feminist content.[3] In answering feminist critics of political liberalism, we aim to show something more radical: not only is it possible to show political liberalism *can* be feminist insofar as particular political conceptions of justice can have feminist content, but, also, political liberalism's core commitments actually *restrict* all reasonable political conceptions of justice to those that secure genuine substantive equality for all, including women (and other marginalized groups). And so, we claim, political liberalism is a feminist liberalism.

To make good on this claim, we consider why some maintain that political liberalism cannot secure substantive equality for women. Next we examine attempts by Sharon Lloyd, Amy Baehr, and Martha Nussbaum to demonstrate the feminist potential of political liberalism. We claim that insofar as Lloyd and Baehr attempt only to demonstrate that political liberals can accept particular political conceptions of justice that contain substantive feminist content, they miss the full feminist potential of political liberalism as such. And we claim that, while Nussbaum recognizes that political liberalism's idea of equal citizenship limits the comprehensive doctrines that count as reasonable, she does not address how political liberalism's core ideas constrain all reasonable political conceptions of justice in a way that secures substantive equality for all citizens, which is what we aim to do. We argue that political liberalism's criterion of reciprocity limits reasonable political conceptions of justice to those that eliminate social conditions of domination and subordination relevant to reasonable democratic deliberation among equal citizens and that the criterion of reciprocity requires the social conditions necessary for recognition respect among persons as equal citizens. As a result we claim that the criterion of reciprocity limits reasonable political conceptions of justice to those that provide genuine equality for women along various dimensions of social life central to equal citizenship.

---

criticism in her "Back toward a Comprehensive Liberalism?" See also Hay, *Kantianism, Liberalism and Feminism.*

[3] Lloyd, "Family Justice and Social Justice" and "Toward a Liberal Theory of Sexual Equality"; Baehr, "Perfectionism, Feminism and Public Reason" and "Feminist Receptions of the Original Position"; Nussbaum, "The Future of Feminist Liberalism."

II. Feminist Criticism of Political Liberalism

Why do some feminists claim that political liberalism maintains its position as a *political* liberalism at the expense of securing substantive equality for women?[4] First consider how political liberalism differs from comprehensive liberalism. Here we follow Rawls. A comprehensive liberalism is a liberal theory that grounds principles of justice in moral, religious, or other values that are not limited to citizens' interests as such and that concern claims about how things are, what is right, and what is true. By contrast, political liberalism begins from the fact of reasonable pluralism[5]—the claim that in a free democratic society, reasonable people will accept contrary and irreconcilable but, nonetheless, reasonable comprehensive doctrines. Reasonable comprehensive doctrines result from the exercise of theoretical and practical reason, and they usually relate to a "tradition of thought or doctrine."[6] Furthermore, because reasonable comprehensive doctrines are those that are accepted by reasonable persons, they must be consistent with the criteria for reasonable personhood; reasonable persons, inter alia, accept the burdens of judgment and how the burdens of judgment restrict public reason, accept the claim that political power should not be used to limit reasonable comprehensive doctrines, and offer terms for social cooperation that are justified to others as free and equal citizens.[7] Given the fact of reasonable pluralism, political liberals consider how a just, democratic society is possible.[8] Its possibility, they maintain, depends on the satisfaction of the liberal principle of legitimacy, which is the claim that the exercise of political power is justified only if it stems from political principles that are reasonably justified to those subject to them viewed as free and equal citizens.[9] The principles are not merely rational for individuals to accept given their situation. Rather, as discussed in chapter 2, principles of basic justice

---

[4] Rawls certainly intends his theory of justice to secure some kind of substantive equality for citizens, as opposed to merely formal equality. This is evidenced by various features of his political conception of justice, justice as fairness, including its guarantee of the fair value of political liberties, fair equality of opportunity, and the difference principle (JF, pp. 148–152).

[5] JF, pp. 36–37.

[6] PL, p. 59.

[7] PL, pp. 59, 61, 60, 49.

[8] PL, p. xx.

[9] Compare with IPRR, p. 578.

and constitutional essentials must be justified by values and reasons that persons *share* as free and equal citizens.[10] These values and reasons are understood to be political values and reasons, and they are limited to citizens' interests in securing their standing as free and equal citizens relative to others. Citizens regard political values and principles as reasonable and need not affirm them as true or right. Also, central to political liberalism is its criterion of reciprocity and its conception of citizenship, which we will discuss below. It is these ideas, we think, that hold the key to addressing certain feminist criticisms of political liberalism and that actually constrain the set of reasonable political conceptions of justice for a politically liberal democratic state to those that will yield genuine substantive equality for women (and other marginalized groups). But we should not get ahead of ourselves, as we need an account of the alleged tension or incompatibility between women's substantive equality and *political* liberalism.[11]

Susan Okin characterizes the problem as follows: political liberals accept a wide range of comprehensive doctrines as reasonable (including all the major religions) and permit families and other private associations to organize as they see fit as long as they do not violate the principles of political justice. Some of these doctrines contain elements that suppose the legitimacy of gender hierarchies or essential gender differences. Under certain conditions, (some) persons' acceptance of these sexist yet reasonable comprehensive doctrines can effectively prevent women from enjoying real social, economic, and political equality with men because any political conception of justice that is shared by persons viewed as free and equal citizens will not be sufficient to protect women from gender inequality.[12]

---

[10] This concerns political liberalism's idea of public reason. See IPRR and our discussion of the idea of public reason in chapters 2 and 3.

[11] We will not attempt to note all feminist concerns about Rawls's political philosophy, but, instead, we focus on *some* that challenge the compatibility of women's substantive equality and *political* liberalism. Nussbaum notes a number of feminist concerns about Rawls's theory in her "Rawls and Feminism"; also see her "The Future of Feminist Liberalism." For an exceptionally thorough statement and analysis of the feminist criticisms of Rawls's work, see Abbey, *The Return of Feminist Liberalism*.

[12] Okin, "Political Liberalism, Justice and Gender" and "Justice and Gender." Okin also claims that sexist comprehensive doctrines can preclude children's development of the two moral powers. But, as Lloyd argues, whether certain sexist comprehensive doctrines would prevent children from developing the two moral powers to the necessary degree in a Rawlsian society is an empirical question. See Lloyd, "Family Justice and Social Justice." If

Central to this concern is the idea that political liberalism (at least as it stands) lacks the theoretical resources necessary to secure substantive equality for women. Thus, the claim is that political liberalism is not a feminist liberalism. We aim to show the contrary and to do so by developing certain core ideas at the heart of *political* liberalism. Importantly, other feminists—Amy Baehr, S. A. Lloyd, and Martha Nussbaum, in particular—have argued that political liberalism can yield feminist conclusions.[13] But we think these feminists have failed to show how *political* liberalism's core ideas restrict all reasonable political conceptions of justice to those that secure substantive equality for women. To be fair, neither Baehr, Lloyd, nor Nussbaum aims to show the feminist potential of political liberalism without reference to a particular political conception of justice. Hence, our project differs from theirs in that we intend to show that political liberalism's criterion of reciprocity entails a principle of nondomination and a principle of recognition respect, which restrict all reasonable political conceptions of justice in important ways; hence, here we do not defend a particular political conception of justice as one that will secure substantive equality for women.

So it will be clear how our project differs from that of Lloyd, Baehr, and Nussbaum, we briefly describe their work. Baehr and Lloyd argue that political liberals can address substantive equality for women through the use of public reason arguments. However, both Lloyd and Baehr show only that political liberalism is compatible with political conceptions of justice that have feminist content; neither shows that political liberalism as such requires it. Consider Lloyd. She is concerned with "equality in the distribution of the benefits and burdens of social cooperation," and she offers a particular conception of public goods.[14] The political conception of justice she ultimately develops is very similar to Rawls's, with the following caveat concerning sex equality: "If women bear a disproportionate share of social burdens (and/or enjoy a proportionately inferior share of social benefits) according to publicly recognized criteria of value, then they are

---

some citizens' beliefs and actions in accordance with such doctrines worked to thwart the development of the two moral powers in children, someone sympathetic to Rawls's theory would be on firm ground for insisting on children's protection, although we cannot address here what sorts of measures would be appropriate.

[13] Lloyd, "Family Justice and Social Justice" and "Toward a Liberal Theory of Sexual Equality"; Baehr, "Perfectionism, Feminism and Public Reason"; Nussbaum, "Rawls and Feminism."

[14] Lloyd, "Toward a Liberal Theory of Sexual Equality," pp. 65, 69.

subequals."[15] Baehr interprets this caveat as an *antidiscrimination* principle according to which "gender not affect the distribution of *any* of the [public] goods."[16] This principle would entail, for example, that if women are disadvantaged relative to men in terms of social primary goods such as income and wealth, then society should be restructured to prevent this. We are sympathetic to Lloyd's particular conception of what justice requires; we do not criticize the content of her political conception of justice. However, even if Lloyd's arguments are successful, she shows only that a particular political conception of justice (a modified version of justice as fairness) can generate feminist content but not that political liberalism as such requires it.

Now consider Baehr. Although she argues that feminism (or, to be more precise, some feminist conception of the good) cannot itself be a public political philosophy insofar as it rests on substantive ideals about the good life, she aims to show "some of the feminist content of a public political philosophy."[17] To this end, she assesses political liberalism's ability to deliver feminist content by combining certain aspects of Rawls's justice as fairness with features of Lloyd's political conception of justice. In particular, she seems to adopt much of Rawls's method, including the original position and the veil of ignorance, to argue for Lloyd's antidiscrimination principle, and then she assesses feminist concerns such as the commodification of sex from this point of view.[18] However, decision procedures for political principles such as the original position (and its veil of ignorance), specific accounts of public goods, and political principles themselves are all features of particular political conceptions of justice, and political conceptions of justice will vary in their accounts of these features. Like Lloyd, if her arguments are successful, Baehr shows that a particular political conception of justice can have feminist content and not that political liberalism as such requires it.

Nussbaum's claims go further than either Baehr's or Lloyd's as she suggests that certain ideas at the core of political liberalism can protect women from injustice. In "Rawls and Feminism," she notes that the idea

---

[15] Lloyd, "Toward a Liberal Theory of Sexual Equality," pp. 69–70.

[16] Baehr, "Perfectionism, Feminism and Public Reason," quoting p. 209, but see her full discussion of this point, pp. 208–212.

[17] Baehr, "Perfectionism, Feminism and Public Reason," p. 195.

[18] Baehr, "Perfectionism, Feminism and Public Reason," p. 211.

of equal citizenship is central to political liberalism and that any reasonable comprehensive doctrine must "grant the full equal citizenship of women" and "impose no barriers to women's exercise of those civic functions."[19] Any comprehensive doctrine that fails to do this is unreasonable. We think that Nussbaum is correct to suggest the feminist potential of political liberalism's conception of equal citizenship; however, Nussbaum does not develop in any detail how this conception of equal citizenship (apart from her particular political conception of justice) can be employed to secure sex equality.

Of course, Nussbaum proposes a particular political conception of justice—a capabilities approach—which, if defensible by political values and the object of an overlapping consensus of comprehensive doctrines, would certainly address many issues relevant to women's substantive equality. Her capabilities approach specifies certain human capabilities as "implicit in the idea of a life worthy of human dignity" and as the "source of political principles for a liberal pluralistic society."[20] Among the numerous capabilities part of her approach are "being able to have good health," being "secure against violent assault," and "being able to participate effectively in political choices that govern one's life."[21] Such capabilities are certainly central to women's equality.

It is not our aim to criticize Nussbaum's particular political conception of justice, to assess whether it can be justified using political values, or to determine the extent to which it delivers sex equality. Indeed, we think her political conception of justice (or a somewhat revised version of it) is certainly part of the family of reasonable political conceptions of justice for a politically liberal, well-ordered society. Rather, our project is to step back from particular political conceptions of justice altogether and examine and develop political liberalism's criterion of reciprocity to show its substantive content and the constraints it puts on any reasonable political conception of justice. We claim the criterion of reciprocity limits reasonable political conceptions of justice to those that provide genuine equality for women along various dimensions of social life central to equal citizenship.

---

[19] Nussbaum, "Rawls and Feminism," p. 510.

[20] Nussbaum, *Frontiers of Justice*, p. 70 and see her *Women and Human Development*.

[21] Nussbaum, *Frontiers of Justice*, pp. 76–77.

III. Reciprocity, Citizenship, and Equality

To show that political liberalism is a feminist liberalism, we now consider how political liberalism's ideas of reciprocity and of equal citizenship limit reasonable political conceptions of justice to only those that include principles that yield substantive equality for all, including women (and other marginalized groups). We begin by discussing political liberalism's criterion of reciprocity.[22]

According to Rawls, the criterion of reciprocity requires that when persons advance principles of basic justice or constitutional essentials, "those proposing them must also think it at least reasonable for others to accept them as free and equal citizens, and not dominated or manipulated, or under the pressure of an inferior political or social position."[23] We claim that the criterion of reciprocity calls for (1) the eradication of social conditions of domination and subordination relevant to democratic deliberation and participation among equal citizens and (2) the provision of the social conditions of recognition respect. As a result we claim that the criterion of reciprocity limits reasonable political conceptions of justice to those that provide genuine equality for women along all the dimensions of social life central to equal citizenship.

The criterion of reciprocity expresses the normative core of political liberalism and is the ideal by which citizens are to engage with one another in their deliberations about matters of basic justice and constitutional essentials. The deliberations of citizens under the constraints of the reciprocity condition determine the very terms of social cooperation in a democratic state. Importantly, the criterion of reciprocity is not a mere formal constraint on deliberation. It imposes substantive content

---

[22] We understand political liberalism's criterion of reciprocity, as proposed by Rawls, to be similar to Anderson's conception of democratic equality. Anderson claims, "Negatively, egalitarians seek to abolish oppression—that is, forms of social relationship by which some people dominate, exploit, marginalize, demean, and inflict violence on others. . . . Positively, egalitarians seek a social order in which persons stand in relations of equality." And, as we note below, she argues that "democratic equality regards two people as equal when each accepts the obligation to justify their actions by principles acceptable to each other, and in which they take mutual consultation, reciprocation, and recognition for granted" ("What's the Point of Equality?," p. 313). Anderson, however, does not state a connection between the view she develops and Rawls's criterion of reciprocity. The view of reciprocity we develop is specifically for political liberalism, and we use it to show how political liberals can address feminist concerns.

[23] IPRR, p. 578.

on political conceptions of justice, and political conceptions of justice that lack that content are not reasonable.

Rawls claims that "there are numerous reasonable political conceptions of justice, and "the limiting feature of these forms is the criterion of reciprocity, viewed as applied between free and equal citizens, themselves seen as reasonable and rational."[24] The substantive content that Rawls believes reciprocity imposes on any reasonable political conception of justice includes "a list of certain basic rights, liberties, and opportunities," "special priority to those rights, liberties, and opportunities, especially with respect to the claims of the general good and perfectionist values," and "measures ensuring for all citizens adequate all-purpose means to make effective use of their freedoms."[25] To explain the limiting nature of the criterion of reciprocity, Rawls remarks, "For what reasons can both satisfy the criterion of reciprocity and justify denying to some person religious liberty, holding others as slaves, imposing a property qualification on the right to vote, or denying the right of suffrage to women?"[26] Hence, Rawls thinks that when we try to determine principles for a liberal, democratic state that we think are reasonable for persons as free and equal citizens to accept, certain kinds of things (e.g., slavery) cannot be justified to persons viewed as having the normative status of free and equal citizens, and other things must be accepted (e.g., certain rights and liberties, such as freedom of association).

We think that the substantive content for reasonable political conceptions of justice that the criterion of reciprocity generates goes significantly beyond what Rawls imagines for two reasons. First, the sort of reasoning that Rawls uses to generate the list of features that will be characteristic of any reasonable political conception of justice can be employed to justify access to other social goods, including social goods that have been of particular concern to feminists. We will demonstrate this below. And, second, the criterion of reciprocity itself has negative and positive aims with respect to the social conditions for reasonable democratic deliberation among persons viewed as free and equal citizens. The social conditions for reasonable democratic deliberation should be secured by any reasonable political conception of justice, and these conditions place

---

[24] IPRR, p. 581.

[25] IPRR, pp. 581–582.

[26] IPRR, p. 579.

significant restraints on any reasonable political conceptions of justice. Demonstrating the latter point is our main concern, and the point with which we begin.

We propose that reciprocity as an ideal of justification has negative and positive aims. Negatively—so that persons can avoid addressing others as dominated, manipulated or under the pressure of an inferior social position—it requires the elimination of pervasive social hierarchies that thwart the give and take of public reasons among free and equal citizens. Positively, it requires the social conditions necessary for recognition respect among persons viewed as free and equal citizens.[27] These negative and positive aims of reciprocity are not always easily separable, since eliminating the social conditions of domination among individuals helps to create the conditions for recognition respect among persons. In what follows, we develop in more detail our view of the negative and positive aims of reciprocity and note some of the laws and policies that, under certain social conditions, are important to realizing reciprocity.[28]

When women participate in public, political life or the labor market or in various other spheres of social life, they must often overcome gender norms and expectations or succeed in spite of them. In other words, gender norms and expectations often result in women operating under the pressure of an inferior social position. Such social subordination, in turn, interferes with or obstructs equality of standing and, hence, undermines the conditions for reciprocity. In what follows, we argue that such subordination must be addressed in order to secure the conditions for reciprocity and equality among citizens.

In our earlier work on this topic, we considered examples of how pervasive social hierarchies can interfere with the give and take of reasons among free and equal citizens and more generally interfere with individuals' ability to view others as free and equal citizens.[29] In particular,

---

[27] Here we rely on the idea of recognition respect as it has been developed in the work of Darwall. See, e.g., Darwall's *The Second-Person Standpoint*, pp. 119–147.

[28] Our account develops Watson's understanding of reciprocity in her "Constituting Politics." She argues that reciprocity requires (1) that a citizen have the ability to formulate an identity as an equal citizen, (2) that a citizen be regarded by others as an equal citizen, and (3) that a citizen be able to engage in the exchange of reasons as an equal citizen.

[29] Watson considers other examples in her "Constituting Politics." Also, one might object that members of socially dominant groups often are subject to a kind of problematic reductionism. For example, a wealthy, white male arguing for tax cuts or, say, against affirmative action might be criticized on the grounds that he defends such a position only due to his

we focused on examples of the ways in which social hierarchies function to undermine the authority of members of socially subordinated groups as reason givers in their interactions with socially dominant groups. Since developing those arguments, we became aware of Miranda Fricker's excellent work *Epistemic Injustice*.[30] Fricker provides a systematic analysis of a central phenomenon we had in mind, which she calls "testimonial injustice."

Testimonial injustice predominantly occurs when a speaker is afforded a credibility deficit, by a hearer or hearers, on the basis of prejudicial stereotypes grounded in the speaker's social identity.[31] Whether consciously or unconsciously, persons draw on schema of social identities to form judgments about the quality or veracity of other's claims, and in some cases this can lead to an unjust assessment of the worthiness of the claims being put forward by persons occupying socially inferior positions grounded in their group-based identities. Fricker is especially concerned, as are we, with systematic testimonial injustice. Moreover, we are concerned with the way such systematic testimonial injustice undermines equal citizenship.[32]

For example, consider Anita Hill's testimony during Clarence Thomas's Senate confirmation hearings prior to his Supreme Court appointment. Hill, who was a law professor at the time, testified that Thomas sexually harassed her when he was her supervisor at both the Department of Education and the Equal Employment Opportunity Commission. She

---

group membership; that is, only a white, wealthy male would make such an argument. Are his reasons dismissed because of his group membership, and is he simply reduced to his group status if he is criticized on such grounds? We need not deny that members of dominant groups are sometimes reduced to their group status and that this, too, presents an obstacle to reciprocity. However, insofar as membership in a dominant group confers systematic advantages to persons, an individual's standing as an equal citizen is not compromised by such group membership. Moreover, working to remove the social conditions that create and maintain socially oppressive hierarchies and undermine reciprocity will also eliminate the conditions that lead to reductionism of persons in socially dominant groups. We thank Matt Zwolinski for the raising this concern.

[30] Fricker, *Epistemic Injustice*.

[31] Fricker, *Epistemic Injustice*, pp. 17, 20–21.

[32] In her essay "Epistemic Justice as a Condition of Political Freedom," Fricker argues that an account of freedom as nondomination, a view she sees as generically liberal, entails that epistemic justice is "a constitutive condition of non-domination." Fricker's view was developed after our work on this topic, but we find important overlap. As a point of distinction, however, we emphasize nondomination as central to substantive equality, and we think that such equality is necessary for political freedom.

took a polygraph, which supported her claims. Nonetheless, politicians, the media, and many citizens doubted Hill's credibility more broadly. Thomas was confirmed.

This case, we think, is a paradigm case of testimonial injustice. Her identity as an African American women undermined her credibility, and this is despite the fact she was a graduate of Yale Law School, an accomplished attorney, and a law professor. Of course this case is complicated by the intersection of race and gender, which works against Hill and amplified the defense of Thomas. The dismissal, by many, of Hill's testimony (here not meant in the legal sense) must be understood in the context of a society in which for centuries African American women's testimony about sexual violence was dismissed or not recognized, as men (most significantly, white men) were thought to be entitled to sexual access to African American women.[33] Important, too, is the socially constructed controlling image of some African American women as sexually promiscuous and as sexual aggressors.[34] Kimberlé Crenshaw forcefully makes this point:

> Rape and sexual abuse in the work context, now termed sexual harassment, has been a condition of Black women's work-life for centuries. Forced sexual access to Black women was institutionalized in slavery and was central to its reproduction. Rape and other sexual abuses were justified by the myth that Black women were sexually voracious and indiscriminate and that they readily copulated with animals, most frequently represented to be apes and monkeys. Indeed, their very anatomy was often objectified.[35]

Thomas's political conservatism made him a favorite of the political Right, but his race, too, is important to an analysis of this case. Indeed, the fact that Anita Hill and Clarence Thomas were both black shaped the defense of Thomas. (And, certainly, if Hill had been white, this case would have been quite different.) Again, Crenshaw highlights the way

---

[33] For an account of the connections between sexual harassment and slavery, see Davis, "Slavery and the Roots of Sexual Harassment." For an analysis of the role of racism in sexual harassment patterns, see Hernández, "The Racism of Sexual Harassment."

[34] See Collins, *Black Sexual Politics* and "Mammies, Matriarchs and Other Controlling Images" in *Black Feminist Thought*.

[35] Crenshaw, "Race, Gender, and Sexual Harassment," p. 1469.

that race functioned in this context to effectively silence and dismiss Hill's testimony:

> The Hearings have also revealed that shared racial identity does not render anyone immune to the myths and stereotypes that distort the sexual images of Black women. Orlando Patterson, a highly acclaimed Harvard professor, argued in the aftermath of the Confirmation Hearings that even if testimony about Thomas's gross pornography-laden harassment was actually true, Thomas was justified in lying about it given that such behavior was recognizable (and apparently acceptable) to Black women as simply a style of "down home courting."[36]

Additionally, Hill, as we know, was attacked for being a race traitor— accusing a prominent, successful black man of sexual harassment was claimed, by some, to be a betrayal of the black community. As such, Hill and other women of color routinely face a double bind in which gender and race are pitted against one another: loyalty to women is claimed to "entail" a betrayal to race and loyalty to race to entail a betrayal to women.[37]

Hence, testimonial injustice is a serious wrong that affects persons in their various interactions in social life, including interactions in the labor market, the political sphere, and family life. When stereotypes related to gender, race, and other aspects of social identity (or the intersection of multiple such categories) result in hearers systematically discounting speakers' testimony, the standing of persons as free and equal citizens is frustrated or undermined.

Perhaps the most salient examples of testimonial injustice that women encounter are the kinds of challenges and disbelief they receive upon reporting the crime of rape.[38] Rape myths are prevalent in our society, and police and/or university officials are not immune from their force in assessing the claims of rape victims. As Jon Krakauer documents in his recent exposé *Missoula*, about the ineffectual (and sometimes corrupt) investigations of claims of rape at the University of Montana and the subsequent Department of Justice investigation, police routinely vetted the

---

[36] Crenshaw, "Race, Gender, and Sexual Harassment," p. 1471.

[37] Crenshaw, "Race, Gender, and Sexual Harassment," p. 1471.

[38] See, e.g., Wood, " 'Get Home Safe.' "

veracity of rape claims by asking victims if they had a boyfriend, surmising that if the answer was yes it was probable that the accusation was false.[39] The Department of Justice reported:

> Our investigation has uncovered evidence indicating that the County Attorney's Office engages in a pattern or practice of gender discrimination in violation of the Equal Protection Clause of the Fourteenth Amendment to the United States Constitution and relevant statutes. In particular, there are strong indications that the decisions of the County Attorney's Office regarding the investigation and prosecution of sexual assaults and rape, particularly non-stranger assaults and rapes, are influenced by gender bias and gender stereotyping and adversely affect women in Missoula.[40]

While this is a welcome result, and remedial action by the Missoula County Attorney's office is now required and underway, there are no doubt similar practices in many places that have undermined women's ability to seek justice and, so, failed to treat them as equal citizens.

Consider how this relates to the negative aim of reciprocity that requires the elimination of social hierarchies that are incompatible with all persons' ability to be viewed as free and equal citizens and protection from domination. Again, reasonable persons offer others terms of cooperation they sincerely believe others will share as equal citizens.[41] Hence, reasonable political conceptions of justice are only those that reasonable persons believe are justified to others as free and equal citizens and not as individuals who occupy a subordinate status. This excludes conditions that fail to secure nondomination for persons as free and equal citizens.

Again, the ideal of reciprocity is central to explaining how justice is possible in a society characterized by the fact of reasonable pluralism, and this ideal requires that fundamental principles of justice be justified to all members of society viewed as free and equal citizens. Political legitimacy itself, Rawls says, is "based on the criterion of reciprocity: our exercise of political power is proper only when we sincerely believe that the reasons we

---

[39] Krakauer, *Missoula*, p. 54.

[40] See the report here: U.S. Department of Justice, letter to Fred Van Valkenburg, February 14, 2014, http://www.justice.gov/sites/default/files/crt/legacy/2014/02/19/missoula_ltr_2-14-14.pdf.

[41] PL, p. 49.

would offer for our political actions—were we to state them as government officials—are sufficient, and we also reasonably think that other citizens might also reasonably accept those reasons."[42] When social hierarchies are pervasive, they compromise some persons' ability to be viewed as equal citizens by others and thwart reciprocity and justice. Furthermore, these hierarchies can interfere with the exercise of basic liberties, fair equality of opportunity, and the fair value of political liberties. The last requires that "the worth of political liberties to all citizens, whatever their social or economic position, must be approximately equal, or at least sufficiently equal, in the sense that everyone has a fair opportunity to hold public office and to influence the outcome of political decisions."[43] Hence, in order for any set of principles of basic justice to be reasonable, they must preclude social hierarchies that threaten persons' ability to stand as equal citizens and be so regarded by others.

Importantly, our interpretation of reciprocity is central to the stability of a politically liberal, well-ordered society characterized by the fact of reasonable pluralism. The stability of a conception of justice concerns both whether those raised in a society structured by a reasonable political conception of justice will develop a sense of justice so as to act in accordance with the political conception and whether the political conception can achieve an overlapping consensus of reasonable comprehensive doctrines.[44] Our conception of reciprocity is fundamental to stability in the following way. The stability of society depends on the fulfillment of the liberal principle of legitimacy, which, again, requires that the exercise of political power is justified only if it stems from political principles that are shared by persons viewed as free and equal citizens. Rawls says that the principle of legitimacy is "based on the criterion of reciprocity."[45] When systematic social hierarchies are in place, even if not directly as a result of state action, the legitimacy of the state may be undermined. As we have argued, systematic social hierarchies can thwart public reasoning among free and equal citizens. What persons accept given an inferior social position is not the same as what they find reasonably justified as free and equal citizens.

---

[42] IPRR, p. 578.

[43] PL, p. 327.

[44] PL, p. 141.

[45] IPRR, p. 578.

Conditions of nondomination further promote stability in a number of ways: they increase the confidence of citizens that they are the political equals of others; they prevent systematic abuse of positions of social privilege; they underwrite the authority of all citizens (particularly, members of socially subordinated groups) to engage in the political process as equals and enjoy the substance of their rights as citizens. Hence, the eradication of social conditions of domination and subordination relevant to the exchange of public reasons among free and equal citizens is necessary for stability.[46]

The criterion of reciprocity does not require the elimination of gender altogether or certain other social identities. It does not even require the elimination of all possible hierarchical notions of gender or social identities. To be precise, it requires the elimination of social positions (created by norms, expectations, etc.) that compromise persons' ability to be viewed as free and equal citizens and have standing as equal citizens. Arguably, gender systems would have to be radically revised but not necessarily eliminated. The negative aim of the criterion of reciprocity, then, requires nondomination or freedom from social positions that compromise persons' ability to be viewed by others as free and equal citizens and that interfere with their standing as free and equal citizens. On our view, reciprocity entails a principle of nondomination.

The positive aim of reciprocity concerns the social conditions necessary for individuals to advance fundamental principles of justice under conditions which they believe it is reasonable for others to accept as free and equal citizens. We said that these social conditions are, essentially, the social conditions necessary for recognition respect among persons as citizens.[47] Stephen Darwall argues that *recognition respect* for persons fundamentally involves acknowledgment of an individual's standing or

---

[46] Thanks to Peter Vallentyne for pressing this point.

[47] For discussion of the role of respect for persons in political liberalism, see, e.g., Larmore, "The Moral Basis of Political Liberalism"; Neufeld, "Civic Respect, Political Liberalism"; and Boettcher, "Respect, Recognition." Larmore claims that a principle of respect for persons is the moral basis of political liberalism; Neufeld claims that political liberalism's criterion of reciprocity is based on equal civic respect for persons, which is a kind of recognition respect; and Boettcher claims that the basis for political liberalism's account of public reason is mutual respect, understood as recognition respect. We thank Neufeld for these references and for suggesting that our claim of the connection between reciprocity and recognition respect is further supported by this literature. See also our discussion of respect and the criterion of reciprocity in chapter 2.

authority as a person.[48] Hence, recognition respect for persons as citizens involves acknowledgment of an individual's standing or authority
as a citizen. Such respect is central to the criterion of reciprocity. A citizen must offer other citizens terms for cooperation that are reasonable
because she acknowledges that others have authority as equal citizens
to demand reasonable justifications for principles of basic justice and
constitutional essentials. Persons' standing as equal citizens, importantly, also gives them the right to make claims of justice on others and
to promote their conception of the good consistent with the demands
of justice. In public, political debate, this means that citizens should
take other citizens to have a legitimate right to make claims, to propose
principles and policies, and to offer justifications for their views. In the
public, political sphere, citizens should not disparage, degrade, or hu-
miliate others who disagree with their political views, have a different
comprehensive conception of the good, or have a social identity that
they dislike or find objectionable. These are moral requirements, not
legal ones.

There are two types of problems associated with pervasive social
hierarchies that undermine the conditions necessary for recognition
respect, which is central to the positive aim of reciprocity. We will call
one type of problem *the problem of authority* and the other *the problem of
advancing claims of justice*. The problem of authority occurs when members
of a social group fail to garner recognition respect from other citizens and
cannot participate in public, political deliberation on a basis of equality.
Members of the social group are not regarded as fully equal citizens by
others; they are not acknowledged to have the *authority* to make claims
on others as equal citizens. The second type of problem occurs when, because of their subordinated position, members of a group are unable to
advance their claims of justice as equal citizens. We clarify the nature of
these problems below.[49]

Equal authority among citizens is central to the criterion of reciprocity.
Such authority is fundamentally about the kind of political relationship
that exists among members of society. In a politically liberal society,
citizens must stand in a relation of *equal authority*. This idea is akin to

---

[48] Darwall, *The Second-Person Standpoint*, pp. 119–147.

[49] The problem of authority results in the problem of individuals not being able to advance
claims of justice, but it can have other causes, too.

Elizabeth Anderson's idea of democratic equality. She says that "democratic equality regards two people as equal when each accepts the obligation to justify their actions by principles acceptable to the other, and in which they take mutual consultation, reciprocation and recognition for granted."[50] Persons' acceptance of the obligation to justify their actions by principles acceptable to others depends on the idea of equal authority. Anderson stresses that the primary interest of democratic egalitarianism is that citizens have a certain kind of relationship relative to other citizens in society; in her view, the distribution of goods in society is secondary to this. Recognition respect for persons as citizens requires the recognition of persons' mutual equal authority as citizens in the public, political realm and in civil society more generally. Democratic societies' acknowledgment of the importance of recognition respect among citizens in civil society is reflected in civil rights legislation. Consider, for example, the U.S. Civil Rights Act of 1964. This legislation, inter alia, forbade racial discrimination in employment and public accommodations and desegregated public schools. The legislation was central to securing better employment and educational opportunities as well as providing access (or better access) to public accommodations for African Americans and other groups. But it also *affirmed* the standing of African Americans as equal citizens and recognized their *authority* to demand respect from others. Civil rights legislation can be central to securing the background conditions for reciprocity in society.

Each person's ability to advance a claim of justice as an equal citizen is also essential for reciprocity among citizens. This requires both (1) that persons as citizen claim-makers regard themselves in a certain kind of way and have the self-worth and self-respect required to advance claims of justice and (2) that others not only recognize the equal authority of citizen claim-makers but that they give proper hearing to the claims of other citizens. With respect to how persons must understand themselves, Rawls asserts that central to citizenship is that persons see themselves as "self-authenticating sources of valid claims."[51] Of importance for our purposes is that persons must think that, like other citizens, and regardless of their social positions or social identities, they have legitimate claims of justice and are entitled to promote their conception of the good, provided

---

[50] Anderson, "What's the Point of Equality?," p. 313.

[51] PL, p. 32.

this is done in a way that is consistent with other citizens' freedom to do the same. All persons have a political identity, which is their identity as free and equal citizens, as well as various social identities, which are the identities that persons assume or are assigned by social institutions. Being able to formulate an identity as an equal citizen requires that a person's social identities do not undermine his or her identity as a free and equal citizen. As noted above, if a person is a member of an oppressed group, then his or her ability to form an identity as an equal citizen can be compromised.[52] Reciprocity requires that background institutions be such that all reasonable persons can form an identity as an equal citizen. Hence, socially hierarchical identities cannot result in second-class citizenship for members of socially dominated groups; this is incompatible with democratic equality.

Pervasive social hierarchies can also prevent the claims of some persons from receiving a proper hearing as the claims of equal citizens. Charles Mills discusses this problem in *The Racial Contract*. There Mills describes the ways in which systematic oppression serves to distort the moral ontology and epistemology of both dominant and subordinate classes. In the case of racial inequality as present in the modern political landscape, Mills argues that to be a full member of political society, to be "white," one must come to learn and accept a "set of mistaken perceptions" that validate white political and epistemic authority. But he also says that this cognitive distortion is not easily exposed to members of dominant groups because it "precludes self-transparency and genuine understanding of social realities."[53] Of course, this is just the point that for social hierarchies to remain stable and functioning, they must find ideological support that seems to justify in some way the inequality, and when such ideologies are pervasive, such as racism and sexism, members of dominant groups, especially, are often blinded to the ideologies' causes and solutions. As such ideologies operate in the background culture, or even the foreground,

---

[52] Calhoun makes this point in her discussion of the status of gays and lesbians in American society. She claims that "equating *being* a homosexual with immorality produces a novel civic status: the citizen-deviant. Because all things gay or lesbian are routinely coupled, in legal and lay imaginations, with sodomy, child molestation, solicitation, promiscuity or some other category of immorality, nothing one does *as* a gay man or lesbian is untainted by the specter of immorality. . . . Constructed as citizen-deviants, gay men and lesbians occupy a shadowy territory neither fully outside nor fully inside civil society" (*Feminism, the Family*, pp. 104–105).

[53] Mills, *The Racial Contract*, p. 18.

claims of injustice by subordinate groups—claims for equal treatment or equal respect—fail to register as legitimate within the dominant moral discourse. The positive aim of reciprocity, then, requires the provision of social conditions in which persons as citizens relate to each other as equal authorities and in which persons advance claims of justice as equal citizens. Call this reciprocity's principle of recognition respect.

We imagine that reasonable conceptions of justice can vary in how the social conditions of recognition respect are captured in principles of justice. However, surely part of what the social conditions of recognition respect would require in any political liberal society is a certain kind of civic education. In addition to knowing their rights, liberties, and responsibilities as citizens, persons must appreciate that their entitlements and responsibilities and those of others stem from their standing or authority. Persons must appreciate their legitimate right to participate in democratic deliberation and civil society. Furthermore, as Rawls asserts, persons must understand that as citizens they are regarded as free in the sense that even if they modify or abandon their conception of the good, they retain their entitlements and responsibilities as citizens. Likewise persons' various social identities do not change the entitlements of persons as citizens.[54]

Other types of law and policy will be necessary in certain societies to satisfy reciprocity's principle of recognition respect. In hierarchically gendered societies in which women as such are targeted for violence, legislation like the Violence against Women Act (VAWA) as passed by the U.S. Congress, or some similar act, is necessary. This act had immense potential for not only addressing actual violence against women in the United States but also for affirming women's status as equal citizens. The VAWA recognized a "Federal civil rights cause of action for victims of crimes of violence motivated by gender," and it declared that "all persons within the United States shall have the right to be free from crimes of violence motivated by gender."[55] This legislation allowed victims of gender-based violence to sue perpetrators for compensatory and punitive damages, injunctive and declaratory relief, and more. As Catharine MacKinnon notes, not only did the VAWA recognize gender violence as sex inequality, but it also gave power to victims insofar as victims had the power to bring causes

---

[54] PL, p. 30.

[55] Violence of Women Act of 1994, 42 U.S.C. §13981 (1994).

of action and, thereby, affirm their own status as citizens.[56] Although the U.S. Supreme Court nullified the most substantive parts of this legislation,[57] in its original form it is precisely the kind of legislation that can help secure and sustain conditions of reciprocity among citizens.[58] Similarly, feminist arguments to the effect that pornography, prostitution, rape, domestic battery, and so forth undermine women's equality (and so should be considered civil rights violations) deserve serious consideration.[59] We will develop such an argument regarding prostitution in the next chapter.

Importantly, in any politically liberal society there will be numerous political conceptions of justice; the basic structure will be organized in accordance with (at least) one member from the family of reasonable political conceptions. In public discussions of political conceptions of justice, persons must assess the merits of various political conceptions of justice with respect to how well they secure the social conditions necessary for reciprocity. Some political conceptions of justice will no doubt fail to secure these conditions. Persons can object to such conceptions of justice as unreasonable.

Above we also noted that Rawls thinks the criterion of reciprocity imposes substantive demands on reasonable political conceptions of justice in another way. He claims that insofar as we try to determine principles for a democratic state that we think are reasonably justified to persons as free and equal citizens, certain kinds of things cannot possibly be so justified and other things must be accepted. We noted that Rawls proposes a list of three features that he thinks must be part of *any* reasonable political conception of justice. Again, those features include (1) certain rights, liberties, and opportunities; (2) priority for these rights, liberties, and opportunities; and (3) security for all persons to sufficient all-purpose means to pursue their conception of the good. Rawls stresses that there are different understandings of the "ideas of citizens as free and equal persons and of society as a fair system of cooperation over time," and as a result political conceptions can vary in how the above features are specified

---

[56] MacKinnon discusses the potential of the Violence against Women Act for affirming women's citizenship in her "Disputing Male Sovereignty."

[57] *United States v. Morrison*, 120 S. Ct. 1740 (2000).

[58] Watson makes a similar argument in favor of regulating pornography as a sex equality issue in her "Pornography and Public Reason."

[59] See, e.g., MacKinnon's arguments in *Women's Lives, Men's Laws*.

and with respect to "how they order, or balance, political principles and values."[60] Even so, he takes the features noted above as central to any reasonable political conception of justice, given the sort of reasons that could "satisfy the criterion of reciprocity." Here we suggest that the features of any reasonable political conception of justice that follow from what could possibly satisfy the criterion of reciprocity go beyond those enumerated by Rawls and that these features include ones that concern substantive equality for women.

In any society characterized as a fair system of cooperation over time, the "orderly production and reproduction of society and its culture from one generation to the next"[61] is of fundamental concern. Indeed, it is a fundamental interest of every person as a citizen that she is reasonably cared for as a child,[62] that is, that her physical and emotional needs are met and that others provide for her moral development and her education so she can be prepared for the responsibilities of citizenship and to pursue her conception of the good when she reaches maturity. Women have done and continue to do most of the work caring for children and as a result have been disadvantaged relative to men in their ability to participate in the labor market, the political sphere, and civil society. However, because it is a fundamental interest of every person that she receives care as a child and because this work is necessary for the continuation of society over time, this work should be regarded as socially obligatory work for which we are all collectively responsible. And those who perform this work should not be disadvantaged relative to other citizens with respect to their ability to participate in the various spheres of social life central to citizenship.[63] Recall that Rawls regards slavery, denying religious liberty, and

---

[60] IPRR, p. 582.

[61] The quoted passage is from Rawls, and he claims that "the orderly production and reproduction of society and its culture from one generation to the next" is why the family is part of the basic structure (IPRR, p. 595).

[62] In fact, it is clearly a fundamental interest of every person as a citizen that he or she is cared for in any time of dependency over the course of a life. As Kittay, Nussbaum, and others have noted, Rawls has not adequately addressed issues of justice relating to dependency and disability. We cannot adequately address here how the criterion of reciprocity bears on these issues, but we hope to take this up in future work. On Rawls's failure to address issues of justice relating to dependency and disability, see, e.g., Kittay, *Love's Labor* and Nussbaum, *Frontiers of Justice*.

[63] See Fraser's antimarginalization principle in "After the Family Wage: A Postindustrial Thought Experiment," in *Justice Interruptus*, p. 48.

certain voting qualifications as simply incompatible with the criterion of reciprocity. So, too, we claim is any distribution of socially obligatory work that privileges some citizens over others in spheres of social life central to citizenship. How could any citizen reasonably think that a distribution of socially obligatory work that significantly disadvantages a group of citizens in their ability to participate in the labor market, civil society, and the political sphere is reasonably justified? We discuss the gendered division of labor in more detail in chapter 8.

Recall that some worry that the core commitments of political liberalism will not guarantee substantive equality for women in a so-called well-ordered, politically liberal society.[64] Again, political liberals accept the fact of reasonable pluralism and view a wide range of comprehensive doctrines as reasonable, including ones that are sexist according to some feminist comprehensive doctrines. The thought is that a political conception of justice that is justified by political values and beliefs and that could be the object of an overlapping consensus of reasonable comprehensive doctrines is likely to leave unaddressed many of the obstacles to substantive equality women face.

We think our view effectively responds to this worry. Although our view does not entail that comprehensive doctrines that contain some sexist elements (according to some) will necessarily be unreasonable, we think the criterion of reciprocity places substantive demands on any reasonable political conception of justice. Hence, political liberalism's criterion of reciprocity can curtail the power of comprehensive doctrines to perpetuate the subordination of women with respect to the dimensions of social life central to equal citizenship and deliver the social goods necessary for equal citizenship. This is as much as any liberal view can do.

We have argued that the criterion of reciprocity requires the elimination of social positions that undermine persons' ability to be free and equal citizens. One might wonder what our view entails with respect to the ways in which the state can legitimately address the social subordination of some groups. For example, can the state directly attack gender norms that are part of a comprehensive doctrine?[65] As we have indicated, we think the state can enact social policy aimed at structuring society in accordance with the criterion of reciprocity. If women as such are

---

[64] Okin, for example, stresses this worry.

[65] We thank an anonymous reviewer for urging us to clarify our view on this issue.

targeted for violence, it will be necessary for the state to make violence against women a civil rights violation. If practices such as prostitution subordinate women, the state can prohibit them or regulate them in ways consistent with equality.[66] Furthermore, suppose the state offers parental leave to new parents, but gender norms are such that only women use this leave. If this results in gendered norms and expectations in the economy that disadvantage women's participation as equal citizens, the state can condition maximum leave periods on sequential work leaves by both parents, absent special circumstances. Of course, sometimes the way in which the state can address certain practices is limited by freedom of expression.

Consider proposals for banning burkas in public places.[67] One reason for such proposals is that the burka can be thought to express the sentiment that women should be invisible in public or have no public presence. Even if this is true, under most conditions, banning the burka in public places would be an unacceptable violation of freedom of expression.[68] Furthermore, the equal status of women as citizens in the public, political sphere and in civil society can be addressed by other social policy. Given the importance of freedom of expression, prohibitions on the expression of both reasonable and unreasonable comprehensive doctrines is justifiable only in the most extreme conditions.[69] Comprehensive doctrines will be both expressed and critiqued in the background culture of society. However, public reason should be limited to political values when principles of basic justice and constitutional essentials are at issue, and public reason condemns comprehensive doctrines that reject the central features of political liberalism. Rawls says, "Central to the idea of public reason is that it neither criticizes nor attacks any comprehensive doctrine, religious or nonreligious, except insofar as that doctrine is incompatible with the essentials of public reason and a democratic polity."[70]

---

[66] For example, the state may criminalize consumption of prostitution (i.e., the "johns") or distribution of prostitution (i.e., "the pimps") while decriminalizing prostitution itself (i.e., the women in most cases) in order to address the sex inequality at stake here. See chapter 7.

[67] We thank Eddy Nahmias for raising this example and Andrew Altman for discussion.

[68] See Nussbaum, "Veiled Threats?"

[69] See Nussbaum's discussion of this point in Rawls in her "Rawls and Feminism," p. 509.

[70] IPRR, p. 574.

IV. Not a Partially Comprehensive Liberalism

Here we will offer an initial defense of our view from the charge that our account is actually a partially comprehensive liberalism, not a political liberalism. We will return to this concern at the conclusion of the book, when our full view is clear. Recall, for now, that we claim that the criterion of reciprocity requires (1) the eradication of social conditions of domination and subordination relevant to democratic deliberation among equal citizens and (2) the provision of the social conditions of recognition respect. Consider two ways that one might make the charge that our view is a partially comprehensive liberalism. One might claim that because the view we develop requires all reasonable comprehensive doctrines to be compatible with accepting the substantive demands of the principle of nondomination and the principle of recognition respect, the range of comprehensive doctrines that will be *reasonable* on our account will be quite narrow. And this is not consistent with the spirit of political liberalism, which begins with the recognition of "a pluralism of incompatible yet reasonable comprehensive doctrines."[71] That is, political liberals view a wide range of comprehensive doctrines as reasonable, including the main comprehensive doctrines that currently characterize modern, democratic societies. Our view, it may be said, is inconsistent with this. Or one might object that the substantive content that we attribute to the criterion of reciprocity is not part of the political culture of democratic states or that we develop the ideas that are part of the political cultural in controversial ways.

To begin, while we think that any reasonable comprehensive doctrine must be compatible with reciprocity's principle of nondomination and principle of recognition respect, we think that most comprehensive doctrines in modern democratic states are so compatible or are revisable such that they are.[72] And, as a result, we think that political conceptions

---

[71] PL, p. xvi. Again, Abbey expresses this concern about our view; see note 1 of this chapter.

[72] Perhaps this claim is contentious. A significant number of Americans accept religious doctrines according to which women should be subordinated to men in the church and the home. Whether persons who accept such views can accept the central tenets of political liberalism depends on whether these persons believe that women are *equal citizens* with men and should enjoy the same entitlements as men as citizens. If they don't, they are unreasonable. Similarly, according to some persons who accept various religious doctrines, same-sex marriage is wrong and should not be legal, although marriage between a man and a women should be legally recognized and protected by the state. They justify their view in accordance with religious doctrine. People with such views are unreasonable and their

of justice constrained by the criterion of reciprocity could be the object of an overlapping consensus among reasonable comprehensive doctrines.

While we cannot demonstrate here the compatibility between particular comprehensive doctrines and our conception of reciprocity, clarifying our view a bit should help make the case. The demands of the principle of nondomination and the principle of recognition respect concern persons standing as free and equal citizens and the social conditions necessary for this. Persons' social positions and socially ascribed or assumed identities should not affect their standing as citizens. Belief in gender differences (or even gender hierarchy in religious authority) can be part of a reasonable comprehensive doctrine so long as the doctrine is compatible with the recognition of all persons as equal citizens in the substantive sense outlined above, and admittedly this would require revision of various comprehensive doctrines currently held by some citizens. We do not see why believing, for example, that God requires a kind of gender hierarchy in the church and home necessarily prevents individuals from also recognizing that persons regardless of sex are equal citizens and have certain entitlements and responsibilities.

That said, political liberals do accept a particular notion of the normative priority of citizenship, given their conception of freedom.[73] Citizens are free in the sense that persons regard themselves as citizens who are capable of modifying or abandoning their conception of the good and that they understand that they have rights, liberties, and responsibilities as citizens, irrespective of their other identities or associations.[74] Citizens are also free in the sense of being self-authenticating sources of valid claims. This means that persons in a politically liberal society are viewed as ends and as such can legitimately press claims on others in connection with their beliefs, values, and ideas of the good life.[75]

Thus, a person's identity as a citizen has normative priority over her other identities in the following ways: (1) from the point of view of the

---

doctrines, as they are or as these people understand them, are unreasonable in this respect. Perhaps they are revisable to be reasonable comprehensive doctrines. Thanks to reviewers for pressing us on this.

[73] Abbey makes the point about the normative priority of citizenship in "Back toward a Comprehensive Liberalism?," though she argues that emphasizing this priority is a problem for political liberalism.

[74] PL, p. 30.

[75] PL, p. 32.

state, a person, regardless of her beliefs, affiliations, or social identities, always enjoys certain rights, liberties, and responsibilities as a *citizen,* and because persons are citizens (and for no other additional reason), they can legitimately make claims on others to promote their idea of the good life, *and* (2) from her own point of view and the point of view of other citizens, a person is always owed respect as a *citizen,* regardless of her beliefs, affiliations, or social identities, and because she is a citizen, has standing to promote her interests (provided she is reasonable). This means that her rights and liberties as a citizen cannot be denied by others and that she cannot sell, exchange, or otherwise divest herself of her rights and responsibilities as a citizen (even if she chooses not to enjoy them). One's identity as a citizen, then, has normative priority over other identities just in the sense that no matter what one's other identities are, one's identity as citizen always gives one a certain standing and rights, liberties, and responsibilities. This does not mean a person must understand citizenship as the most important part of her identity or as who she fundamentally is.

We also believe the conception of reciprocity we develop is part of the public, political culture of modern, democratic states. Concern with nondomination and recognition respect is at the heart of the various civil rights movements that have characterized democratic states in the past hundred years. Claims about discrimination on the basis of sex, race, disability, and sexuality are about access to certain social goods, but they fundamentally reflect concern for persons' standing as free and equal citizens with others and the elimination of oppression.

Thus, although feminists have doubted political liberalism's ability to secure substantive equality for women, this doubt is misplaced. Political liberalism's criterion of reciprocity places substantive demands on any reasonable political conception of justice, as any reasonable political conception of justice must secure social conditions of nondomination and recognition respect among citizens. Hence, political liberalism is a feminist liberalism. In the next three chapters, we further develop and make good on this claim by examining three central areas of life in which women's social and political inequality is pervasive: prostitution, the gendered division of labor, and marriage.

7

Public Reason and Prostitution

Social inequality does not first exist in the abstract, in search of a basis or polarization or natural joint to carve or asymmetry to which to attach. It exists in the social reality of its particulars, such as the social dominance of men through which women are subjected. Sex equality as a norm comes into being through the resistance of women as a people to their subjection. The equality principle, in this approach, is properly comprised of the practical necessities for ending inequality in each of its real forms.

—CATHARINE A. MACKINNON, *Women's Lives, Men's Laws*

I. Introduction

Up until now, we have been concerned to work out the details of a particular conception of public reason for political liberalism and to argue that our interpretation of political liberalism is also a feminist political liberalism.[1] In the remainder of the book, we develop specific policy proposals for how our vision of a feminist political liberalism can address substantive issues of gender inequality that have endured in modern, liberal democracies and threaten to endure even in a politically liberal, well-ordered society. In so doing, we employ the substantive conception of free and equal citizenship that we argued is central to political liberalism. We give public reason arguments for our proposals that draw on that account. We want to show that our account of exclusive public reason does not burden or exclude feminist arguments in public reason, at least insofar as such arguments can be made by appealing to the conception of free and equal citizenship we think is central to political liberalism. In fact, such

---

[1] As noted in the preface, Watson is the sole author of this chapter, although Hartley provided enormously helpful feedback, far beyond what one would hope for from a colleague simply giving feedback. Conversations with Catharine MacKinnon have greatly improved this chapter; she pressed, objected, and demanded clarity over and over again. In addition, Elizabeth Barnes, Susan Brison, Craig Agule, Carol Hay, and Blain Neufeld generously provided comments and criticism. Any confusions or mistakes that remain are entirely my own.

a conception of free and equal citizenship provides powerful grounds for advocating for substantive sex equality.

Here we argue that arguments for legalization or decriminalization of prostitution should be rejected on sex equality grounds. We emphasize the centrality of the rights to bodily integrity and sexual autonomy on a basis of equality as central to citizenship. None of our arguments incorporates a view of sex or sexuality in a particular moralized sense; that is, we do not claim that sex itself is morally special or should be reserved for meaningful intimate relationships, nor do we adopt some similar conservative or partial view about how individuals should regard or value sex.

Feminist activists and scholars have long identified sexuality as a primary site of gender inequality and the subordination of women— whether through critiques of dominant forms of heterosexuality and its accompanying narratives of romance, or critiques of motherhood and its narratives of self-sacrifice, or critiques of ideals of sexual purity and sexual restraint that apply to ideals of femininity, or through critiques of legal and social norms effectively licensing rape, and much else having to do with the way that social and legal structures enact asymmetrical norms of sexuality that serve to subordinate women. However, even feminists remain deeply divided about the precise details of such critiques and, importantly, over the proper response to ending forms of sex-based subordination.

The contemporary debate among feminists over prostitution is a particular site of such contestation.[2] One indication of the depth of division is the lack of agreement over what to even call the practices of buying and selling sex. Some advocate for referring to the practice historically known as "prostitution" as "sex work." The arguments supporting the use of the terms "sex work" and "sex worker" are complex and varied, but they center around the claim that such work is not in itself oppressive and that the primary obstacles to equality for persons engaged in "sex work" concern social stigma and failure to treat "sex work" as work. In contrast, many feminists continue to use the term "prostitution" to refer to the institution of the buying and selling of sex, for it captures the exploitative and unequal nature of the practices central to their critique.[3] Moreover, it includes

---

[2] For a survey of various feminist approaches to prostitution, see Spector, *Prostitution and Pornography*.

[3] See, e.g., MacKinnon, *Women's Lives, Men's Laws*; Pateman, *The Sexual Contract*; Jeffreys, *The Idea of Prostitution*; Raymond, *Not a Choice*; Anderson, *Value in Ethics and Economics*; Satz, *Why Some Things Should Not Be For Sale*.

within it recognition of the fact that prostitution is a gendered practice—overwhelmingly, it is *women* in prostitution. Thus, there is no neutral term, no neutral starting point from which to begin a discussion of the institution of buying and selling sex, for to choose a term is to choose a side in the debate.

As our arguments will make clear, we favor an abolitionist model, in which the goal of state regulation is to end prostitution as we now know it. Thus, we will use the term "prostitution" rather than "sex work."[4] In addition, "sex work" is used much more broadly than is prostitution, for "sex work" refers to a range of activities, including pornography, stripping, and phone and webcam sex, and so on. We aim to consider only prostitution here, not the broader set of activities that fall under the umbrella of "sex work".

A further challenge concerns what to call the people who sell sex.[5] Advocates of legalization or decriminalization as well as some women active in prostitution insist on "sex worker" rather than "prostitute," as they regard the use of "prostitute" as disrespectful and claim usage of that word denies the "agency" of women in prostitution. While it is no doubt a good idea, in general, to refer to persons by using the terms they prefer, there are important reasons to reject the term "sex worker" in discussions of systems of prostitution. First, though there are those who insist on this term, they do not represent all persons or women in prostitution. Moreover, the insistence on this term often comes from those active in prostitution or those making money from prostitution (the pimps and brothel owners). In contrast, women who have exited prostitution, in many cases, reject the term "sex worker" in favor of "prostitute" or

---

[4] In other contexts, Watson has used "sex work" to critique the practice of the buying and selling of sex. In those contexts, Watson aimed to directly address arguments offered by advocates of legalization and decriminalization where using their terms was central to the argument. See Watson, "Why Sex Work Isn't Work."

[5] As noted in the Swedish Institute's "Selected Extracts of the Swedish Government Report," "What to call persons who are involved in prostitution is a sensitive issue. The report uses the term sex buyer and the expression to buy sex. On the other hand, the terms sex seller and to sell sex were avoided because they give the impression that prostitution is a business transaction between two equal parties, a scenario that, according to the report, very rarely corresponds to reality. At times, the report uses the word prostitute to designate the person who is exploited sexually. However, the phrases person who is exploited in prostitution and person with experience of prostitution also occur in the text. Regardless of the choice of words, it is important to stress that this is not about what the persons involved are but rather what they do" (p. 3).

"prostituted persons."[6] Second, the use of "sex worker" already begs important questions, questions that this chapter aims to address, such as: Is so-called "sex work" just like other forms of work? Can persons who sell sex as a "job" enjoy the same kinds of worker health and safety protections other workers enjoy as basic human rights? Is it possible to apply standard employment law and other relevant civil rights laws where selling sex is the "job"? Third, after a full assessment of the arguments for legalization or decriminalization and direct engagement with the material reality of the lives of women in systems of prostitution, it is clear that prostitution is a system of gendered inequality; using the word "prostitute" rather than "sex worker" is central to keeping that fact at the forefront.[7]

As feminist political liberals, we hold that arguments that rest on a particular conception of the "good" of sex or of the role of sex in a broader conception of the good are illegitimate grounds for state policy. Political liberals must reject arguments that are grounded in claims about sexual chastity or purity or the unique and intrinsic value of sex in a particular account of the good life. Thus, in our view, only public reason arguments are acceptable arguments for consideration in whether and how to regulate the buying and selling of sex, as the issues raised by prostitution concern matters of basic justice. This means that arguments in favor of regulation or against such regulation must be such that they rest on political values and do not draw upon controversial and particular normative accounts of the value of sex or sexuality as such. Rather, public reason arguments require appealing to the interests of persons as free and equal citizens and offering an interpretation of what, in a particular case, freedom and equality necessitate. This interpretation of what liberalism demands has led many to think that the liberal position ought to be some form of legalization or decriminalization.[8] We disagree.

We give a sex equality argument against decriminalization and legalization (often thought to be the quintessential liberal positions) and, instead, argue in favor of what is known as the "Nordic model"—understood broadly as a state policy that fully decriminalizes the selling of sex yet criminalizes the buying of sex while adopting substantive social supports

---

[6] See, e.g., Moran, *Paid For*.

[7] Of course the reader will have to wait for the arguments that support that conclusion; nonetheless, we do think our arguments bear out this claim.

[8] See, e.g., Nussbaum, "Whether from Reason or Prejudice."

to enable persons in prostitution to exit prostitution.[9] We craft our arguments drawing on a rich body of empirical data concerning different models of regulation and facts about the conditions of persons living in prostitution. In this sense, this entire argument is an exercise in nonideal theory. However, as many of our arguments concern the intrinsic features of prostitution, they equally apply in any politically liberal, well-ordered society. The normative basis for our arguments is the particular account of free and equal citizenship we have argued for thus far. We give what we take to be powerful public reason arguments both against legalization and full decriminalization and in favor of the Nordic model.

II. Some Basic Facts about Prostitution and Legal Approaches to It

Of course as with any complex social phenomenon and debates concerning state/legal policy addressing it, part of the dispute concerns just what the facts are, which ones are salient, and how to interpret them. This is true in debates about prostitution. However, there are some fairly uncontroversial facts and starting points that various positions within the debate acknowledge. First, it is nearly universally acknowledged that the primary reason persons enter into prostitution is extreme economic deprivation.[10] Sometimes this is phrased in terms of economic necessity, sometimes in terms of survival. What is clear is that the overwhelming

---

[9] A brief description of the Nordic model as a sex equality model can be found on Equality Now's website. MacKinnon pioneered a full defense of the Nordic model as a sex equality model, as she developed the legal model. See her early formulation of the central ideas in "Prostitution and Civil Rights," in *Women's Lives, Men's Laws*, pp. 151–161; and her most recent and developed defense, "Trafficking, Prostitution, and Inequality."

[10] A variety of sources confirm this, across a range of perspectives on whether prostitution should be legalized, decriminalized, or criminalized in some form. See, for example, a study conducted by the Policy Department on Citizen's Rights and Constitutional Affairs for the European Parliament, "Sexual Exploitation and Prostitution and Its Impact on Gender Equality." See also Thukral, Ditmore, and Murphy, "Behind Closed Doors," citing "financial vulnerability" and "economic deprivation" as the overwhelming reason for entry into prostitution in a study of "indoor" sex work in New York City (p. 10); see also All-Party Parliamentary Group on Prostitution and the Global Sex Trade, "Shifting the Burden," citing "poverty" as the primary reason for entry into prostitution for 74% of indoor workers (p. 31). Other routes into prostitution cited by the report include experience of sexual abuse as a child, drug and alcohol abuse, and being in the foster care system as a female child. The authors conclude, "More often than not, prostitution is entered out of desperation arising from a number of situation-specific factors" (p. 33).

majority of persons in prostitution enter into it as a means of "last resort" to secure some level of economic security and meet their or their family's basic needs. Although there are rare exceptions, persons with a decent level of economic security don't enter into prostitution. Second, the over-whelming majority of persons in prostitution are women and girl children. Moreover, women of color, First Nations women, and trans women, that is, women who are vulnerable across various axes of inequality, are overrepresented in prostitution.[11] Third, women in prostitution are subject to an array of harms—violence, rape, and exposure to sexually transmitted diseases (STDs), to name the most prevalent.[12] Fourth, the pathways into prostitution involve layers of vulnerability and inequality. For example, common pathways to prostitution include a history of childhood sexual abuse, homelessness, attempts to flee domestic abuse, recruitment or force by a male partner, the low status of women in some cultures, and, again, economic desperation.[13]

Less universally accepted is the claim that the criminalization of prostitution serves to make persons in prostitution worse off in nearly every respect,[14] though among those who aim to improve the lives of women in prostitution, whatever their orientation toward legalization,

---

[11] See Farley et al., "Garden of Truth." See also Aboriginal Women's Action Network, "Aboriginal Women's Statement on Legal Prostitution."

[12] This is acknowledged by nation-states in which prostitution is legal or decriminalized, as is documented by their health and safety manuals. It is also a central theme of those who organize as "sex workers" and produce their own health and safety manuals. See, for example, Akers and Evans, *Occupational Health and Safety Handbook*, published by St. James Infirmary. St. James Infirmary "is an Occupational Safety & Health Clinic for Sex Workers founded by activists from COYOTE (Call Off Your Old Tired Ethics) and the Exotic Dancers Alliance in collaboration with the STD Prevention and Control Section of the San Francisco Department of Public Health." In addition, in Germany, where prostitution is legal, a governmental report states, "For example, one cannot ignore the empirical findings that show that those working in this industry are subject to considerable, empirically verifiable, psychological and physical threats. Prostitution is generally a physically and psychologically demanding, risky and dangerous business in which particularly vulnerable groups frequently engage. This was confirmed by a survey of a subpopulation of prostitutes during a study into the situation, safety and health of women in Germany that was commissioned by the Federal Ministry of Family Affairs, Senior Citizens, Women and Youth. This group suffered considerably more childhood violence, sexual violence, violence in relationships and violence in the workplace" (Germany, Federal Ministry for Family Affairs, Senior Citizens, Women and Youth, "Report by the Federal Government," p. 11).

[13] See, e.g., Leidholdt, "Prostitution and Trafficking in Women," p. 171; MacKinnon, "Trafficking, Prostitution, and Inequality," pp. 276–281.

[14] MacKinnon, *Sex Equality*, pp. 1553–1554.

decriminalization, or the Nordic model, this claim is universally recognized. "Criminalization" refers to a system of state regulation in which both the buying and the selling of sex are illegal and subject to criminal penalties, whether fines or incarceration or both. Under criminalization regimes, women (the prostitutes) are arrested and jailed at a disproportionate rate relative to the buyers (the men).[15] In addition, police corruption is pervasive: police extort, threaten, and coerce women in prostitution into giving them sexual access.[16] Women in prostitution fear engagement with the police such that they are much less likely to report violence or rape or other forms of harassment to police, effectively leaving them without a basic resource for safety and security that other citizens enjoy.[17] A criminal record follows women throughout their lives and limits other opportunities for employment should they decide to exit prostitution. Regimes of criminalization also function to undermine or limit access to stable and secure housing and health care.[18] Women with convictions for prostitution are disadvantaged in child custody disputes.[19] Moreover, they are doubly criminals if they fail to report and pay taxes.

Those who reject the arguments for criminalization as unsound or illiberal may be inclined to think that legalization is both philosophically and practically superior. Legalization involves removing all criminal sanctions connected with the practice of prostitution (for both buyers and sellers), but it also involves a system of state regulation. Often, it also involves permitting brothels as businesses. This moves beyond legally permitting the buying and selling of sex between individuals to allowing third parties to "exploit the prostitution" of others. Such a system of regulation includes the issuing of brothel licenses, the registration of prostitutes, setting legal age limits, and restricting "employment" from immigrants, for example.[20] Legalization often includes additional regulations, such as zoning laws, the mandating of condom usage, and other so-called occupational health

---

[15] MacKinnon, *Sex Equality*, pp. 1553–1554.

[16] MacKinnon, *Sex Equality*, pp. 1553–1554.

[17] MacKinnon, *Sex Equality*, pp. 1553–1554. See also "Statement on Prostitution and Human Rights," in Pheterson, *A Vindication of the Rights of Whores*, p. 105.

[18] See Matthews et al., *Exiting Prostitution*.

[19] See Ahrens, "Not in Front of the Children."

[20] See Barnett and Casavant, "Prostitution."

and safety standards, including mandatory STD testing (but only for prostitutes, not johns).[21]

Arguments in favor of legalization appeal to various considerations, including the claim that state regulation will provide safe and uniform working conditions, reduce coercion, reduce violence, reduce criminally run brothels (associated with organized crime), as well as provide access to state resources such as health care and social security.[22] Moreover, some advocates of legalization argue that reducing stigma associated with prostitution ought to be a central aim of any approach to prostitution; proponents of legalization often claim, though without any real evidence, that legalization will reduce the social stigma associated with prostitution.[23] Of course, all of these considerations are consequentialist in that they appeal to increased utility for prostitutes themselves (and arguably by extension improved utility for the buyers). Beyond these consequentialist considerations, those in favor of legalization argue there simply are no good nonmoralistic reasons for criminalization, and they think that legalization is an improvement (reduces more harms) that mere decriminalization.[24]

Advocates of decriminalization argue for the removal of criminal laws concerning prostitution, but not necessarily adding terms for (legal) regulation. In practice, nation-states that have decriminalized prostitution accompany such legislation with various regulations rather than complete lack of regulation.[25] Proponents of decriminalization include various sex worker advocacy groups and some human rights organizations, such as Amnesty International, as well as other political organizations, and of

---

[21] Barnett and Casavant, "Prostitution."

[22] The Netherlands is prime example. However, in their own governmental report, issued five years after the lift of the brothel ban, they conclude the situation of women in prostitution is worse than it was prior to the lift. See Netherlands, Scientific Research and Documentation Center, "Prostitution in the Netherlands."

[23] One might observe that while stripping and pornography have long been legal in the United States, the mere fact of their being legal doesn't seem to have reduced the social stigma of persons engaged in pornography or stripping, though it does seem to have reduced the stigma directed at consumers.

[24] See, e.g., Weitzer, *Legalizing Prostitution.*

[25] Barnett and Casavant, "Prostitution," pp. 4–9, as for example in Australia and New Zealand. See also New Zealand Parliamentary Counsel Office, Prostitution Reform Act.

course various academics.[26] Those who advocate for decriminalization share the critique of criminalization discussed above but argue against legalization primarily on the grounds that it entails extensive state control over the women in prostitution in ways that deny them "autonomy" and "agency" and perpetuates a new set of distinct harms.

The shared premises among those who advocate for legalization and decriminalization include the claim that criminalization reflects an illicit moralism that should have no role in a liberal society and the claim that prostitution has always existed, and will always exist; thus they share the aim of developing an approach to prostitution that is claimed to reduce harms experienced by persons in prostitution. Such approaches are often referred to as "harm reduction models."[27] The key disagreement is over whether legalization or decriminalization is more effective as a model of harm reduction.

A distinct argument that presents itself as a sex equality approach to prostitution concludes that decriminalizing the selling of sex while criminalizing the buying of sex is the most effective means to combating the harms of prostitution while affirming the equality of women.[28] This is known as the Nordic model. The Nordic model was first adopted in Sweden in 1999. It has since been adopted by Norway, Iceland, Northern Ireland, and France, and a similar kind of law was passed in Canada (in 2014). The European Parliament passed a resolution in 2014 recommending member states consider the Nordic model.[29] The model is premised upon the claim that reducing or eliminating demand for commercial sex is essential to reducing or eliminating sexual exploitation (whether through

---

[26] Amnesty International, "Amnesty International Publishes Policy and Research." "Movement activists generally do not support legalization that allows state oversight and licensing of workers. Regulation, they believe, would not benefit workers and could harshly punish those who refuse to be 'pimped' by the state. Historically, official supervision has imposed mandatory health inspections on workers (but not on clients) and usually designated prostitution zones controlled by the police" (Chateauvert, *Sex Workers Unite*, p. 4). See also Shrage, "Prostitution and the Case for Decriminalization."

[27] For a discussion of harm reduction models and arguments, see Matthews, *Prostitution, Politics and Policy*, pp. 83–88; Weitzer, *Legalizing Prostitution*, especially chapter 4, pp. 72–101; Chateauvert, *Sex Workers Unite*, p. 17 (where harm reduction is framed as a human rights approach).

[28] See MacKinnon, "Trafficking, Prostitution, and Inequality."

[29] See European Parliament, "European Parliament Resolution."

sex trafficking or prostitution) and securing the material conditions of free and equal citizenship for women.

It is framed as a sex equality approach because it begins its analysis by taking the fact of the gendered structure of prostitution, in which women are overwhelmingly the sellers and men the buyers (as part of a larger pattern of gender inequality), as central to the subsequent analysis of the inequalities that lead to and stem from prostitution as a social institution. Moreover, it is grounded in an intersectional analysis of these inequalities, recognizing that there is a *hierarchy* within prostitution itself. Women of color, First Nations women, trans women, and women in so-called third-world nations are both overrepresented in prostitution (and sex trafficking) and subordinated relative to others within prostitution (including earning less, having less negotiating power when it comes to condom usage, and having less mobility within the "profession").[30]

From an empirically grounded analysis of the hierarchically gendered structure of systems of prostitution, the Nordic model was developed by asking: What legal approach is best suited to end such gendered inequality and bring about *more* gender equality? Thus, its orienting purpose is to address *this specific* form of gender inequality while simultaneously creating conditions to increase gender equality. In order to make the case that the Nordic model does this better than the alternatives (legalization or decriminalization), a thorough analysis of such alternatives is necessary. Advocates of the law have done this work. Here we provide additional arguments that support their conclusions, exposing the flaws and gender-unequal consequences of both legalization and decriminalization.

III. Public Reason and Prostitution

Any public reason argument will necessarily draw on a conception of free and equal citizenship in conjunction with a particular reasonable political conception of justice. We have not defended any particular reasonable political conception of justice, given that we aim to specify the commitments of political liberalism as compatible with a family of such conceptions. However, we have argued for a substantive interpretation of the reciprocity condition such that a commitment to substantive sex equality follows from

---

[30] MacKinnon, "Trafficking, Prostitution, and Inequality," pp. 277–278.

it and must be a part of any reasonable political conception of justice. The claims we defend are that reciprocity (a limiting condition on all reasonable political conceptions of justice) requires the elimination of pervasive social hierarchies that thwart the give and take of reasons among persons as free and equal citizens and securing the social conditions necessary for recognition respect. As we said in developing these ideas in chapter 6, this means the state has an obligation to eradicate practices of domination and subordination that interfere in the enjoyment of the status of free and equal citizenship on a basis of equality, and the state has an obligation to secure conditions of nondomination for groups that are subjected to hierarchical forms of inequality; this entails a substantive commitment to sex equality.[31]

Each of the positions we've been discussing—legalization, decriminalization, and the Nordic model— claims to emphasize the values of women's sexual agency and sexual autonomy as a part of the basic rights of persons (as citizens). Each view interprets the demands of respecting such agency in different ways, of course. And each view frames itself in terms of equality as well, of course again, emphasizing different claims to equality as well as different interpretations of what equality demands. Each view emphasizes equal access to fair working conditions and opportunities as well as the basic entitlements of citizenship—fair compensation, protection from violence and basic security of the person, access to health care and other essential social services—though, again, each view differs on the means for securing these rights and goods for persons in prostitution. We will now turn to each view to reconstruct and evaluate its main claims.

As stated above, advocates of legalization aim to establish a legal framework of regulation that treats sex work as a form of work just like other forms of employment that are currently recognized. One journalist expresses the view this way:

> There is a political usefulness in *calling* all of this "sex work," while also insisting that it varies considerably over time and place. To do so is to insist that those who do sex work, in all of their workplaces and in varied conditions, deserve the rights and respect accorded to workers in any other industry.[32]

---

[31] See chapter 6.

[32] Grant, "Let's Call Sex Work What It Is."

And further, she criticizes those who object to calling prostitution, or other commercial sex acts, "sex work," saying:

> What sex work opponents actually have in mind when they cringe at the idea that sex work could be "a job like any other" is that sex work does not—and cannot—resemble their work. When anti–sex work crusaders think of "jobs," they're thinking of their more respected labor administering social projects, conducting research and lobbying. To consider sex work to be on the same level as that work breaks down the divisions that elevate some forms of labor while denigrating others.[33]

Views like this are often invoked to support arguments for legalization.

A central question any system of legalization has to confront is whether to permit pimping—that is, whether it is going to not just allow the selling of sex but also allow persons to profit from others' selling sex. Though, of course, in legalization regimes "pimps" are transformed into "business owners." In the Netherlands, this was accomplished when the brothel ban was lifted in 2000. (Interestingly, this legislation was called "lifting the ban on *exploiting* the prostitution of others.")[34] In all places in which prostitution is currently legal, brothels are also permitted (thus, pimping is permitted). This raises a second central question: whether persons in prostitution are properly understood as employees, in the common legal sense of the term. It is worth noting that nowhere prostitution is legal are prostitutes treated, legally, as employees *just like other employees*. One primary reason for this is establishing an employee-employer relationship between brothel owners and prostitutes is recognized to cede unacceptable control to brothel owners and thus restrict the sexual autonomy of prostitutes.[35] For example, a conventional employee-employer relationship could undermine the right of prostitutes to refuse particular clients, to set their own prices and negotiate directly with clients, and to negotiate particular sex acts. In addition, legalization as such comes with mandated health screenings and surveillance of sex workers' bodies in ways that sex

---

[33] Grant, "Let's Call Sex Work What It Is."

[34] My emphasis.

[35] See Netherlands, Scientific Research and Documentation Center, "Prostitution in the Netherlands"; Barnett and Casavant, "Prostitution"; and Germany, Federal Ministry for Family Affairs, Senior Citizens, Women and Youth, "Report by the Federal Government."

workers themselves object to as invasive, punitive, and premised upon the belief that prostitutes are vectors of disease in need of control. Notably, there is no symmetrical screening and surveillance of buyers' bodies.

There are further problems with the conventional employee-employer model that haven't been adequately recognized by advocates of legalization. One central claim among such advocates is that "sex work is work" like any other kind of work and should be subject to the same regulations. However, this simply isn't possible.[36] The German government acknowledges this explicitly, even though many advocates of legalization refuse to similarly concede that sex work cannot be treated just like any other job. A governmental report stated, "However, prostitution was not to become a 'job like any other.' The employer's right to issue instructions was largely restricted in favour of prostitutes' right to sexual self-determination. No prostitute is to be obliged to serve a particular client or to engage in certain sexual practices against her will."[37] This is a crucial concession and serves our argument: sex cannot be treated like any other job without removing prostitutes' right to sexual autonomy and bodily integrity. Thus, an exception, at least, must be made for a right to refusal. (Though, this is not enough to support systems of legalization.) However, what this concession does show is that sex is distinct, different, and perhaps unique—not because of a moralized conception of sex or sexuality but because of the centrality of the right to bodily integrity.

As Watson has argued elsewhere, various laws and regulations that we think are justified in employment contexts simply cannot be enforced in the context of prostitution.[38] For example, occupational health and safety standards developed for occupations (primarily medical or research work) in which employees are at risk for exposure to blood-borne pathogens or infectious diseases are extremely demanding, as they should be, and place worker safety at the center of regulation development. Such regulations, supported by nation-state-specific legislation as well as international human rights instruments, require personal protection equipment such

---

[36] Germany, Federal Ministry for Family Affairs, Senior Citizens, Women and Youth, "Report by the Federal Government," p. 9.

[37] Germany, Federal Ministry for Family Affairs, Senior Citizens, Women and Youth, "Report by the Federal Government," p. 9.

[38] Watson, "Why Sex Work Isn't Work."

as gloves, face shields, and in some cases full body coverage.[39] Obviously, such safety equipment is compatible with performing the tasks central to doing the job in these contexts, unlike in commercial sex. However, a limit on what kinds of tasks are permissible in such contexts includes adherence to safety practices. While "sex workers" (in prostitution) have developed their own occupational health and safety manuals and these have impacted legislation, many of their standards are mere recommendations. (For example, the New Zealand OHS guide for "the sex industry" recommends that "workers doing outcalls should carry a small torch [flashlight] to be used in the event of there being unsatisfactory lighting for a thorough examination of a client in the client's home, hotel room, car, etc.," and "checking the client for visible signs of sexually transmissible infections is strongly advised.") The only substantive requirement to emerge is the requirement of condom usage.[40] Aside from the fact that this requirement is often violated,[41] condoms simply do not offer sufficient protection from infectious diseases, whether primarily sexual or not, nor do they address other health and safety concerns common in prostitution. Pregnancy, rape, and violence are all "occupational hazards" in prostitution. Other common threats to health and safety in sex work include repetitive stress injuries especially to the genitals and anus, bladder infections, chronic cystitis, and

---

[39] The International Labor Organization, "C155: Occupational Health and Safety Convention," states, "1. Employers shall be required to ensure that, so far as is reasonably practicable, the workplaces, machinery, equipment and processes under their control are safe and *without risk to health*. 2. Employers shall be required to ensure that, so far as is reasonably practicable, the chemical, physical and biological substances and agents under their control are *without risk to health when the appropriate measures of protection are taken*. 3. Employers shall be required to provide, where necessary, adequate protective clothing and protective equipment to prevent, so far as is reasonably practicable, risk of accidents or of adverse effects on health" (Article 6, my emphasis). Nation-state-specific interpretations of these human rights vary. For example, in New Zealand, where prostitution is decriminalized, Occupational Health and Safety Standards require that "all workers, no matter what industry they work in, have the *right not to suffer harm* through carrying out normal requirements of their work" (New Zealand Department of Labour, Occupational Safety and Health Service, "A Guide," p. 17). And, in the United States, the U.S. Department of Labor, Occupational Health and Safety Act of 1970, says, "The law requires employers to provide their employees with working conditions that *are free of known dangers*" (italics are ours for emphasis).

[40] New Zealand Department of Labour, Occupational Safety and Health Service, "A Guide," p. 21.

[41] New Zealand Department of Labour, Occupational Safety and Health Service, "A Guide," p. 37, notes, "Unfortunately, incidents occur where workers are force by clients to have sex without a condom against their will (i.e., rape)."

kidney infections.[42] In addition, female sex workers are at increased risk of cervical dysplasia and cervical cancer.[43] HPV, the cause of cervical cancer, cannot be prevented with condom use alone. (The vaccine is effective for some strains of HPV, but not all, and not all cancer-causing strains.) All of these facts document exposure to known risks and dangers to health and safety; they are intrinsic to the job and are not minimal. It simply is not possible to develop sufficient regulations to meet occupational health and safety standards applicable to all other areas of employment (where the requirement is that working conditions eliminate "all known risks") and permit the acts essential to prostitution.[44]

This is true in other areas of the law as well, such as sexual harassment and civil rights. In brief, sexual harassment laws as they now stand are simply incompatible with prostitution. Central to sexual harassment law is the claim that employer's demands for sex in exchange for benefits is incompatible with women's equality. Sex as a condition of employment is a form of sex discrimination under current U.S. law.[45] Thus, either a

---

[42] New Zealand Department of Labour, Occupational Safety and Health Service, "A Guide," discusses repetitive stress injuries and advises sex workers to change positions or activities in order to avoid them (p. 41).

[43] Farley, *Prostitution and Trafficking in Nevada*, p. 46.

[44] Of course there are other "dangerous jobs" that entail various risks. As noted in Watson, "Why Sex Work Isn't Work," "According to the National Bureau of Labor Statistics report on fatal job injuries in 2011, fishers and logging are the most dangerous jobs in the U.S. (as measured by fatalities). In 2011, the fatal injury rates of fishers (127.3) and loggers (104.0) were approximately 25 times higher than the national fatal occupational injury rate of 3.5 per 100,000 full-time equivalent workers. Pilots, farmers, roofers, and drivers/sales workers and truck drivers also had fatal injury rates that exceeded the all-worker rate of 3.5 fatal occupational injuries per 100,000 full-time equivalent workers." See Pegula and Janocha, "Death on the Job." By contrast, the death rate of women in prostitution is 40 times higher than of women not in prostitution. In a study of women in prostitution in Colorado, researchers calculated a crude morality rate of 391 per 100,000 and a homicide rate among active "prostitutes" as 229 per 100,000. See Potterat et al., "Mortality in a Long-Term Open Cohort of Prostitute Women." Based on this study, the death rate of women in prostitution is just over three times higher than that of fishers, and nearly four times higher than that of loggers, the two most dangerous jobs in the United States (fn15). However, the inherent risk in prostitution of violation of bodily integrity as a part of the job distinguishes it from even other very risky occupations.

[45] After extensive research, we could find no example of a sexual harassment suit in the context of prostitution in Nevada. This is likely a result of the fact that sex workers in Nevada brothels are required to sign a contract that includes various clauses aiming to protect the brothel owners from litigation. For example, such contracts include a statement that there is no employment relationship (such workers are "independent contractors"); they include an indemnification clause (prohibiting sex workers from holding brothels liable for virtually any harms they may suffer in the context of sex work); and they include an agreement

carve-out (exemption) will be required to square selling sex with current law or both a carve-out for current law and new legislation that aims to define sexual harassment in this specific context—where sex is a condition of employment—would be required. In either case, women in prostitution will not have full access to the power and protection of sexual harassment law on a basis of equality with other workers.[46]

Reflection about enforcing civil rights laws prohibiting discrimination in public services produces the counterintuitive result that such laws protect prospective clients and not women in prostitution. This is true whether prostitutes are considered employees or independent contractors—for both are required to abide by antidiscrimination laws. Refusing service to a member of a protected group on grounds of age, race, disability status, and even sex is a civil rights violation. Perhaps an exception could be written into the law for sex. (For, perhaps, allowing persons in prostitution to deny service to same-sex customers seems different from allowing them to deny "services" to other groups?) Though it isn't obvious that any clear and defensible line can be drawn between sex status and other groups protected by discrimination law (unless one conflates one's actual sexual preferences, for heterosexual sex, with one's "job" description, but under the arguments for sex work, why should we do that?). In any case, the point here is that supposing, for example, any particular prostitute simply wanted to exclude persons over the age of 65 from her "services," this would actually violate the civil rights of the person being denied "service."

This highlights a critical tension between treating sex work as work like any other form of work and securing the rights to bodily integrity and sexual autonomy and of persons engaged in such work. Prostitutes themselves advocate for the importance of sexual autonomy and agency in the

---

to arbitration clause (waiving of right to jury trial/agreement to arbitration: arbitration is "final" and "binding" upon parties and "sole and exclusive remedy of the parties"). And "independent contractor hereby agrees and acknowledges that by submitting to arbitration, she is waiving her right to a jury trial." This ensures privacy/confidentiality, which is important to the brothels and to their advantage. Dennis Hoff (famous pimp-owner of many brothels in Nevada) sued one of the sex workers ("Jimi Lynn") for failure to abide by the gifts clause in her contract (where workers are required to pay the brothel 50% of the cash value of any gifts), and in the course of that litigation her contract was leaked. See Barrett Enterprises Group, "Moonlite Bunny Ranch."

[46] See Watson, "Why Sex Work Isn't Work."

course of their work—which includes the right to refuse anyone, at any time, for any reason.[47]

Moreover, reconciling civil rights protections for persons with disabilities and securing sexual autonomy for sex workers presents a distinct set of challenges. Persons with HIV-positive status, both as potential clients and as workers, are protected under the Americans with Disabilities Act; discrimination against such persons as seekers of services and as employees is prohibited. This raises the question of whether prostitutes could, consistent with the ADA, refuse sexual services to an HIV-positive client or forbid HIV-positive persons from selling sex. The full argument for this claim is complex. Elsewhere Watson argues:

> If this sounds far fetched, consider that persons with disabilities, including STIs [sexually transmitted infections], are covered under the Americans with Disabilities Act (ADA) and that the standard for refusal of service as explained by the Department of Justice is: "In almost every instance, the answer to this question is no. Persons with disabilities may be excluded from the activities or services of a private or public entity because of a health concern only if they pose a significant risk to the health or safety of others, known as a 'direct threat,' that cannot be *eliminated or reduced to an acceptable level by reasonable modifications* to the entity's policies, practices, or procedures. The determination that a person poses a significant risk to the health or safety of others may not be based on generalizations or stereotypes about a particular disability; it must be based on an *individualized assessment of the person with the disability* that relies on current medical evidence." All the arguments in favor of the legalization of sex work rely on the claim that the risks of contracting an STI can be reduced to an acceptable level so as to protect worker health and safety. If we accept these latter arguments, then there seems to be no justification for singling out HIV positive persons, either as clients or "workers" for exclusion.[48]

---

[47] Such a right is formally written into the law in the Netherlands, Germany, and New Zealand, although ample evidence, as documented in the text, shows such a right is merely formal.

[48] Watson and Flannigan, *Debating Sex Work.*

Again, perhaps such reconciliation may develop, but it at least will require treating prostitutes *differently from other workers*, creating exceptions in the law, and arguably such exemptions will deny persons in prostitution equal protection and rights as compared with other sound worker protections.

Thus, given the nature of the work (in prostitution), our arguments force the following conclusion: so-called "sex work" isn't like other forms of work, and indeed there is something unique about sex (and not in a moralized sense that is objectionable) that should inform how we think about what state regulations (if any) are appropriate to the buying and selling of sex.

What is unique about sex is that exercising control over the conditions, manner, and persons with whom one has sex is central to one's ability to maintain one's bodily integrity. Securing the conditions for control over one's bodily integrity is necessarily prior to, and required for, the exercise and enjoyment of any other rights. Places in which prostitution is legalized do, indeed, have exemptions, exceptions, and carve-outs that treat prostitution as different from other kinds of work. Such exceptions generally written into the law include the legal right to refuse sex with any particular client, though the ability to actually exercise this right in brothel conditions is another matter. Advocates of legalization may celebrate these kinds of exemptions, but supporting them just underscores that prostitution ("sex work," in their terms) is not a job like any other. That is an indefensible position. But these exceptions are not enough to secure equal working conditions for women in prostitution, for they require exempting women in prostitution from worker protections designed for the purposes of securing equality in the workplace.

One might think that a system of legalization in which women in prostitution are treated as independent contractors would resolve many of the issues we have raised for an employee-employer model of "sex work", for unlike an employee-employer relationship, independent contractors have greater autonomy in at least one sense: they have more direct control over their working conditions. Yet many of the same problems remain: the arguments we have given concerning occupational health and safety standards, sexual harassment law, and civil rights all apply equally where persons are independent contractors. In sum, it seems clear that a system of legalization simply cannot secure sexual autonomy, rights to security of the body and bodily integrity, and equality (as compared with the protections other citizens enjoy as workers).

Perhaps decriminalization will fare better. Current regimes of decriminalization do not adopt a completely laissez-faire attitude toward prostitution. Many of the regulations present in nation-states that legalize prostitution are similarly present in nation-states that decriminalize it. For example, New South Wales (Australia) and New Zealand both decriminalized prostitution (in 1979 and 2003, respectively), yet both have laws that specifically regulate the industry. New South Wales has minimal regulation,[49] whereas New Zealand has much more extensive regulations, including the licensing of brothels and health and safety requirements.[50] Of course, this is the result of political compromise. Arguments for decriminalization have been successful only where advocates promised to address sex trafficking and concerns about public health. Advocates of quasi-legalization (decriminalization with some regulations) will face the same set of objections just raised against legalization concerning their ability to secure both the sexual autonomy of women in prostitution as well as the conditions under which they have the ability to maintain their bodily integrity and equality with other legally recognized forms of work.

Beyond these arguments that aim to show the legal inconsistencies and tensions in legalization and decriminalization, the practical realities show that because of their unequal, subordinated social status, women in prostitution are unable to exercise and enjoy the purported protections that advocates of legalization or decriminalization claim to offer. For example, even in legalization regimes, nonlegal forms of prostitution flourish alongside legal forms, and the most vulnerable women are locked into the nonlegal forms.[51] Pimps persist (pimps as third parties to whom prostitutes make payments, as distinct from brothel owners).[52] Central employment protections are not available in practice, leaving women in

---

[49] In New South Wales, brothels are legal but subject to council planning approval. Escorts are unregulated, and street prostitution is permitted with some restrictions, such as that it must not be done near schools, churches, and hospitals. Presently, New South Wales is considering legislation to expand regulation. See NSW Parliamentary Research Service, "Brothel Regulation in NSW."

[50] New Zealand Parliamentary Counsel Office, Prostitution Reform Act.

[51] Netherlands, Scientific Research and Documentation Center, "Prostitution in the Netherlands."

[52] Netherlands, Scientific Research and Documentation Center, "Prostitution in the Netherlands."

prostitution vulnerable. Exit is difficult.[53] Ability to refuse in practice is minimal. Coercion into prostitution continues. A Netherlands report five years after the lift of the brothel ban concludes, "The extent of emotional well-being has declined between 2001 and 2006 with regard to all measured aspects. This matches the finding that the extent of distress has become higher, and the use of sedatives has increased."[54] Working conditions have not improved in Germany and the Netherlands, according to governmental reports.[55] And as the Netherlands report notes, legalization has done nothing to improve the asymmetries of power that prostitutes face; employers have significant power, and given that the work is done in private, there are "more opportunities for abuse of power" than in other work contexts.[56]

For all the reasons given above, neither legalization nor decriminalization (in which both the buyers and the sellers are equally decriminalized) is compatible with securing the freedom and equality of persons in prostitution as equal citizens. In addition, both legalization and decriminalization leave *demand* unaddressed. In so doing, they fail to address the primary mechanism that drives supply—the supply of women—which is demand. Moreover, legalizing or decriminalizing prostitution without creating meaningful opportunities for alternative options to earn a decent living ensures that those without such options will continue to find prostitution their best option.

---

[53] "When prostitutes make the decision to leave prostitution they often find themselves confronted by a multitude of problems. Along with financial and/or family problems, health problems linked to prostitution and stress from violence, in some cases experienced early in life, nearly half of those wanting to leave prostitution find themselves in a situation that is further compounded by the fact that they have little school education or vocational training. The preconditions for leaving the profession are not favourable" (Germany, Federal Ministry for Family Affairs, Senior Citizens, Women and Youth, "Report by the Federal Government," p. 33).

[54] Netherlands, Scientific Research and Documentation Center, "Prostitution in the Netherlands."

[55] "However, all in all, the results of the empirical study show that only little has been done up until now to improve working conditions. . . . Since those operating brothel-like establishments make business decisions like other traders or businessmen/women based on business management criteria, it is not surprising that working conditions are not improved unless they also fulfill the economic interests of the operator" (Germany, Federal Ministry for Family Affairs, Senior Citizens, Women and Youth, "Report by the Federal Government," p. 63).

[56] Netherlands, Scientific Research and Documentation Center, "Prostitution in the Netherlands."

Moreover, the report cites evidence of a shift in attitudes among persons about buying sex, and similarly a shift in demand—the target of the legislation.[68]

Because the Nordic model was developed by making the gendered structure of prostitution and trafficking central to its analysis, it starts with the acknowledgment that women are overwhelmingly the persons in prostitution (the sellers) and that men are overwhelmingly the buyers (and pimps). Moreover, it begins with the acknowledgment that this fact is both a result of inequality and a cause of further inequality. Thus, as explained earlier, it is a sex equality approach to prostitution. Its advocates recognize that decriminalization of the sellers (the women) is, under current conditions, the most equal approach (for as we noted above, criminalization disproportionately harms women in prostitution and legalization does not improve their overall conditions comparatively). However, its advocates argue that continued criminalization of the men (the buyers and pimps) is essential to promoting sex equality, for this is the most effective means to demand reduction, without which inequality and exploitation flourish. In addition, state support for exit is essential to the model; advocates recognize that without meaningful and robust alternatives to prostitution, women will continue to be disproportionately trapped in systems of prostitution. Such state support for exit should be very robust—perhaps even more robust than they are currently in nation-states with the Nordic model.

Contrary to many criticisms of feminist opposition to legalized or fully decriminalized prostitution, the Nordic model does not draw on or incorporate a view of sex or sexuality in a particular moralized sense; that is, it does not claim that sex itself is morally special or should be reserved for

---

order to determine how the ban has been applied in practice by the police, prosecutors and courts. As to the matter of the effects of the ban, the inquiry compared the incidence and forms of prostitution in Sweden today with circumstances prior to the ban's introduction. In addition, it compared the circumstances in Sweden with those in five other comparable countries—Norway, Denmark, Finland, Iceland and the Netherlands" (Swedish Institute, "Selected Extracts").

[68] The report states, "This means that a change has occurred in attitudes toward purchasing sexual services, which coincides with its criminalization. This change in attitude must be interpreted in such a way that the ban itself has had a normative effect, and that this can be expected to last, considering that the support is greatest among the young" (Swedish Institute, "Selected Extracts").

Thus far in our argument, we have considered prostitution independently from sex trafficking. Of course, strictly speaking as concepts, they are distinct. As a practical matter, they are intimately related and often indistinguishable.[57] The UN Special Rapporteur on Trafficking in Persons makes this point: "For the most part, prostitution as actually practiced in the world usually does satisfy the elements of trafficking."[58] Catharine MacKinnon has also provided powerful evidence and arguments that, as a practical matter, the conditions under which women enter into and remain in prostitution (severe and pervasive sex inequality) satisfy the elements of sex trafficking (notably "sexual exploitation through abuse of power or as condition of vulnerability").[59]

This reality is often elided in discussions of prostitution, where prostitution is usually characterized as the selling of sex on a voluntary basis. Sex trafficking, in contrast, is usually thought to involve the force, fraud, or coercion of persons into selling sex. Many people think that sex trafficking involves movement of persons for purposes of prostitution (movement across international or national borders).[60] However, this isn't a part of legal definitions of sex trafficking. Though legal definitions vary somewhat, they all basically coalesce around the exploitation of persons for prostitution through force, fraud, or coercion.[61]

---

[57] According to the European Parliament briefing paper "European Parliament Resolution," "The most conservative official statistics suggest that 1 in 7 prostitutes in Europe are victims of trafficking, while some Member States estimated that between 60% and 90% of those in their respective national prostitution markets have been trafficked. Moreover, the data available confirm that most trafficking in Europe is for the purposes of sexual exploitation, principally of women and girls."

[58] European Parliament, "European Parliament Resolution."

[59] MacKinnon, "Trafficking, Prostitution, and Inequality." p. 299.

[60] As MacKinnon makes clear, "Movement across jurisdictional lines is not, and has not been, an element of the international definition of trafficking since at least 1949" ("Trafficking, Prostitution, and Inequality," p. 299).

[61] The United Nations Protocol to Prevent, Suppress and Punish Trafficking in Persons, Especially Women and Children, the "Palermo Protocol," defines trafficking: " 'Trafficking in persons' shall mean the recruitment, transportation, transfer, harbouring or receipt of persons, by means of the threat or use of force or other forms of coercion, of abduction, of fraud, of deception, of the abuse of power or of a position of vulnerability or of the giving or receiving of payments or benefits to achieve the consent of a person having control over another person, for the purpose of exploitation. Exploitation shall include, at a minimum, the exploitation of the prostitution of others or other forms of sexual exploitation, forced labour or services, slavery or practices similar to slavery, servitude or the removal of organs." The U.S. Congress, Victims of Trafficking and Violence Protection Act offers the following definition of "severe trafficking": "A commercial sex act is induced by force, fraud, or coercion,

There is vast empirical evidence that where prostitution (defined as a voluntary selling of sex) is either legalized or decriminalized, sex trafficking (force, fraud, or coercion) flourishes and grows. In turn, demand grows. And in turn, more trafficking occurs to supply the demand. Niklas Jakobsson and Andreas Kotsdam analyzed the relationship between nation-state laws (in Europe) concerning prostitution and sex trafficking. They "find that trafficking of women for commercial exploitation is least prevalent in countries where prostitution is illegal, most prevalent in countries where prostitution is legalized, and in between in those countries where prostitution is legal but procuring is illegal."[62] Additionally, as a briefing paper for the European Parliament emphasizes, "several studies made in recent years suggest, indeed, that the legislation on prostitution [discussing legalization in Germany and the Netherlands] increases the flow of trafficking for sexual exploitation, while the working conditions of prostitutes and the level of violence have not improved—according to government reports."[63] And even more, in a paper analyzing 150 countries, the authors conclude, "On average, countries where prostitution is legal experience larger reported human trafficking inflows."[64]

Thus, effective strategies for addressing the potential for exploitation in prostitution and trafficking for purposes of sexual exploitation must address demand. In assessing the Nordic model, the EU briefing paper notes that it "seems to have effectively reduced demand and deterred traffickers."[65] Similar conclusions are drawn in other studies.[66] The Swedish government report assessing the model 10 years after the passage

---

or in which the person induced to perform such an act has not attained 18 years of age." Interestingly, trafficking (as opposed to severe trafficking) is defined as "sex trafficking": "the recruitment, harboring, transportation, provision, or obtaining of a person for the purpose of a commercial sex act." Thus, as legally defined, all users of prostitutes are sex traffickers, though not of the severe kind distinguished above.

[62] Jakobsson and Kotsdam, "The Law and Economics of International Sex Slavery," quoting abstract.

[63] See European Parliament, Directorate-General for Internal Policies, "Sexual Exploitation and Prostitution."

[64] Seo-Young, Dreher, and Neumayer, "Does Legalized Prostitution Increase Human Trafficking?," quoting abstract.

[65] See European Parliament, "European Parliament Resolution."

[66] See European Parliament, "European Parliament Resolution."

of the new law that criminalizes the buying but not the selling of sex, concludes:

> Since the introduction of the ban on the purchase of sexual serv-
> ices, street prostitution in Sweden has been reduced by half. This
> reduction may be considered to be a direct result of the criminaliza-
> tion of sex purchases. In a comparison, we have noted that the prev-
> alence of street prostitution was about the same in the three capital
> cities of Norway, Denmark and Sweden before the ban on the pur-
> chase of sexual services was introduced here, but the number of
> women in street prostitution in both Norway and Denmark subse-
> quently increased dramatically. In 2008, the number of people in
> street prostitution in both Norway and Denmark was estimated to
> be three times higher than in Sweden. In light of the great economic
> and social similarities that exist among these three countries, it is
> reasonable to assume that the reduction in street prostitution in
> Sweden is a direct result of criminalization.
>
> In the last five years, Internet prostitution has increased in
> Sweden, Denmark and Norway. However, the scale of this form of
> prostitution is more extensive in our neighboring countries, and
> there is nothing to indicate that a greater increase in prostitution
> over the Internet has occurred in Sweden than in these comparable
> countries. This indicates that the ban has not led to a change in
> arenas, that is, from street prostitution to the Internet, in Sweden.
> In light of this it should be possible to conclude that the reduction
> of street prostitution by half that took place in Sweden represents
> a real reduction in prostitution here and that this reduction is also
> mainly a result of the criminalization of sex purchases.
>
> There is nothing to indicate that the prevalence of indoor pros-
> titution that is not marketed through advertisements in magazines
> and on the Internet, for instance, prostitution in massage parlors,
> sex clubs and hotels, and in restaurant and nightclub settings,
> has increased in recent years. Nor is there any information that
> suggests that prostitutes formerly exploited on the streets are now
> involved in indoor prostitution.[67]

---

[67] An English translation of the key findings of the report describes the methodology of the committee tasked with evaluating the effects of the new law (Nordic model): "With regard to the application of the ban, the committee examined reports of crime and sentences in

meaningful intimate relationships, nor does it adopt some similar conservative or partial view about how individuals should value sex. Rather, it
rests on a view about the substantive demands of sex-equal citizenship, in
which gender-based hierarchies that shape women's life prospects in employment, health, basic safety of the person, and the enjoyment of equal
standing with their co-citizens are simply intolerable. Thus, it is a public
reason argument.

Arguments for the decriminalization or legalization of "sex work" are
often thought to be the quintessential liberal positions. One thought that
permeates this argument is that there is no nonmoralistic argument for
restricting or prohibiting markets in sex among adults. That is, some think
that any argument that aims to restrict or eliminate markets in sex among
"consenting" adults must be premised on a moralized view about sex (such
as that it is always wrong to sell sex because there is something special
about sex, as opposed to selling, say, nonsexual labor). Another thought
that permeates many liberal reflections on legalization is that prohibition
is a form of paternalism that is unacceptable in liberal states committed to
the view that the state should allow individuals to engage in harmful behavior when those harms are primarily borne by the individuals involved.[69]

Generally, liberals accept arguments for state regulation and enforcement of the kinds of worker health and safety regulations demanded by
human rights instruments cited above on the grounds that they promote
the twin liberal values of freedom and equality. The work relation—the
employee-employer relation—is an unequal relationship; employers have
significantly more power, and individual employees alone lack sufficient
power to negotiate fair and just conditions of work. Labor unions (even
"sex worker" unions) are premised upon the recognition of the fact that
collective bargaining is one way to ensure greater equality in the employee-
employer relationship.[70] Government regulations that set minimum
standards for fair terms of employment are another way to collectively
address the power imbalance between employers and employees. What
we have tried to show here is that the values of securing worker health,

---

[69] For an argument that some forms of prohibition are both paternalistic and nonetheless
justifiable by liberal principles, see de Marneffe, *Liberalism and Prostitution*.

[70] Although it is worth noting that brothel owners and pimps in fact run many sex worker
unions and collectives. See Farley, "Bad for the Body," pp. 1091–1092.

safety, and rights to sexual autonomy and bodily integrity on a basis of equality with other forms of work are not achievable under a legalization (or decriminalization) regime.

A commitment to sex equality requires securing the conditions for women to enjoy and exercise the full rights of citizenship on a basis of equality. Legalization or full decriminalization of prostitution is not compatible with the realization of sex equality either in conceptualization or in actual practice. Rather, as we have argued here, the Nordic model is the best approach to prostitution for women and for those committed to making sex equality real.

Social Norms, Choice, and Work

Any just and fair solution to the urgent problem of women's and children's vulnerability must encourage and facilitate the equal sharing by men and women of paid and unpaid work, of productive and reproductive labor.

—SUSAN M. OKIN, *Justice, Gender and the Family*

I. Introduction

Despite antidiscrimination laws in education and employment and sexual harassment laws,[1] the gendered division of labor with respect to both paid and unpaid work is a persistent fact in modern liberal democracies.[2] Data from the United States demonstrate this. According to the U.S. Bureau of Labor Statistics, in 2015, 56.7% of women participated in the labor force, compared to 69.1% of men.[3] However, 25% of employed women worked part-time jobs, while just 12% of employed men did. Furthermore, women earned just 81% of men's "median weekly earnings." The data show that income still varies considerably by race, too, again, despite laws prohibiting race-based discrimination. For example, Asian women and white women earned more than black women and Hispanic women; however, black women and Hispanic women took home about 90% of the earnings of black men and Hispanic men, respectively. Of course, the smaller gap between black men and women and Hispanic men and women is due in part to men in these groups earning less.

---

[1] Of course, many women who are sexually harassed don't report it, for reasons that are perfectly understandable given their situations. See, e.g., Miller, "It's Not Just Fox."

[2] As noted in the preface, Hartley is the sole author of this chapter. She thanks Watson for generous feedback on multiple drafts of the chapter, and she thanks Gina Schouten and Kathryn Joyce for very helpful comments, too.

[3] U.S. Bureau of Labor Statistics, "Women in the Labor Force."

Marriage and motherhood were also key factors affecting women's earnings. Using data from the U.S. Bureau of Labor Statistics, Michelle Budig stresses:

> Unmarried women earn 96 cents to an unmarried man's dollar, and childless women (including married and unmarried) earn 93 cents on a childless man's dollar. In contrast, wives and mothers fare far less well. Even among full-time workers, married mothers with at least one child under age 18 earn 76 cents on a married father's dollar. Single mothers earn 83.1 cents to a single custodial father's dollar (that single moms are much less likely to be employed full-time relative to single dads is masked by this estimate among full-time workers).[4]

More recently, a 2015 study reported that mothers earn 71.4% of fathers' earnings.[5]

There is also an inequitable division of unpaid work between men and women as groups. Consider unpaid dependent care work.[6] Women remain the primary caregivers for children and for adults who depend on others for help in meeting their basic needs.[7] According to the 2015 American Time Use Survey, in households with children under six, women spent more than twice as much time on an average day with physical care for children.[8] Women were also the majority of unpaid eldercare providers (56%), and women spent more time on the days they provided care than men doing this work (3.5 hours to 2.9).[9] The Family Caregiver Alliance, a nonprofit organization that aims "to improve the quality of life for caregivers and those they care for through information, services, and

---

[4] Budig, "The Fatherhood Bonus." Budig's research shows that parenthood increases the earnings of most fathers, and women's earnings decrease with each child. However, her research reveals that the "fatherhood bonus" benefits the most advantaged men the most and that the "motherhood penalty" hurts the least advantaged women the most.

[5] Institute for Women's Policy Research, "Mothers Earn Just 71 Percent of What Fathers Earn."

[6] Women also do much of the paid work that relates to the caring of dependents. This work is often underpaid and performed without the needed material and social support, but we cannot address this here.

[7] See, e.g., Heymann, *The Widening Gap*; Crittenden, *The Price of Motherhood*.

[8] U.S. Bureau of Labor Statistics, "American Time Use Survey, 2015."

[9] U.S. Bureau of Labor Statistics, "Unpaid Eldercare in the United States."

advocacy," documents the disproportionate amount of eldercare women provide:

> An estimated 66% of caregivers are female. The average caregiver is a 49 year old woman, caring for her 60 year old mother who does not live with her. She is married and employed. Although men also provide assistance to family members, female caregivers may spend as much as 50% more time providing care than male caregivers.[10]

Furthermore, women spend more time each day doing housework. According to the 2015 American Time Use Survey, "On an average day, women spent more than twice as much time preparing food and drink and doing interior cleaning, and over three times as much time doing laundry as men did."[11]

The primary caregivers of dependents, most of whom are women, face a number of challenges. In the United States, there is no federal law requiring paid leave. A number of jobs in the U.S. labor market lack paid leave, sufficient paid leave, or sufficient flexibility for meeting caring responsibilities for others. So those who combine unpaid caregiving with labor market participation must often reduce their labor market hours or take less demanding positions; some caregivers choose to work in the labor market part time. Those who choose less demanding positions or part-time paid work often suffer from reduced earnings, reduced benefits, lost opportunities for advancement, and positions with little power and prestige.[12] Meeting caregiving responsibilities can also result in losing a promotion or even a job. Many caregivers who work in the labor market and, certainly, those who provide caregiving full time are financially dependent on others for the goods they need for themselves and those for whom they care. Since women are often the primary caregivers of dependents, caregiving makes many women dependent on others for financial security. Out of concern for the well-being of those for whom they care, some women who are financially dependent on their spouses or partners tolerate

---

[10] Family Caregiver Alliance, "Women and Caregiving."

[11] U.S. Bureau of Labor Statistics, "American Time Use Survey, 2015."

[12] See, e.g., Heymann, *The Widening Gap*; Williams, *Unbending Gender*; Slaughter, "Why Women Still Can't Have It All."

behavior that they would otherwise not if they were in a better position to leave a marriage or other relationship, including, for example, physical abuse, verbal abuse, adultery, and demeaning spending allowances and/or other forms of economic abuse. But even in relationships in which women never face such deplorable spousal or partner behavior, the fact of inequality between the spouses and partners influences the distribution of goods within the household and how couples relate to each other—how much they will ask of their partner and the sorts of things they judge worth complaining about.[13] Marital relationships or other long-term relationships that do end in divorce or separation leave women and their dependents vulnerable to poverty.

Are these substantive inequalities injustices that the state ought to remedy in some way? And can political liberals recognize such inequalities as injustices and appropriately address them? Again, in modern democratic states, there are equal basic rights and liberties for all citizens and antidiscrimination laws in education and employment. The gendered division of labor is at least partially the result of men and women making different choices about work and family life, even if such choices stem from social norms about gender. The choices that women make relative to men's disadvantage them in various ways: such choices lead them to earn less, enjoy less power and prestige in the labor market, be less able to participate in the political sphere on an equal basis, make them to some degree financially dependent on others, and leave them at a bargaining disadvantage and vulnerable in certain personal relationships. But if women make these choices against a background of certain rights, liberties, opportunities, and protection from discrimination, on what grounds and under what circumstances could or should the state intervene? After all, political liberals accept the fact of reasonable pluralism, and reasonable people will make difference choices with different outcomes, given their views of the good. Different choices alone do not indicate injustice. As Brian Barry stresses:

> The egalitarian liberal position is that justice requires equal rights and opportunities but not necessarily equal outcomes defined over groups. It is certainly true that many liberals have as a matter of fact hoped that, once women had the same rights and

---

[13] On the latter point, see Crittenden, *The Price of Motherhood*, pp. 113–114.

opportunities as men, there would be a long run tendency for the profile of choices made by women and the profile of choices made by men to converge. But what must be emphasized is that it is perfectly possible to believe that justice demands equal rights and opportunities for men and women while at the same time neither hoping nor expecting that this will result in the career choices of women tending to become statistically indistinguishable from those of men.[14]

In contrast, many feminists urge us to think critically about the circumstances in which men and women make choices about both paid and unpaid work.[15] Clare Chambers claims that liberals, generally, are too quick to take "individuals' choices as the determinant of justice."[16] She rejects the claim that choice itself is a "normative transformer" in the sense of transforming the object of choice from potentially suspect to warranted. Rather, she emphasizes that choices and options are socially constructed: (1) social norms shape preferences and, thereby, choices, and (2) social norms restrict options. As a result, she claims that when a "choice in question harms the chooser in relation to those who choose differently" and when "there are identifiable pressures on the choosing group to make that choice," then the state may need to intervene for the sake of equality and freedom.[17] Some women, for example, choose low-paying, flexible jobs or forgo labor market participation altogether in order to care for dependents and are disadvantaged as a result; their choice is certainly made under considerable pressure given norms for women regarding caring for dependents. In Chambers's view, state intervention is appropriate.

Gina Schouten, like Chambers, argues that political liberalism's ability to secure equality and justice for women depends on whether political liberals can address certain sexist or morally objectionable social

---

[14] Barry, *Culture and Equality*, p. 92. Chambers calls attention to and goes on to challenge this important claim from Barry in her *Sex, Culture, and Justice.*

[15] This recognition is a common theme in recent work on the gendered division of labor. See, e.g., Chambers, *Sex, Culture and Justice*; Schouten, "Is the Gendered Division of Labor a Problem of Distribution?"

[16] Chambers, *Sex, Culture, and Justice*, p. 118.

[17] Chambers, *Sex, Culture, and Justice*, p. 120.

norms that affect women's choices and options. And both Chambers and Schouten view the current gendered division of labor, in particular, as partly the result of women's choices in the context of objectionable social norms that shape women's preferences, structure social institutions, and restrict women's options. Chambers thinks that political liberals simply lack the resources to address this problem. Specifically, she claims that political liberals fail to take first-order autonomy to be important for justice and that the protection of this sort of autonomy is necessary to secure equality for women.[18] Schouten, on the other hand, argues that in some circumstances political liberals must support political interventions aimed at undermining the gendered division of labor, but she claims that our own strategy, which she calls the "Incompatibility Strategy," fails.[19] In previous work,[20] we claim that insofar as the gendered division of labor is incompatible with free and equal citizenship for women, political liberals can and must adopt many of the policies feminists propose for its elimination (in nonideal societies and well-ordered societies, too).

In this chapter, we build on our argument for the claim that political liberalism is a feminist liberalism by focusing on how and when political liberals can and must address the social norms in the background culture of society that shape the choices and options of men and women and subordinate or disadvantage women. Most of our discussion in this chapter focuses on the gendered division of labor, but we think that our claims here can be used to provide a framework for other issues of concern to feminists, such as when the state can interfere with other cultural practices that threaten women's equality. In short, we aim to clarify, develop, and defend our view regarding when and how political liberals can rectify inequality and the disadvantages that women face when work is gendered. We reply to the work of both Chambers and Schouten in order to address their important challenges and better explain the commitments of political liberals.

---

[18] Chambers, *Sex, Culture, and Justice*, pp. 159–201.

[19] For Schouten's argument that in some circumstances political liberalism requires gender egalitarian intervention in the division of labor, see "Citizenship, Reciprocity." For Schouten's critique of our strategy for the justification of gender egalitarian interventions in the division of labor, see "Does the Gendered Division of Labor Undermine Citizenship?"

[20] See Hartley and Watson, "Is a Feminist Political Liberalism Possible?" and "Feminism, Religion and Shared Reasons."

II. Political Liberalism and Autonomy

For this discussion, we assume that the gendered division of labor is partly due to different choices made by men and women and that these choices are crucial to sustaining this division of labor that disadvantages women. Of course, these choices are made when institutions are structured in a certain way and when gender norms influence people's choices and options. We also assume that there are various policies the state could enact to affect individuals' choices—policies that would alter persons' preferences and options by changing the structure of the institutions in which the choices are made—and we assume that these policies would result in a more egalitarian division of labor in both paid and unpaid work between men and women. These policies include, for example, short-term paid leave to care for dependents, state-supported day care and aftercare, shorter work weeks, more flexible work hours, and job sharing. On what grounds, though, could political liberals justify such policies?

II.1 Chambers on Political Liberalism and Autonomy

As noted above, Chambers thinks that political liberals are "peculiarly ill-equipped to deal with injustices resulting from culture and choice."[21] Central to her argument is the claim that political liberals regard only "second-order autonomy"—not "first-order autonomy"—as a concern of justice and, so, a concern of the liberal state. According to Chambers, first-order autonomy requires that an individual "critically examines rules and norms and follows only those that she endorses." Second-order autonomy requires that an individual "chooses and endorses the overall conception of the good that she follows."[22] The distinction is meant to capture two levels of reflective endorsement. An example will help to clarify these distinct senses of autonomy and Chambers's worry about political liberalism. Consider a Catholic who endorses Catholicism as a way of life and who commits herself to the infallibility of the pope's teachings, which she follows without question. She is second-order autonomous insofar as she reflectively endorses Catholicism as a way of life, but she is not first-order autonomous, as she follows the pope's particular teachings (e.g., specific rules and instructions) on the basis of his authority (which she defers to

---

[21] Chambers, *Sex, Culture and Justice*, p. 160.

[22] Chambers, *Sex, Culture, and Justice*, pp. 160–161.

as part of the way of life she endorses) and not her own reflective endorsement of the particular rules.

Chambers says that political liberals recognize the importance of second-order autonomy through their insistence that the moral power of having the capacity to form, revise, and pursue a rational conception of the good is a fundamental interest of persons as citizens. One aspect of this moral power as Rawls defines it is the ability to revise one's conception of the good, and Chambers says that the capacity for first-order autonomy is "expressed in Rawls's claim that individuals must be able to 'revise' their conception of the good."[23] Despite Chambers's recognition that one of the moral powers includes the capacity to revise a conception of the good, she claims that political liberals think only securing citizens' second-order autonomy is necessary for justice. This is so, she claims, because being second-order autonomous means that "individuals must be free to use their second-order autonomy to alienate their first-order autonomy."[24] In the example above, the individual alienates her first-order autonomy to unquestioningly follow the dictates of the pope.

According to Chambers, there are two problems with taking only second-order autonomy to be a concern of justice. The first problem concerns the fact that social norms limit preferences, and preferences are used in the construction of institutions and the framing and shaping of options. Gendered social norms, then, lead to gendered and constrained opportunities, and this is true even when, formally, there are equal options.[25] So if the gendered division of labor is partly the result of different choices of men and women, then we should consider that gender norms may heavily influence individuals' preferences, constrain options available to individuals as members of different groups, and result in problematic inequality or disadvantage for one group relative to another. There are circumstances, surely, when the state should intervene. This concern suggests that liberals should be concerned both with the choices that are part of a way of life and the very possibility of second-order autonomy at all.

---

[23] Chambers, *Sex, Culture, and Justice*, p. 162.

[24] Chambers, *Sex, Culture, and Justice*, p. 165.

[25] Chambers, *Sex, Culture, and Justice*, p. 161. Chambers stresses that Nussbaum makes this case in her own work. See Nussbaum's *Sex and Social Justice* and *Women and Human Development*.

According to Chambers, a second problem with taking only second-order autonomy to be a concern of justice is that some conceptions of the good ("ways of life") or "specific choices within a life" are harmful or result in inequalities or both.[26] That is, to follow certain social norms and receive certain benefits, individuals must sometimes take courses of action that involve physical, mental, or material harm or social subordination.[27]

To show how problematic it is to privilege second-order autonomy over first-order autonomy, Chambers discusses the practice of female genital mutilation (FGM). While it may seem odd for us to discuss FGM in the midst of a discussion of social norms and the gendered division of labor, FGM is a paradigmatic example of a cultural practice that is part of a gendered way of life and that is utterly unacceptable for anyone committed to equal citizenship for women. By starting with this case, the relevant commitments of political liberalism for addressing social norms and choice will be apparent, and, so, how to address other cases like the gendered division of labor will be clearer. Here, though, is the problem: Chambers thinks FGM should be banned under any conditions, and she thinks that, given their commitments, political liberals cannot justify a ban on FGM in some circumstances.

According to Chambers, the liberal state should recognize that if certain practices are significantly harmful or pose significant risk of harm and if compliance with the practice is required to comply with a social norm (that is unjust or maintains/perpetuates social inequality) and to receive a benefit, then the state should ban the practice.[28] In her view, FGM clearly warrants a ban; so, too, do breast implants. As makeup is less harmful, a ban would not be appropriate, but other measures would, such as a state media campaign.

II.2 Response to Chambers

To begin our response to Chambers, we note that Chambers's description of political liberalism is too crude. Whether in a nonideal society or in a well-ordered, politically liberal society, political liberals do not view choice as a normative transformer in all circumstances. Political liberals

---

[26] Chambers, *Sex, Culture and Justice*, p. 161.

[27] Chambers, *Sex, Culture, and Justice*, p. 173.

[28] Chambers, *Sex, Culture, and Justice*, pp. 195–196.

are fundamentally concerned with all persons standing in a relationship of free and equal citizenship in a liberal democratic society viewed as a shared cooperative enterprise. They endorse a substantive notion of equality, as we argued in chapter 6, and they think that the basic structure must be set up in accordance with principles and constitutional essentials that secure equal citizenship for all. When social norms in the background culture influence choice and limit options in such a way as to undermine persons' standing as free and equal citizens, then the state can intervene and sometimes must intervene, regardless of persons' preferences and endorsement of a way of life or aspects thereof.

We also note that political liberals can straightforwardly condemn FGM. An interagency statement from the United Nations declares:

> Communities that practice female genital mutilation report a variety of social and religious reasons for continuing with it. Seen from a human rights perspective, the practice reflects deep-rooted inequality between the sexes, and constitutes an extreme form of discrimination against women. Female genital mutilation is nearly always carried out on minors and is therefore a violation of the rights of the child. The practice also violates the rights to health, security and physical integrity of the person, the right to be free from torture and cruel inhuman or degrading treatment, and the right to life when the procedure results in death.[29]

FGM is a severe practice of sex subordination through the mutilation of the body of girls and women that is used to control women's sexuality so that they will be suitable for male sexual consumption. It is mainly practiced on girls, who are simply unable to consent, or women under coercive or forced conditions. The procedure itself is dangerous, practiced under unsafe conditions by individuals who are not health professionals, and carries lifelong health risks (both physical and psychological). As political liberals are fundamentally committed to securing the conditions for free and equal citizenship for all persons, they can condemn this practice anywhere as a violation of women's fundamental rights.

Chambers, though, asks us to *imagine* conditions under which *adult* women seek genital procedures involving symbolic cutting and flesh

---

[29] World Health Organization, "Eliminating Female Genital Mutilation."

removal but in an entirely different social context. Imagine a well-ordered, politically liberal society, in which all persons receive an education to prepare them for citizenship (have knowledge of their rights and entitlements and various opportunities they might pursue). In a community within that society certain female genital procedures are associated with sexual purity and fittingness for marriage and are, no doubt, tied to views about gender objectionable from the point of view of many feminists. Suppose women seek such procedures informed of the fact that such procedures have permanent consequences and long-term risk, even when performed in licensed facilities by licensed professionals. It is under these circumstances in which Chambers claims that political liberals cannot support a ban on FGM.

It is difficult to respond to Chambers on this point. What we are asked to imagine is simply not FGM, as that is practiced under very specific conditions in which women are subordinated to men and do not enjoy the same status as men as members of society; this is utterly unacceptable to political liberals. What we must imagine here, instead, are female genital procedures (involving symbolic cutting or flesh removal) in a wholly different context. We think it is highly unlikely that such procedures would be sought. Given the extraordinary difference in context in which we could begin to imagine political liberals permitting such female genital procedures, we could draw comparisons to purely cosmetic labiaplasty and so-called vaginal rejuvenation procedures available in the West.

In recent years more women in the United States have sought these procedures than ever before.[30] Women who seek such procedures certainly face considerable pressure to meet beauty norms, and the women who choose these procedures are willing to risk harms of infection, decreased sexual pleasure, long-term pain, and scars for the sake of what they believe will be a more attractive appearance and, presumably, other benefits associated with that. The American College of Obstetricians and Gynecologists issued in 2007 (and reaffirmed in 2017) a committee opinion warning of the lack of data about the safety and consequences of the procedure and of "deceptive" attempts by marketers to suggest that vaginal rejuvenation,

---

[30] Halloway, "The Search for the Perfect Vagina." The American Society of Plastic Surgeons reports that there was a 39% rise in labiaplasty between 2015 and 2016 (Horton, "Stats Show Labiaplasty Is Becoming More Popular").

designer vaginoplasty, revirgination, or G-spot amplification procedures are "accepted and routine surgical practices."[31]

What of such procedures in a well-ordered, politically liberal society? Again, it depends on the circumstances of the society. Certainly, feminists should lead campaigns in the background culture to bring attention to the unknown health and safety risks of these procedures and to promote healthy body images for women and girls; indeed, information about health—diet, exercise, normal and abnormal differences among human beings—should be part of the basic education provided to all children. The state can ban medical and cosmetic procedures if they are unsafe or too risky, although it is not yet clear if vaginal cosmetic surgeries are sufficiently risky or harmful to meet this standard. The state, of course, can regulate such procedures given its concern with health and human safety, including requiring patients be made aware of risks and/or receive counseling.

Consider a different sort of case in which, due to social norms and in order to obtain a benefit, some women may wish to sell sex. As noted in chapter 7, it is not possible to protect persons in prostitution in the way that other workers are protected from health and safety risks; it is not clear how to reconcile meaningful respect for sexual autonomy with civil rights laws (protecting the right of prostitutes to refuse sex while protecting clients from discrimination on the basis of membership in a protected class); it is not clear how to design laws to protect prostitutes from sexual harassment or from violence and coercion; and in any society in which women are sexually objectified (which is part of the background culture of all current societies and could be part of the background culture of a well-ordered society) and in which the purchasing of sex is legalized, prostitution will contribute to and perpetuate a view of women that threatens the standing of women as free and equal citizens. Given the risk of harm and threats to bodily integrity to those who sell sex and the threat to equal citizenship for all women and girls, the case is overdetermined. Political liberals can advocate for state intervention in the name of equality. As discussed in chapter 7, we endorse the Nordic model for state regulation of prostitution.

Now recall the first problem that Chambers notes with taking second-order autonomy (and not first-order autonomy) as the concern

---

[31] Committee on Gynecologic Practice, "Vaginal 'Rejuvenation' and Cosmetic Vaginal Procedures."

of justice: social norms limit preferences and are used in the construction of institutions. Gendered social norms, then, lead to gendered and constrained opportunities, even when, formally, there are equal options. Again, note that the current gendered labor market is partly the result of men and women making different choices about labor market participation and caring for dependents. A recent survey by Pew Research is telling of current social norms in the United States. Consider:

> In a 2012 Pew Research survey, the vast majority of Americans (79%) rejected the notion that women should return to their traditional role in society. Yet when they were asked what is best for young children, very few adults (16%) said that having a mother that works full time is the "ideal situation." Some 42% said that having a mother who works part time is ideal and 33% said what is best for young children is to have a mother who doesn't work at all. Even among full-time working moms, only about one-in-five (22%) said that having a full-time working mother is ideal for young children. . . . About half (47%) said working part time is ideal for these women, while 33% said not working at all would be the best situation.[32]

In this survey, Americans had a very different view about the ideal situation for dads: "Fully seven-in-ten adults said working full time would be ideal." Insofar as different social norms hold for men and women when it comes to labor market participation and caring for dependents, men and women will have different preferences, which affect their options. Can political liberals intervene for the sake of equality and justice?

In the United States, as Joan Williams and others have argued, the overwhelming majority of the best jobs in the labor market and most other jobs assume that workers do not have primary responsibility for dependents.[33] The hours and other work requirements (traveling, relocation, scheduled meetings, leave policies, etc.) are simply too demanding for individuals to be both full-time participants in the labor market and the primary caretakers of dependents. However, the matter would be quite different in a society well-ordered by a political conception of

---

[32] Parker, "Women More Than Men Adjust Their Careers."

[33] See, e.g., Williams, *Unbending Gender*.

justice. Political liberals view society as a system of cooperation over time, and principles of basic justice and constitutional essentials must be justifiable to persons viewed as free and equal citizens. As Rawls says, of central concern is the "orderly production and reproduction of society and its culture from one generation to the next."[34] Indeed, it is a fundamental interest of every person as a citizen that she is reasonably cared for as a child and in any time of dependency (although Rawls does not adequately address this).[35] Women have done and continue to do most of the work caring for children and other dependents, and as a result have been disadvantaged relative to men in their ability to participate in the labor market, the political sphere, and civil society. However, as it is a fundamental interest of every person that she receives care in times of dependency and as it is fundamental to the continuation of society that this work be performed, this work should be regarded as socially obligatory work for which we are all collectively responsible. We do not think any other view is consistent with the recognition of persons as free and equal citizens.

While it need not be the case that caring for dependents is equally distributed among those able to perform the work in society, it must be the case that those who perform this work should not be disadvantaged relative to other citizens with respect to their ability to participate in the various spheres of social life central to citizenship.[36] We take these spheres of life central to citizenship to include the labor market, the political sphere, civil society, and the family (understood in the "political" sense as an institution for caretaking relationships of various sorts). If caretakers are disadvantaged with respect to their ability to participate in any sphere of life central to citizenship due to their performance of socially necessary work for which members of society are collectively responsible, then caretakers are not equal citizens with others.

One might say caretaking work simply needs to be recognized as work as valuable as labor market participation and appropriately

---

[34] The quoted passage is from Rawls, and he claims that "the orderly production and reproduction of society and its culture from one generation to the next" is why the family is part of the basic structure (IPRR, p. 595).

[35] See, e.g., Kittay, *Love's Labor*; Nussbaum, *Frontiers of Justice*. We believe political liberals can adequately address this but do not discuss it here.

[36] See Fraser's antimarginalization principle in her "After the Family Wage" in *Justice Interruptus*, p. 48.

compensated for as such (for example, by state-provided caregiver allowances, together with other benefits comparable to labor market jobs). Individuals can choose labor market participation or full-time care work. This won't do. There are two principal reasons.[37] First, as a matter of how life in modern democratic societies has developed, the labor market and the family are distinctive institutions with peculiar purposes, relationships, sources of satisfaction/dissatisfaction, opportunity for recognition and power beyond one's personal sphere, creativity, and frustration. One does not substitute for the other. From the point of view of the state, the labor market is one aspect of the economy (the economy also includes socially necessary unpaid work), in which individuals work together, by selling their labor, to produce many of the discrete and distributable goods and services that are needed by citizens. It allows individuals to develop and employ their talents and skills and form distinctive, transactional relationships, both of which contribute to the social bases of self-respect.

Now consider the institution of the family. Political liberals recognize that as part of their comprehensive doctrines individuals may have peculiar conceptions of the family. However, political liberals must recognize a political institution—the family in the political sense—for the support of intimate caring relationships, given that material care in times of dependency is among the needs of all persons,[38] that caring relationships are central to the healthy emotional, cognitive, and moral development of children, and, too, that intimate caring relationships are needed for adults to exercise their moral powers.[39] Relationships in the family are distinctive: they are intimate and personal and involve a different kind of vulnerability than most other relationships. Being able to participate in both the family and the labor market is important for citizenship, as is, again, being able to participate in the political sphere and in civil society. It is not publicly justifiable for society to be structured so that some individuals—because they are providing the socially necessary work of caregiving—are marginalized from institutions central to citizenship.

---

[37] See Fraser's "After the Family Wage" and, in particular, her critical discussion of the caregiver parity model.

[38] Kittay, *Love's Labor*; Nussbaum, *Frontiers of Justice*.

[39] Brake, *Minimizing Marriage*.

There is another problem with the idea that caretaking work simply needs to be recognized as work as valuable as labor market participation and compensated for appropriately.[40] Here imagine that "compensated for appropriately" means that caregivers are not disadvantaged in terms of income and wealth and in terms of power and status in the family, civil society, and the political sphere (although the latter would be extraordinarily difficult to bring about). Insofar as gendered social norms about caring and other work are deeply entrenched, they will be persistent. We should expect gender specialization to continue in which women are the primary caregivers of dependents and men prioritize their labor market participation; this kind of gender specialization constrains the real opportunities of men and women. Chambers forcefully argues, "Social norms set out what may be chosen, and place conditions on what must be done in order to receive certain benefits."[41] Rawls says that fair equality of opportunity requires that "supposing that there is a distribution of native endowments, those who have the same level of talent and abilities and the same willingness to use these gifts should have the same prospects of success regardless of their social class of origin, the class into which they are born and develop until the age of reason."[42] In a society in which there are gendered social norms about prioritizing caregiving and labor market participation, men and women may not have the same *willingness* to use equivalent talents and skills. Yet, as Chambers might say, the reason for this may be that men and women are in the grip of powerful social norms that shape their desires and preferences and that limit their options at least insofar as their self-worth partly depends on external recognition. Desires and preferences are, of course, always adaptive to the social world. However, when social norms overwhelmingly steer members of one social group to one of the spheres of life central to citizenship and overwhelmingly steer members of another social group to a another sphere of life central to citizenship, then the state should be concerned that persons do not genuinely enjoy fair equality of opportunity.

---

[40] This discussion is important to answering Schouten's worry about the harms of gender specialization that don't stem from gender hierarchy.

[41] Chambers, *Sex, Culture, and Justice*, pp. 172–173.

[42] JF, p. 44.

Such social group–based preferences should call into question the extent to which persons enjoy the conditions for second-order autonomy, too. Hence, given concern for both fair equality of opportunity and second-order autonomy, the state should make it possible for those primarily responsible for caring for dependents to be full-time participants in the labor market and give incentives for caregiving to be shared among adult members of a household. The policies noted earlier, such as paid family leave with incentives for sharing caregiving work among adult household members, a shortened work week, state-supported day care and aftercare, are key.

However, even though we think that the labor market must be restructured to allow the primary caregivers of dependents to be participants in the labor market on par with others when it comes to opportunities for income, promotion, and power in the workplace, we recognize that some individuals will still choose to perform caregiving full time or part time in the family. Sometimes this will be the most efficient way for a caregiver to meet the needs of the person or persons being cared for (e.g., a parent with a child who has unusually demanding needs or a person who is caring for multiple dependents, such as young children and an elderly parent or relative); sometimes it will be because of a person's view of the good. Arguably, if persons choose to perform caregiving work full time, even if the labor market is structured to assume that its participants are caregivers of dependents, those who perform this work should not be vulnerable to others in order to meet their needs. Caregivers perform socially necessary work, and they are entitled to recognition and support for it and to job retraining when their care work is complete.

Recall, again, Chambers's worry stated more generally: social norms limit preferences and options, and this reveals a problem with political liberals taking only second-order autonomy to be important for justice. We tried to show that in the case of the gendered division of labor, when social norms operate in such a way that equal citizenship is threatened or compromised, political liberals can and must intervene, absent countervailing considerations to the contrary. This holds for other practices and institutions that result from gendered social norms that frustrate equal citizenship, too. In short, for political liberals, a substantive conception of equal citizenship determines the limits of choice.

III. Citizenship, Gender Hierarchy, and the Division of Labor

III.1 The Incompatibility Strategy and the Gendered Division of Labor

Schouten challenges our attempt to show that political liberals can adequately address important issues of sex equality when it comes to the gendered division of labor.[43] We have argued—here and elsewhere—that justice requires that many of the policies that feminists favor to end the gendered division of labor can or must be adopted in our own circumstances and in an ideal society, too, insofar as the gendered division of labor is incompatible with free and equal citizenship. Schouten dubs our view the Incompatibility Strategy, which we think is fitting. She claims that given our strategy, we, heretofore, have an unmet argumentative burden and, too, that we are unable to address *nonhierarchical* aspects of the gendered division of labor that should be of central concern to feminists. We take up her charges to better explain and defend our view.

Consider her charge of our unmet argumentative burden. First, Schouten notes that given our strategy, "we need to establish *not just* that the groups in subordinate roles in the GDL [gendered division of labor] have their interests frustrated" but that the "GDL *itself* does the frustrating."[44] As she says, in the justification of laws and policies for specific domains, "it matters what aspects of gender are actually incompatible with citizenship," and to justify interventions in the labor market and recognition and support for caregivers, we need to show that the gendered division of work frustrates equal citizenship. Second, she claims that we need to show that the "incompatibility between the GDL and citizenship" is *systematic* in order to support the kinds of policies we suggest are central to sex equality such as paid family leave, equal pay for part-time work, and affordable day care/aftercare.[45] Schouten admits that the gendered division of labor is systematic, but she questions whether its effects on citizenship are systematic. Finally, Schouten says that the criterion of reciprocity "does not demand that the interests of citizenship be maximally promoted" and that we need to show that "the *balance of citizenship reasons*

---

[43] Schouten, "Does the Gendered Division of Labor Undermine Citizenship?"

[44] Schouten, "Does the Gendered Division of Labor Undermine Citizenship?," p. 296.

[45] Schouten, "Does the Gendered Division of Labor Undermine Citizenship?," p. 296.

tells in favor of interventions: that the citizenship interests in remedying the hierarchy of the GDL *outweigh* the citizenship interests in avoiding political intrusions to change the relative costliness of gender egalitarian and gender *in*egalitarian domestic arrangements."[46]

Now consider Schouten's second charge, which is that our strategy does not address *nonhierarchical* aspects of the gendered division of labor that should be of central concern to feminists. Schouten claims, "We can imagine a society in which gendered norms incline men and women systematically toward *different* background identities, but in which those identities are not arranged in a hierarchy of income, status and power."[47] So imagine again that gender norms incline men to participation in the paid labor market and women to caregiving but that social policy is such that women are compensated for their caregiving work and not disadvantaged in terms of income, status, and power. Two problems may still persist as a matter of nonhierarchical gender that should be addressed by the state as a matter of justice. First, Schouten claims, "there are harms resulting from men and women being systematically obstructed from *combining* serious commitments to caring for others with similarly serious commitments to attainment in the world of paid labor."[48] Many people want to combine paid labor market work with caregiving because they view both as satisfying and important and, Schouten says, "made more valuable when complemented by the other." Second, Schouten stresses the harms of *gendered* specialization: "Social norms differentiate between men and women and push them into social roles that might not best suit their interests and temperament."[49] These harms, Schouten says, are independent of gender hierarchy of the gendered division of labor, as income, power, status, and other social goods could be held equally between paid labor market participants and caregivers of dependents. And she says, "While the harms of presumed specialization are caused by the foreclosing of genuine opportunities to combine two worthy life projects, the harms of *gendered* presumed specialization are caused by the social context against which individuals

---

[46] Schouten, "Does the Gendered Division of Labor Undermine Citizenship?," p. 297.

[47] Schouten, "Does the Gendered Division of Labor Undermine Citizenship?," p. 299.

[48] Schouten, "Does the Gendered Division of Labor Undermine Citizenship?," p. 300.

[49] Schouten, "Does the Gendered Division of Labor Undermine Citizenship?," p. 301.

choose how to specialize, given that they cannot realistically choose *not* to specialize."[50]

III.2 Defending the Incompatibility Strategy

In response to Schouten, we emphasize that we understand political liberalism to be premised on a relational theory of equality. What is of fundamental importance is that persons stand in a relationship of free and equal citizenship in a liberal democratic society viewed as a shared cooperative enterprise. According to relational theories of equality, as Anderson says, "certain patterns in the distribution of goods may be instrumental to securing such relationships, follow from them or be constitutive of them," but what is of primary importance is "the relationships within which the goods are distributed."[51] Hence, it is not the case that just because there may be a certain (equitable) division of distributable goods (income, wealth, and power) in society, all persons stand as free and equal citizens.

If some persons are effectively marginalized from participation in any of the spheres central to citizenship because of society's structure, or if the ability to participate in all such spheres is effectively precluded due to the way that social norms constrain choice and form and shape institutions, then free and equal citizenship is frustrated. As we argued in our response to Chambers above, in modern, liberal democratic states, there are distinct spheres of life central to citizenship: the political sphere, civil society, the labor market, and the family. Persons have interests as free and equal citizens in the goods, activities, and relationships that are distinctive of each sphere and in the ability to participate in each sphere. Given persons' interests as citizens, the ability to effectively participate in one sphere does not make up for being effectively excluded from another. Our point is not that some or most persons, given their views of the good, would *like* to be able to participate in these spheres of life. Rather, our claim is that it is among the needs of persons as free and equal citizens that they be able to participate in certain spheres.

We cannot trace here all the interests of persons as citizens in each sphere; we assume that the interests of persons as citizens in the political sphere and civil society, which includes places of public accommodation,

---

[50] Schouten, "Does the Gendered Division of Labor Undermine Citizenship?," p. 301.

[51] Anderson, "What's the Point of Equality?," pp. 313–314.

are more familiar. We stated in our reply to Chambers that the labor market and the family have distinct purposes. Again, in the labor market, persons work together to produce many of the goods and services needed by individuals to meet their basic needs and to pursue their view of the good. It permits individuals to exercise their talents and skills and to engage in transactional relationships as means to their goals or ends-in-themselves. The ability to participate in the labor market (if one is able) is also important for a person's sense of self-worth, insofar as the kind of distinctive relationships and opportunities it offers affirms persons' contributions to society as a collective enterprise. For political purposes, the family can be understood as an institution or framework for intimate personal relationships involving the material and emotional care that is in the interests of persons as citizens. Again, this includes physical care in any time of dependency, emotional and moral caretaking for minor children, and the emotional care normally needed by adults to be in good health and to be able to exercise the moral powers.

With this in mind, we turn to Schouten's specific claims. Recall Schouten's worry that our strategy does not allow us to address problematic nonhierarchical aspects of gender. She says that if we imagine a society in which social norms incline men to labor market participation and women to caregiving, then if the society is structured so that caregivers are not disadvantaged in the distribution of income, status, and power in society, then our strategy cannot address this kind of problematic gender specialization. To begin, we find it implausible that in any society with pervasive gender specialization such that women were inclined to be caregivers and men were inclined to be labor market participants, women would not be disadvantaged in status and power, even if income was equitable. That aside, on our view, as noted in our response to Chambers, this kind of gender specialization is a problem of frustrated fundamental citizenship interests, and a society in which persons were forced to specialize (regardless of gender) as caregivers or labor market participants is also a society of problematic frustrated citizenship interests. Of course, in the former case, gendered social norms that result in men overwhelmingly prioritizing labor market work and women overwhelmingly prioritizing caregiving add to the injustice of marginalization from a sphere a life central to citizenship, as gender norms about work thwart fair equality of opportunity and raise questions about second-order autonomy. While we hold that among the needs of persons as citizens is the ability to participate in the labor market and the family (as well as civil society and the political sphere), this is not to say that participation in all these spheres must be maximally possible (that is simply not possible), but we hold that persons should be able to participate in all the spheres relevant to citizenship to a significant degree.

So, while the inability to combine labor market work and caregiving is not necessarily a problem of hierarchy or gender injustice (although it is usually both), it is at least a problem of systematic marginalization and exclusion that undermines citizenship, which we think political liberals must address. We also want to acknowledge that it is certainly possible that in a well-ordered, politically liberal society with the reforms we imagine (short-term paid leave for dependent care, state-supported day care and aftercare, shorter work weeks, more flexible work hours when possible, job sharing, etc.) there will still be some gender specialization in the labor market and in the family that is due to individual choice given certain social norms. Although as feminists we may find this unfortunate or even morally problematic given the ideals of equality that animate our particular views of the good, it may not be to such a degree that citizenship interests are frustrated such that the state can address it.

Now recall Schouten's first challenge, which is that we have an unmet argumentative burden. Schouten notes several aspects of our argument that need to be supported. First, she claims that given our argumentative strategy, we need to show that the gendered division of labor itself systematically undermines citizenship. We think that it clearly does, as we have argued. We very briefly note some conditions of our own society that we take to show this, but note that conditions would be different in any just, well-ordered, politically liberal society. As stressed above, the labor market is structured so that most full-time jobs (and certainly most of the best full-time jobs) assume that workers are not primarily responsible for caring for dependents. Those with dependent care responsibilities—both men and women—struggle to combine full-time labor market participation with dependent care. Given deeply entrenched gender norms about caring (which, in particular, pressure women to be primarily responsible for caring for children), the number of female-headed households, and the demands of paid work, many women take low-paying, more flexible jobs, work part time for proportionally less pay and few benefits, or leave the paid labor market in order to care for dependents. In the case of paid and unpaid work, gendered social norms heavily influence individuals' preferences, and these norms have framed and shaped the labor market, which, too, constrains the real opportunities of individuals who may wish to reject traditional norms. The gendered division of labor, then, systematically undermines equal citizenship. It effectively precludes persons from participation in all the spheres of life central to citizenship and, thereby, frustrates persons' access to their needs and interests as citizens. In our society, the gendered division of labor is a systematic principal mechanism for maintaining and perpetuating gender hierarchy, as the gendered division of labor imposes a framework of choice on persons that results in real inequalities between men and women when it comes to income and wealth, power, and status, and women's dependence on men for access to basic goods.

In conclusion, some feminists have worried that political liberals cannot enact law and policy to undermine sexist or morally objectionable social norms that limit women's choices and options and undermine their equality and freedom. To the contrary, we hold that political liberals offer a particularly attractive view of when such intervention is required, one that secures meaningful equal citizenship for all and that appropriately limits state intervention for the sake of freedom.

9

Political Liberalism and Marriage

At present time, in this state of civilization, what evil could be caused by, first placing women on the most entire equality with men, as to all rights and privileges, civil and political, and then doing way with all laws whatever relating to marriage?

—HARRIET TAYLOR, *"Early Essays on Marriage and Divorce"*

I. Introduction

Rawls is clear that the family is part of the basic structure of society,[1] and the principles of justice apply to it.[2] He also assumes—without argument—that marriage, in some form, will continue to be a vital institution in politically liberal societies. Although feminists have viewed Rawls's inclusion of the family as part of the basic structure as important for gender justice, many have, nonetheless, found his treatment of the family and marriage within his theory unsatisfactory. Consider that Rawls claims that the principles of justice apply to the family as they apply to churches and universities and other associations. He says of the family that the principles of justice should not "apply directly to its internal life" but rather "impose essential constraints on the family as an institution and so guarantee the basic rights and liberties, and the freedom and opportunities of all its members."[3] With respect to marital relationships as part of the family, Rawls says that political conceptions of justice

---

[1] IPRR, p. 595.

[2] This chapter is a revised version of a previously published paper, "Political Liberalism, Marriage and the Family," *Law and Philosophy* (2012) 31: 185–212. That paper was presented at an NEH summer seminar held at Washington University in Saint Louis (2010) and at the 2011 Pacific Division meeting of the American Philosophical Association. We thank audience participants for helpful feedback. We also thank Elizabeth Brake, Claudia Card, Blain Neufeld, Susanne Sreedhar, and anonymous reviewers for generous comments.

[3] IPRR, p. 597.

assume "no particular form" in the sense of "monogamous, heterosexual or otherwise"[4]; what is important is that the family is arranged (through marriage law, too, we suppose) to effectively support its function, which is the "orderly production and reproduction of society and its culture from one generation to the next."[5]

This approach is surely misguided for several reasons.[6] While membership in a church or university is voluntary and exit options are protected, family membership for children is not voluntary,[7] and children are generally removed from their families only in circumstances in which their basic needs are not met (e.g., neglect) or their basic rights are violated (e.g., abuse). And while it is certainly true that most (if not all) comprehensive doctrines will include an ideal of the family or familial relationships, Maxine Eichner claims that Rawls views the family as having a natural function focused on the care and rearing of children and that this natural function exists independent of the state. Such a view, she says, is simply false, as "how families function is inextricably intertwined with both law and social policy."[8] Martha Nussbaum makes a similar point. She remarks that "Rawls tends to treat the family as an organization that has an extrapolitical existence and to ask how far the state may interfere with it."[9] What this misses, Nussbaum stresses, is that while "individuals may call themselves 'a family' if they wish," "they only get to be one, in the sense that is socially recognized, if they satisfy legal tests."[10]

Although we think that Rawls's treatment of the family and discussion of marriage within the family are entirely unacceptable, we think his most general remarks about the family lend themselves to formulating a helpful approach for thinking about political liberalism and the family. Namely, political liberals should consider the interests of persons as free and equal citizens and determine if some political notion of the family is needed to support or protect persons in their status as free and equal

---

[4] IPRR, p. 596n60.

[5] IPRR, p. 595.

[6] Hartley offers the same introduction for how political liberals should think of the family when it comes to the parent-child relationship in her "Political Liberalism and Children."

[7] Nussbaum, "Rawls and Feminism," p. 504.

[8] Eichner, *The Supportive State*, pp. 23–26, quoting p. 25.

[9] Nussbaum, "Rawls and Feminism," pp. 505–506.

[10] Nussbaum, "Rawls and Feminism," p. 505.

citizens. Such interests should be protected and provided for in any reasonable political conception of justice. We think that a political conception of the family is needed to support persons' interests as citizens in certain kinds of intimate caring relationships.[11] All persons need material care in times of dependency, and those who provide this care need recognition and support;[12] children need intimate, personal relationships with caregivers for healthy emotional, cognitive, and moral development; and adults, too, need intimate caring relationships to exercise the two moral powers.[13] Political liberals can recognize the political family for the purposes of effectively supporting and protecting persons in the personal, caring relationships that support these interests of persons as citizens. The family as a political institution is viewed as constructed by the state, and the state doesn't regard the family viewed in this way as having a natural function but as serving socially necessary ones. Of course, as part of their comprehensive doctrines, persons will very likely have their own views and ideals of the family and familial relationships. What is important is that, as a matter of law, citizens regard the family as having political functions, even if they also think certain relationships have another character or purpose in addition to their political purposes.

In this chapter, we focus on marriage and the interests of persons as free and equal citizens that relate to intimate, caring relationships between adults. With respect to whether political liberals can and should recognize legal marriage in any form, the crucial question is this: Can and should political liberals recognize and otherwise support legal marriage given the interests of persons as free and equal citizens? As we have stressed, political liberals hold the view that in modern democratic states persons accept diverse and irreconcilable but reasonable comprehensive doctrines,[14] and they think that in just democratic states, matters of basic justice and constitutional essentials must be justified on the basis of reasons that are shared by persons as free and equal citizens.[15] In short, whether political liberals can or should recognize and support legal marriage as a matter of

---

[11] In developing our approach, we have been deeply impressed by Brake's work on marriage; see her "Minimal Marriage" and *Minimizing Marriage*.

[12] Kittay, *Love's Labor*; Nussbaum, *Frontiers of Justice*.

[13] Brake, *Minimizing Marriage*.

[14] IPRR, p. 573.

[15] See, e.g., IPRR and PL.

basic justice depends on the account of marriage one has in mind and the sort of justification one offers for such marriage. It also depends on the other interests of citizens, which, all things considered, may tell against marriage. Importantly, certain features of political liberalism suggest that we should be skeptical of the prospect of justifying any kind of legally sanctioned marriage in a politically liberal state, even if support for personal relationships is warranted.[16] Views about marriage and its goods seem to stem from persons' particular comprehensive doctrines and not obviously political values or reasons. Indeed, in a politically liberal society, the state takes no view about marital relations (or aspects thereof) as a moral ideal if that ideal does not help secure the fundamental interests of persons as citizens and does not violate law and policy. Hence, we arrive at the heart of the matter: On the basis of what political values and public reasons could any form of legal marriage be justified within political liberalism?

Of course, given the central role that marriage plays in the lives of many persons in contemporary democratic states and its long history as a central social institution, we have reason to expect that at least some aspects of the present institution serve or relate to some fundamental interests of citizens and, hence, make some form(s) of marriage justified within public reason. Certainly, there is, at the very least, good reason to take this seriously. Again, in his discussion of justice and the family, Rawls seems to assume that legal marriage in some form will be part of any politically liberal society,[17] and, although a number of philosophers have discussed political liberalism and the family, the legitimacy of the legal recognition of marriage in a politically liberal society has only recently been questioned.[18] Elizabeth Brake presents a notable exception. She addresses what form of legal marriage, if any, political liberals can and must recognize consistent with political liberalism's core tenets. She argues that "minimal marriage," and no more robust form of marriage,

---

[16] Brake makes this point, although she defends the view that political liberals can and must recognize "minimal marriage" and no more robust form of marriage ("Minimal Marriage," pp. 302–303). See also Brake, *Minimizing Marriage*, pp. 151–154, and chapter 7.

[17] See, e.g., IPRR, pp. 595–601. See also Nussbaum, "Rawls and Feminism," who stresses that Rawls "does not acknowledge the parochial character of the Western nuclear family" (pp. 502–507, quoting p. 504) and her "The Future of Feminist Liberalism," pp. 116–123.

[18] For example, Okin, despite her discussions of political liberalism and the family, does not question the legitimacy of legal marriage for political liberals: "Political Liberalism, Justice"; "Justice and Gender"; "'Forty Acres and a Mule' for Women."

can and must be supported by political liberals, given their conception of public reason and liberal neutrality.[19] More recently Clare Chambers argues against state recognition of marriage in any form; in particular, she claims that the legal recognition of marriage is incompatible with political liberalism's commitment to neutrality.[20] Chambers argues for personal relationship law that is piecemeal and based on practice, as opposed to a legally recognized status. In this chapter, we offer a general account of how political liberals should evaluate the issue of whether the legal recognition of marriage is a matter of basic justice. And we develop and examine some public reason arguments that, given the fundamental interests of citizens, could justify various forms of legal marriage in some contexts.[21] Indeed, we argue that there are strong public reasons that support some forms

---

[19] Brake, "Minimal Marriage," pp. 303–304. See also Brake, *Minimizing Marriage*, chapter 7. In *Untying the Knot*, Tamara Metz argues for the disestablishment of marriage on the grounds that it undermines liberty and equality and that it does not support and protect all those in intimate caring relations. However, Metz argues that the state should protect and support "intimate caring associations" and caregivers; to this end, she claims the state should recognize an intimate caregiving union status with bundled rights and responsibilities as well as protections and material benefits. Although there are important similarities and insights in the work of Metz and Brake, we focus on Brake because she develops her view with the framework of political liberalism in mind, because she separates adult caregiving frameworks from the issues of caregiving frameworks for children and for dependent adults, and because Brake appropriately narrows as well as unbundles the rights, entitlements, and responsibilities viewed as properly associated with adult caregiving. Similarly, Maxine Eichner, in *The Supportive State*, argues that interdependent, caring adult relationships support public goods such as autonomy, human dignity, caretaking and development for children and adults, equal opportunity, and sex equality. She claims the state should "recognize" and "privilege" those adults' caring relationships that support such goods either through a single, formal, legal status of domestic partnership or through a variety of formal, legal domestic partnership statuses based on relationship type. Those with a domestic partnership status would have certain rights and responsibilities to each other, be eligible for benefits from the states, and have rights against third parties. Like Brake's, Eichner's proposal is inclusive of a variety of adult caretaking relationships; however, she bundles domestic partnership rights, entitlements, and responsibilities, and so her view is less flexible than Brake's. It is also not clear the extent to which she narrows marital bundles for domestic partnerships, nor is it clear the legal connections her view permits or could recognize between adult caregiving relationships and frameworks for caring for dependents.

[20] Chambers, *Against Marriage*. Although we had hoped to engage with Chambers's views in this chapter, her book was available only as we finished our manuscript.

[21] Recently, other public reason arguments for civil marriage have been advanced. May argues in "Liberal Neutrality and Civil Marriage" that in certain empirical conditions, given the presumptive permanence of marriage, civil marriage may be consistent with liberal neutrality. Wedgwood argues that marriage is not required for justice but that, in certain conditions, political liberals can recognize legal marriage as consistent with justice. He takes the following points to be central to his claim: (1) "it is a central part of many people's *most fundamental goals and aspirations in life* to participate in the institution of marriage, and a legal institution of civil marriage is the best way for these people to satisfy these aspirations";

of legal marriage in some contexts. In particular, in certain conditions, the recognition of some form of legal marriage may be the best way to protect the fundamental interests of women as equal citizens in freely chosen associations. Or it may be that, in certain conditions, to secure the social conditions necessary for gays, lesbians, and bisexuals to be free and equal citizens, some form of legal marriage can or should be recognized. In addition, we argue that some forms of plural marriage are incompatible with free and equal citizenship, while other forms, in certain contexts, cannot justly be denied the legal recognition and support offered to other types of legally recognized marital relationships. We think a much underappreciated point about political liberalism is that the particular institutions that are justified or required as a matter of basic justice depend in part on the conditions of a particular politically liberal society, as societies characterized by reasonable pluralism can be incredibly diverse. Hence, the actual implications of political liberalism for marriage law cannot be worked out in advance of information about a particular politically liberal society, as the social policy needed to secure equal citizenship in a given society must be context sensitive to be effective.

When considering our position, one might wonder about the extent to which it is simply a defense of a very conventional view. Certainly, most people think the state ought to recognize and regulate marriage, and recently, it is this view that has been challenged. For example, Cass Sunstein and Richard Thaler urge consideration of the privatization of marriage, sometimes called the contract model.[22] Alternatively, Chambers argues for rejecting legal marriage in favor of default directives for personal relationships, permitting only individual modifications that are consistent with justice.[23] She claims that regulations for relationships should be piecemeal, and, so, laws should apply to aspects of relationships; and, again, she thinks that personal relationship law should not be status-based but be practice-based. And Brake, whose proposal we discuss below at length, proposes minimal marriage, which is a kind of personal relationship law involving a status between adults in caregiving relationships but that bears

---

(2) "the institution of marriage does not in itself cause any serious harms"; and (3) "at least *prima facie*, marriage is consistent with justice" ("Is Civil Marriage Illiberal?," p. 39).

[22] Sunstein and Thaler, "Privatizing Marriage."

[23] Chambers, "The Marriage-Free State"; "The Limitations of Contract"; and *Against Marriage*.

little resemblance to traditional marriage.[24] Some argue that only the privatization of marriage or radical marriage reform can free the state from its role in the perpetuation of sexism and heterosexism that is specific to traditional marriage. However, the view we defend is not simply a return to the conventional view. While we think that state-sanctioned marriages may be justified in certain circumstances (or, perhaps, necessary), our arguments for state-sanctioned marriage are sensitive to concerns about equal citizenship for women and sexual minorities. Furthermore, while the kinds of state-sanctioned marriage we think political liberals may recognize in certain contexts are more like conventional marriage than Brake's minimal marriage, any form of marriage recognized in a politically liberal state would differ quite significantly from the institution of marriage in its current form.

II. Political Liberalism, Public Reason, and Marriage

Given the central tenets of political liberalism, we start with this claim: whether political liberals can and should legally recognize and support marriage as a matter of basic justice depends on (1) whether marriage in some form(s) can be understood to be either necessary to or supportive of some fundamental interest(s) of persons as free and equal citizens[25] and, if so, (2) whether the recognition of this form of marriage

---

[24] Brake, "Minimal Marriage" and *Minimizing Marriage*.

[25] What are the fundamental interests of persons as free and equal citizens? For Rawls, citizens' fundamental interests are their higher-order interests "in developing and exercising" their two moral powers and "in securing the conditions under which" their "determinate conception of the good" can be pursued (PL, p. 106). The two moral powers are the capacity to develop, modify, and work toward realizing a rational conception of the good and the capacity for a sense of justice. Political liberals need not accept Rawls's particular account of citizens' fundamental interests. For the purposes of our argument we need not take a position on whether Rawls's particular specification of citizens' higher-order fundamental interests is the correct one. When we discuss the fundamental interests of citizens, we are referring to those interests citizens have within the basic structure and as reflected in constitutional design. For example, we mean citizens' interest in freedom as protected by rights to speech and association or their interest in equality as protected by due process and equal protection. Of course, how one specifies these more particular fundamental interests will ultimately be determined by one's account of the higher-order fundamental interests as well as other factors relevant to constitutional design. For our purposes, we simply need to say that citizens have fundamental interests in their freedom and equality vis-à-vis other citizens and that social policy must protect and promote these interests.

would interfere with citizens' other fundamental interests. Importantly, it may well be the case that some form of marriage supports a fundamental interest of citizens but that the recognition of that form of marriage, all things considered, is not justified. For example, suppose that under certain circumstances the legal recognition of monogamous (same-sex and heterosexual) marriages would support a fundamental interest of citizens. However, it may be that the recognition of that distinctive form of marriage as opposed to something like Brake's minimal marriage would result in problematic disadvantages for those whose interests were not met by those types of marital relationships. In any circumstance, public reasons that support the legal recognition of some form(s) of marriage will have to be considered together with public reasons against recognizing legal marriage of some form(s). And whether any form of marriage is justified in a politically liberal society will depend on various features of the particular society, including the society's other laws and public policies as well as social norms and institutions that are part of the background culture. We now examine some public reason arguments in favor of recognizing legal marriage of some form.

III. Brake's Minimal Marriage and Support for the Social Bases of Adult Caring Relationships

Brake claims that political liberals must recognize "minimal marriage" to appropriately support the social bases of adult caring relationships, and she develops a public reason argument to this end.[26] We agree that Brake's argument is, indeed, a public reason argument, but we reject her claim that appropriately supporting the social bases of adult caring relationships requires the legal recognition and support of minimal marriage in all contexts (and below we will argue that other public reason arguments can justify the recognition of different forms of marriage in some circumstances). Brake's conception of minimal marriage allows consenting adults in caring relationships to exchange various rights relating to the recognition and support of adult caring relationships.[27] A *caring relationship* implies "physical or emotional caretaking or simply

---

[26] Brake, "Minimal Marriage," p. 327; Brake, *Minimizing Marriage*, pp. 167–185.

[27] Brake, "Minimal Marriage," p. 307; Brake, *Minimizing Marriage*, pp. 158–167.

a caring attitude" between individuals and concerns individuals who "know and are known to one another, have ongoing direct contact, and share a history."[28] Proper recognition and support of a caring relationship between legal spouses, on her view, justifies marital rights relating to immigration, caretaking leave, burial and bereavement leave, hospital and prison visitation, joint property, executorship, and emergency decision-making.[29] However, traditional marital rights, which are based on a relationship of economic dependency between spouses, are not part of minimal marriage. Hence, on Brake's view, welfare entitlements do not include spousal benefits, and there are no marital benefits in the tax code.[30] Finally, persons can have multiple legal spouses and select which legal rights to exchange with which spouses, regardless of sex and with no required symmetry of rights with or among spouses.[31]

Some implications of minimal marriage are worth noting. Minors cannot marry anyone, but adult close relatives can marry, including parents and children. The number of individuals one can marry is limited only by the number of individuals with whom one can "genuinely sustain caring relationships."[32] To deal with some potential feasibility problems resulting from the state's acknowledgment of multiple spouses, Brake proposes that for certain rights "minimal marriage could be implemented by giving prospective spouses a list of entitlements, which they could assign as desired, the form indicating numerical limits."[33]

Why does Brake claim that political liberals can and must recognize minimal marriage? First, she argues that the social bases of caring relationships are social primary goods. She distinguishes between material caretaking (e.g., feeding, dressing, grooming, etc.) and attitudinal care, which is part of caring relationships. Caring relationships are "emotionally significant personal relationships between parties who know one another in their particularity, take an interest in each other as persons, interact regularly, and share a history."[34] Adults need material care when

---

[28] Brake, "Minimal Marriage," p. 307; Brake, *Minimizing Marriage*, pp. 158–167.

[29] Brake, "Minimal Marriage," p. 307; Brake, *Minimizing Marriage*, p. 161.

[30] Brake, "Minimal Marriage," p. 308; Brake, *Minimizing Marriage*, p. 161.

[31] Brake, "Minimal Marriage," pp. 303, 307; Brake, *Minimizing Marriage*, p. 161.

[32] Brake, "Minimizing Marriage," p. 310; Brake, *Minimizing Marriage*, pp. 171–185.

[33] Brake, "Minimizing Marriage," p. 310.

[34] Brake, "Minimizing Marriage," p. 327.

unable to care for themselves. Attitudinal care, Brake says, often enhances material care.[35]

Also, central to Brake's argument is that *caring relationships* are among persons' needs as citizens. While the two moral powers (the capacity for a sense of justice and the capacity for a conception of the good) can be exercised in relations that are not caring relationships, Brake stresses that caring relationships "are essential to developing and exercising the moral powers."[36] She claims political liberals should view caring relationships as among the "all-purpose means normally needed" for pursuing reasonable conceptions of the good and like self-respect insofar as both are "psychologically supporting individuals in their life plans."[37]

Brake convincingly argues that the social bases of adult caring relationships are social primary goods. Hence, the question is whether a politically liberal state *must* recognize minimal marriage to support the social bases of adult caring relationships. Brake offers the following argument:

> In the modern world, caring relationships require practical support such as visiting rights, leave, immigration eligibility and relocation assistance; individuals need a way to signal to the vast institutions shaping their lives which relationships should receive these protections. . . . Marital rights signal which relationships such institutions are required to recognize as relevant in visitation, caretaking leave, or spousal hiring and relocation. These entitlements are the social bases of caring relationships.[38]

Essentially, she claims that certain practical supports for caring relationships can be provided only through the state's recognition of minimal marriage.[39]

However, we find this argument unconvincing and think that it is possible in some contexts for the state to provide the social bases of adult caring relationships without recognizing any kind of legal marriage. If

---

[35] Brake, "Minimizing Marriage," p. 327.

[36] Brake, "Minimizing Marriage," p. 328.

[37] Brake "Minimizing Marriage," p. 329 (the first quoted phrase is from PL, pp. 75–76).

[38] Brake, "Minimizing Marriage," p. 331.

[39] Brake, *Minimizing Marriage*, p. 181.

we are right, this undermines Brake's claim that political liberals must recognize minimal marriage. Consider Sunstein and Thaler's discussion of privatizing marriage.[40] They ask us to consider a society in which the state does not recognize legal marriage. In accordance with their comprehensive doctrines (religious, secular, etc.), persons can privately marry and can make legally enforceable contracts consistent with the laws of the democratic state. Certain kinds of relationships are legally impermissible (e.g., incest[41] and child marriage), as are certain types of actions in any relationship (e.g., physical and sexual assault). Persons, though, have a great deal of freedom to determine the terms of their relationships with others. In the society that Sunstein and Thaler ask us to contemplate, when persons privately marry, the state and other institutions can make certain presumptions relating to matters having to do with adult caring relationships (e.g., caretaking and visitation rights), but, through contracts, persons can specify their own arrangements for these matters. And through private contracts,[42] whether persons privately marry or not, persons can specify that others have rights relative to various aspects of their care. Persons can make this information available to others as they choose, or, in the event they are unable to communicate their contractual arrangements, those to whom they have given rights can point to the contractual agreement made between the parties. Adult caregiving is socially supported because the state recognizes and enforces private contracts with respect to interests related to caregiving and makes default presumptions on the basis of private marriage. When a person does not contractually specify rights relative to his or her care, does not privately marry and fall under default laws, and for some reason is not presently able to specify his or her wishes, the state could use evidence of a close personal relationship to determine caregiving rights. This view supports caregiving but is not minimal marriage insofar as the state does not recognize a *legal marital status*, which would involve state authorization of that status and

---

[40] Sunstein and Thaler, "Privatizing Marriage," p. 377.

[41] Should all incest be prohibited in a politically liberal society? For relevant discussion, see Corvino, "Homosexuality and the PIB Argument," pp. 529–532. See also Markel, Collins, and Leib, *Privilege or Punish* (arguing for the decriminalization of mature and consensual incest, adultery, and bigamy).

[42] Another possibility is that the state could introduce unilateral promises as a legally enforceable basis for action. See Markel, Collins, and Leib, *Privilege or Punish*. Thanks to a reviewer for this point.

would involve the enforcement of entitlements on the basis of that status. Rather, a person's entitlements under privatized marriage are enforced as a matter of contract law or based on presumptions about persons' wishes given private marriage; hence, no new legal status is recognized under a system of private marriage.

Brake explicitly rejects the possibility that private contracts can adequately provide the necessary social bases of adult caring relationships. She states that marital rights "exist to support relationships" and that these rights "lie outside of the contract paradigm because their content is shaped by the nature of caring relationships; they designate a status—that of being in a caring relationship—which must be treated as salient in institutional decisions with significant implications for individual lives."[43] Brake notes three types of rights not available by private contract that are part of her account of minimal marriage; these rights are (1) "entitlements to special eligibility for immigration or legal residency," (2) "entitlements against employers for care-taking and bereavement leave," and (3) entitlements to "hospital and prison visiting rights."[44]

Yet, just as Rawls believes that the social bases of self-respect are provided by the distribution of the other social primary goods in accordance with his two principles of justice, it may be that a proper understanding of the social primary goods together with appropriately specified principles for the distribution of these goods will provide for the social bases of adult caring relationships.[45] So minimal marriage may be unnecessary. Consider, first, Brake's claim that the recognition of minimal marriage is necessary for persons to have entitlements against employers for caretaking leave in order to support caring relationships between adults. Although Rawls puts aside matters of justice relating to illness and temporary and permanent impairment,[46] political liberals should recognize that nearly all human beings are members of society entitled to justice and have a claim to care in times of dependency. Furthermore, political liberals should regard the work of caring for persons who are temporarily

---

[43] Brake, "Minimal Marriage," p. 331.

[44] Brake, *Minimizing Marriage*, p. 181.

[45] It is important to note that political liberals need not accept social primary goods as the proper metric of justice nor accept Rawls's principles of justice. Indeed, Nussbaum regards her capabilities approach as a political conception of justice. See, e.g., her *Frontiers of Justice*.

[46] See, e.g., Nussbaum, *Frontiers of Justice*; Kittay, *Love's Labor*.

or permanently dependent on others as socially obligatory work for which members of society are collectively responsible. Although it may not be necessary that all members of society perform this work, those that do should not be disadvantaged relative to other members of society because they perform socially obligatory work, and those who perform this work should be properly respected and compensated. As a matter of justice for dependent members of society and their caregivers, temporary, paid leave from the labor market must be available to those who care for others. Such leave must be in addition to various other measures necessary for the value of caregiving to be properly recognized and for caregivers to be properly supported, and it seems reasonable that the amount of temporary leave a person can take from the labor market in a given year or over a period of years could be subject to some limit. Our point here is simply that Brake's minimal marriage does not seem necessary for persons to have an entitlement to leave from employment in order to provide caregiving in adult caring relationships. A society must recognize the necessity of caregiving for all dependents and support those who do this work; social policy that gives workers an entitlement to temporary work leave to care for others could allow an individual to take leave to care for any dependent member of society. Individuals could take such leave to care for those they are in a caring relationship with, but they could take leave to care for others, too.

Now consider hospital and prison visitation. To the extent that these issues are a matter of basic justice, it seems that freedom of association could provide the necessary basis for hospitals to recognize visitation rights for patients and for prisons to recognize visitation rights for inmates. Consistent with their medical care, hospital patients should be able to receive visitors at their discretion; if unable to communicate their wishes, those with the charge of making medical decisions for the patient can determine visitation. Prisoners, too, insofar as visitation is appropriate for incarceration, should have discretion over visitors. When it comes to hospital and prison visitation, minimal marriage does not seem necessary to provide the rights relevant to the social bases of adult caring relationships.

Finally, Brake claims that to properly support the social bases of adult caring relationships, the state must recognize special eligibility for immigration and legal residency rights for those in adult caring relationships and that minimal marriage is necessary to do this. She stresses that such rights have important consequences when it comes to issues such as in-state tuition and taxation. We, of course, admit that some citizens and residents of a state will no doubt form or have important relationships with persons who are not citizens or residents of their state. These relationships may be of many sorts, including familial, romantic, friendly, or professional. The development and continuation of some relationships may be best facilitated when persons are in close physical proximity to each other, and desired aspects of certain adult relationships (e.g., physical intimacy or providing physical care to a loved one) are available only when persons can live with or near each other. Still, though, is minimal marriage—a formal legal status held by certain citizens—necessary for the state to properly support the social bases of adult caring relationships when it comes to immigration and legal residency? First, note that if open borders are required by justice, then minimal marriage is not necessary for the state to support the social bases of adult caring relationships through immigration and legal residency policy.[47] Arguably, the core commitments of political liberalism as such are not challenged by the prospect of open borders, but we cannot make that argument here. Second, suppose it is justifiable for the state to enact some kind of restrictive—but not closed— immigration and legal residency policy. It does not seem necessary for the state to recognize minimal marriage in order to provide for the social bases of adult caring relationships. The state could recognize a variety of factors as strong grounds for entry. Among these grounds could be a citizen's claim that his or her personal or professional relationship to a foreigner could best or only be facilitated by living in close physical proximity to the person.[48] With respect to personal relationships a citizen could claim, for example, that she could best teach her minor granddaughter family traditions if her granddaughter lived with her or that she could provide physical care to a sick friend if her friend were granted residency. Or, certainly, a citizen could claim that his romantic relationship with another could be made immeasurably easier if the citizen could live near his love. The state could seek evidence to support any of these claims. Certainly, all of these claims that citizens might make could be central to a person's ability to live in accordance with his or her conception of the good. Two of these claims relate to adult caring relationships. We should also note it

---

[47] Brake admits that for cosmopolitans, the state does not need to recognize minimal marriage in order to have immigration and legal residency policies supportive of the social bases of adult caring relationships ("Minimal Marriage," p. 332).

[48] Of course, developing a workable policy to distinguish legitimate claims from fabricated claims would present a serious challenge.

does not seem necessary for the state to make overly intrusive judgments about whose claims are more pressing. Rather a judgment could be made about the reasonableness of a person's claim, and all those with reasonable claims could be in the lottery for immigration or residency. Our point is that if a state's immigration policy is, among other factors, generally based on a citizen's interest in pursuing a relationship that calls for close physical proximity to another (adult or minor), then minimal marriage is not necessary for immigration and legal residency policy to be such as to support the social bases of adult caring relationships. What this shows is that whether a politically liberal society is required as a matter of basic justice to recognize some form of legal marriage is a contextual matter, and it will depend in large part on the particular facts about a society, including other laws and social policy.

IV. Marriage and the Protection of Caregivers in Familial Relationships

To make the point once more that whether political liberals should recognize legal marriage in some form depends on the social conditions of a particular society, consider that legal marriage together with certain marriage laws and policies (including divorce laws) could be a way to protect the adult members of families (e.g., women) from certain vulnerabilities produced by family life.[49] To see how this could occur, consider that in a well-ordered, politically liberal society, some persons may accept comprehensive doctrines that are sexist according to some feminists.[50] Rawls claims that comprehensive doctrines are reasonable[51] as long as they recognize or are consistent with recognizing all citizens as free and equal persons and as such entitled to certain basic rights, liberties, and so on; his view does not require that individuals believe

---

[49] Feminists have often made the point that certain marriage and divorce laws (together with other social reforms) could protect women from vulnerabilities produced by family life. See, e.g., Okin, *Justice, Gender and the Family*, pp. 170–186; Shanley, "Just Marriage," pp. 20–25; Williams, *Unbending Gender*. But see Card, "Against Marriage and Motherhood" and "Gay Divorce."

[50] Okin stresses that some sexist comprehensive doctrines are reasonable for political liberals in her articles "Political Liberalism, Justice" and "Justice and Gender."

[51] For Rawls's discussion of reasonable comprehensive doctrines and reasonable persons, see PL, pp. 59, 49–50. See also Nussbaum, "Rawls and Feminism," p. 510.

there are no sex differences that could justify different sex roles in, say, the church or family. Hence, imagine a society in which, according to some reasonable doctrines, men and women are essentially different by nature and fit for different social roles. Persons who accept these doctrines believe that women are especially fit for family life (in particular, the care of children) and that men are especially fit for participation in the public sphere. In such a politically liberal society, if marriage is privatized and despite that all citizens will be entitled to certain goods of justice, citizens' voluntarily chosen associations may make them vulnerable to disadvantages that concern matters of basic justice. If private marriage makes some citizens vulnerable to such disadvantages, the state can address this. It is possible that certain vulnerabilities created by private marriage and familial associations can be addressed by or guarded against by the recognition of some form of legal marriage. If this is the case, there is a public reason argument for this form of legal marriage. We now develop this point in more detail.

How could private marriage result in problematic vulnerabilities in the sort of society we are imagining? Suppose that numerous persons in the society accept the reasonable comprehensive doctrine noted above and that many persons marry and organize their families such that husbands work in the labor market and wives care for children and other dependents in the home. Let us further specify that political liberals recognize caring for children and other dependents as socially obligatory work for which all members of society are collectively responsible and that, in recognition of this, political liberals accept principles of justice according to which society is structured so that those who perform the work of caring for dependents are not disadvantaged relative to other members of society with respect to their ability to participate in all spheres of social life.[52] Hence, society must be structured so that persons are able to both fully participate in the labor market and provide care to dependents.[53] There are numerous policies the state could enact with this aim in mind. For example, for minors, the state could make available to all parents day care and after-school care. However, many women may choose to forgo labor market participation

---

[52] For an argument that gender equality requires that all members of society be able to perform caregiving work while being able to participate in all spheres of social life, see Fraser, *Justice Interruptus*, p. 48.

[53] Feminists have suggested a number of social policies with this aim. See, e.g., Okin, *Justice, Gender and the Family*; Crittenden, *The Price of Motherhood*; Williams, *Unbending Gender*.

and care for their own children at home; such women are vulnerable to certain disadvantages. Unless they negotiate a generous private contract to protect their interests in the case of private divorce and to recognize their investment in their husbands' career, then, if the private marriage ends, they are likely to see their standard of living fall dramatically. In a politically liberal society, when such relationships end, women will be protected from poverty and guaranteed certain social goods if willing to participate in the labor market, and the criminal law will prohibit physical abuse in any relationship. However, entering the labor market after years of caregiving is difficult. Women may believe they can best protect their financial well-being and that of their dependents by sticking out a bad relationship, even one in which they are at a bargaining disadvantage and in which they tolerate some abusive treatment.[54] In such a society, the value of caregiving work does not seem to be properly registered or compensated.

There are a variety of policies that the state could enact to address this problem. The state could offer those persons who do not work in the labor market but who care for dependents a caregiver allowance. This would both materially compensate caregivers for the socially obligatory work they perform and signify the social value of their work. If the allowance was generous enough, it would not only protect caregivers from poverty but give them bargaining power in relationships such that they need not tolerate abusive behavior from others out of concern for their well-being or the well-being of those for whom they care. But in a gendered society in which many believe that women are fit by nature for caregiving work, this may effectively result in the state perpetuating a view about women as the natural caregivers of dependents, which disadvantages women who do aim to participate in the labor market and possibly compromises liberal neutrality among reasonable comprehensive doctrines.[55]

One might think that in the society we are imagining, the state does not need to do anything at all since if women voluntary choose to forgo

---

[54] Okin famously noted how wives who are economically dependent on husbands are vulnerable to abuse and tolerate behavior they would otherwise object to because of their bargaining disadvantage in their relationship (*Justice, Gender, and the Family*, p. 152).

[55] Fraser argues that a gendered society that attempts to address the disadvantages women face as a result of caring for dependents with a policy such as caregiver allowances "reinforces the view of such work as women's work" and "marginalizes women within the employment sector" ("After the Family Wage," p. 58). Furthermore, she adds, "by reinforcing the association of caregiving with femininity . . . it may also impede women's participation in other spheres of life, such as politics and civil society" (p. 58).

participation in the labor market, given social policy that makes possible combining caregiving work with labor market work and given protection against poverty and a guarantee of certain basic goods if willing to work in the labor market, then women should deal with the consequences of living in accordance with their conception of the good or revise it. Indeed, Rawls says that a political conception of justice includes a "social division of responsibility," which means that given an account of the fundamental principles of justice, persons should "assume responsibility for their ends" and "moderate the claims they make on their social institutions accordingly."[56] Yet, the value of caregiving work as such seems to be called into question in a society that guarantees individuals basic social goods only if they are willing to work in the labor market while performing this work. This message seems to be that, although it is socially necessary work, this kind of contribution to society, by itself, is not important enough to merit protection from poverty, and so on.

This matter is complex, and we cannot begin to resolve it here. We suggest only that, perhaps, marriage law could help and that considerations of vulnerability in private marriage could lead to public reason arguments in support of legal marriage of some kind with various protections for married persons from vulnerabilities. In a politically liberal society, freedom of association and commitment to liberal neutrality among reasonable comprehensive doctrines may lead to families in which some adult members become vulnerable to certain disadvantages that are a matter of justice. While it is possible that these vulnerabilities could be avoided given persons' ability to negotiate private marital contracts, for a variety of reasons persons may fail to privately negotiate appropriate protections against injustice. And although persons must make life plans in consideration of what they can expect as a matter of basic justice, the state should structure society to protect persons' needs as citizens.[57] Hence, even if certain vulnerabilities relating to citizens' needs as such are the result of personal choices and could be avoided given private contract, if law and policy can both preserve freedom and protect against such vulnerabilities, it should, other things being equal. The legal recognition of marriage together with appropriate divorce laws may be able to address certain vulnerabilities created by marriage. Consider Joan

---

[56] PL, p. 189.

[57] See Anderson, "What's the Point of Equality?," p. 289.

Williams's joint-property proposal, which applies to legally married persons with children. She claims that in families in which one adult is the primary wage earner and the other adult is the primary caregiver, the wage earner's participation in the labor market *depends* on the caregiver's work, and "an asset produced by two people should be jointly owned by them."[58] In divorce, a jointly produced asset should be treated as joint property. This means that after divorce the resulting households should enjoy the same standard of living as long as one adult continues to provide the caregiving work that makes the other's labor market work possible and that, in recognition of the fact that performance of caregiving work over time compromises a person's ability to reenter the labor market, continued support for some amount of time after caregiving ends is in order.[59] This sort of proposal addresses some of the problems and vulnerabilities noted above. Adult members of families who provide care for dependent family members and who, as a result, are financially dependent on another adult family member would not have to tolerate abusive treatment from the person who provides financial support out of concern for a decreased standard of living in the case of the dissolution of the marriage. Moreover, the work of the caregiver would receive recognition as socially important insofar as it entitles the caregiver to joint ownership of the labor market participant's wage.

What kind of legal marriage, though, would be supported by this concern? In the case we described, the vulnerability arose in a traditionally gendered marriage. However, the sort of vulnerability we imagined could actually arise in any domestic relationship in which one partner is the sole or primary breadwinner and the other partner is the primary caregiver for dependents in the family. Such vulnerability could also arise in domestic relationships involving more than two partners if one or more partners caring for dependents undermines their bargaining power and leaves them economically vulnerable relative to another partner or partners. Hence, the kind of legal marriage the state would have reason to recognize is a kind of partnership for caring for dependents which protects caregivers in the event of marital dissolution. It would be available to two or more persons (subject to some limit) regardless of the sex of the participants and regardless of whether the persons presently have

---

[58] Williams, *Unbending Gender*, p. 125.

[59] Williams, *Unbending Gender*, p. 129.

dependents. Those who form the union would be subject to certain laws in the event of divorce; for example, it may be that if one partner chooses to forgo labor market participation or work part time in order to care for dependents, it would be appropriate for the state to entitle the caregiver to some share of the breadwinner's earnings (past, present, and future) to properly reflect the caregiver's investment in the breadwinner's career and the contribution of his or her caregiving work to the family.

We cannot fully defend or work out the particular details of this proposal here.[60] We only want to suggest that it is possible that, in a politically liberal society, vulnerabilities created by private marriage and family life could justify legal marriage and divorce laws of some kind aimed at protecting persons' interests as citizens. And we want to stress that it is not only in nonideal societies that legal marriage could be a viable means for protecting women or men as caregivers from certain vulnerabilities. Ideal societies, as understood by Rawls, are well-ordered. They are societies in which (1) "everyone accepts, and knows that everyone else accepts, the very same principles of justice"; (2) it is thought that the basic structure is just by these principles; and (3) citizens accept the principles of justice as just and "generally comply" with the demands of justice.[61] The kind of vulnerability to disadvantage we are imagining could certainly arise in an ideal society so understood.[62] Furthermore, while it may be the case that other laws and policies could also address caregiver vulnerability, legal marriage and divorce may be preferable in a given social context. Our claim is not that legal marriage of some sort is necessary to protect caregivers from vulnerability in a family but simply that, under certain practically realizable conditions, political liberals may be able to support some kind of legal marriage. And, we would like to stress, this argument differs from Brake's insofar as the public reason

---

[60] For example, one important issue that we leave unaddressed is whether the state could offer incentives for this kind of legal marriage.

[61] PL, p. 35.

[62] In her discussion of the state's recognition of marriage in *nonideal* societies, Brake notes that some feminists argue that divorce law can protect women in traditionally gendered families ("Minimal Marriage," p. 335). In transitional societies—that is, those societies not yet ideal—Brake claims that "spousal support liability on grounds of opportunities forgone and contributions to the other's career might be justified by appeal to induced reliance and verbal contracts—mechanisms independently available in contract law," but she notes that "if overall justice does require such transfers, then default rules governing property division on exit from intimate relationships can be enacted independently from marriage" (p. 336).

argument for the legal recognition of marriage is not to provide the social bases of adult caregiving relationships but, rather, to protect caregivers of dependents from problematic vulnerabilities that can result from domestic partnerships.

V. Same-Sex Marriage, Second-Class Citizenship, and Democratic Deliberation

Consider yet another public reason argument that supports the legal recognition of some form of marriage in a political liberal society. Under certain conditions, it may be that the state's power to confer legitimacy on certain relationships through marriage licensing is the best way or an acceptable way to address private discrimination which can compromise the necessary conditions for democratic deliberation. In particular, as we will argue below, in a society in which powerful religious institutions fail to recognize same-sex marriage or condemn it and in which marriage is completely privatized, same-sex couples may be effectively reduced to second-class citizenship. State recognition of a variety of relationships as marital may be able to provide the conditions necessary for equal citizenship.

One might have thought that privatizing marriage could be a central step toward equal citizenship for gays and lesbians. One could argue certainly that the government's recognition, licensing, and authorization of some relationships (monogamous, heterosexual ones) and not others (such as same-sex monogamous relationships or polygamous ones) unjustly discriminates against same-sex couples (and, perhaps, those who desire certain polygamous relationships). Indeed, Sunstein and Thaler claim that privatizing marriage would both respect those who seek same-sex marriage as full citizens and respect religious persons and institutions who oppose same-sex marriage:

> Whatever the precise form of the reform, privatization of marriage would automatically quiet the current battle over same-sex marriage. It would fully recognize, and respect, the autonomy of those religious institutions that do not want to celebrate same-sex unions (or unions of any other kind). It would simultaneously recognize that if same-sex couples want to make commitments to one another, the state should allow them to do so—and should not treat them as

second-class citizens within the eyes of the law. Privatization would eliminate a serious current problem for democratic debate, which is that official marriage is now conflated with religious marriage, in a way that makes alteration in the first seem to threaten the second. It would be highly desirable to have separate terms for what governments do and for what private institutions do.[63]

We think that under certain circumstances privatizing marriage could have this effect. That is, it is possible that privatizing marriage could promote equality by removing the legitimacy-conferring power of state recognition. However, it is easy to imagine circumstances in which privatizing marriage could serve to effectively reduce same-sex couples to second-class citizens. Below we will focus on how this could happen in a politically liberal society.

As noted earlier, political liberals accept a wide range of comprehensive doctrines as reasonable. Freedom of conscience and freedom of association protect citizens' ability to participate in religious institutions. Since these institutions are private associations, members of the institution can deny membership to others on the basis of religious beliefs. Furthermore, within the institution, privileges, positions of power, and the recognition of relationships can be denied to members on the basis of factors such as sex and sexuality. Importantly, religious institutions can be powerful institutions in society. Currently, some religious institutions refuse to recognize same-sex marriage, and it is likely that in an ideal, politically liberal society, many religious institutions would continue to condemn same-sex marriage. If the dominant religious institutions refuse to recognize same-sex marriage and if, in a society with privatized marriage, these religious institutions are the primary institutions from which citizens (even not very religious ones) seek legitimacy and affirmation of their marital commitments, then these institutions will effectively have a monopoly on the affirmation of marital commitment. It is, of course, true that same-sex couples and others *could* make secular marital commitments or seek out religious institutions that will marry them. However, the recognition of a marriage from these institutions may fail to bestow on same-sex relationships the legitimacy that other marriages enjoy. We should stress, too, that, when marriage is privatized and there are no longer any state

---

[63] Sunstein and Thaler, "Privatizing Marriage," p. 379.

entitlements attached to marriage as such, it is the public legitimacy and shared understanding of their commitment that couples will seek from private institutions. As some institutions may have the power to grant more legitimacy than others, the effect could be that private discrimination effectively undermines equal citizenship to the extent that some persons are marked as deviant or inferior and fail to receive the same respect as other citizens.

Should private discrimination against same-sex marriage thwart equal citizenship for gays and lesbians, political liberals are not without recourse. Indeed, political liberalism's criterion of reciprocity requires that persons be able to engage in democratic deliberation as equal citizens. As Rawls describes the criterion of reciprocity, it requires that when persons advance principles of basic justice or constitutional essentials, "those proposing them must also think it at least reasonable for others to accept them as free and equal citizens, and not dominated or manipulated, or under the pressure of an inferior political or social position."[64] Elsewhere we have proposed that the criterion of reciprocity calls for (1) the eradication of social conditions of domination and subordination relevant to democratic deliberation among equal citizens and (2) the provision of the social conditions necessary for mutual respect among equal citizens.[65] If private discrimination results in social hierarchies that affect the ability of gays and lesbians to participate as equal citizens with others in democratic deliberation, then political liberals must take steps to counter the social conditions that undermine some persons' ability to engage in democratic deliberation as equal citizens. It may be that an effective way to counter social hierarchies created through the private discrimination against same-sex marriage is through the state's recognition of a variety of relationships as marital. Religious and other private institutions would, of course, still be free to confer legitimacy on marriages as they wished. Marriage plays an important role in many faiths, and forbidding religious

---

[64] IPRR, p. 578.

[65] We develop and defend this interpretation of Rawls's criterion of reciprocity in chapter 6. We understand Elizabeth Anderson's conception of democratic equality to be similar to Rawls's criterion of reciprocity. Anderson claims, "Negatively, egalitarians seek to abolish oppression—that is, forms of social relationship by which some people dominate, exploit, marginalize, demean, and inflict violence on others. . . . Positively, egalitarians seek a social order in which persons stand in relations of equality" ("What's the Point of Equality?," p. 313).

institutions from private discrimination would be an unacceptable violation of persons' fundamental rights. However, to mitigate the effects of discriminatory practices on citizens, the state could recognize a variety of relationships as marital in the name of equal citizenship.[66] The basic idea is that, in some contexts, the availability of a publicly recognized marital status is central to equal citizenship. The legal recognition of a variety of relationships as marital (same-sex, heterosexual, monogamous, and, perhaps, polygamous) could both confer legitimacy on relationships that are subject to private discrimination and convey a recognizable social meaning for such relationships.

In his discussion of the "fundamental argument for same-sex marriage," Ralph Wedgwood describes the social meaning of marriage as "the web of common knowledge and assumptions about marriage that are shared throughout society."[67] In modern Western society, Wedgwood claims that three aspects are generally thought to be part of the "essential core of the social meaning of marriage." These aspects are "sexual intimacy," "domestic and economic cooperation," and "a voluntary mutual commitment to sustaining this relationship."[68] Wedgwood notes that in modern Western society, it is also assumed that a marriage is between two opposite-sex persons, but he says that monogamy and heterosexuality are not essential to marriage's core meaning. As Wedgwood stresses, without marriage law, the social meaning of marriage will be determined by subcultures or groups.[69] For political liberals, this result would be unproblematic in some circumstances. However, as noted, in other conditions, dominant private institutions could effectively determine the legitimacy and meaning of marriage, and this could threaten equal citizenship. Marriage law would grant legitimacy to certain relationships and provide legal marriages with a social meaning. In a society practically realizable from our own, it is likely that the essential core of the social meaning of marriage would be much like it is today and that nearly all persons who want to marry and who are not allowed to marry by powerful private institutions would be seeking the

---

[66] In chapter 6, we argue that when social inequality threatens or results in political inequality, it is of concern to political liberals.

[67] Wedgwood, "The Fundamental Argument," p. 229.

[68] Wedgwood, "The Fundamental Argument," p. 229.

[69] Wedgwood, "The Fundamental Argument," p. 233.

recognition of a relationship that exemplifies the elements found in the essential core.

Wedgwood claims that the state's recognition of marriage so understood does not presume a conception of marriage in accordance with a particular conception of the good because "the essential social meaning of marriage consists solely in expectations about the sort of relationship that is *typical* of married couples—expectations that are shared by practically everyone, even by those who reject married life as an ideal."[70] Furthermore, he says that the rationale for marriage does not interfere with liberal neutrality as long as the justification for marriage does not stem from some particular conception of the good.[71] Importantly on Wedgwood's view, if marriage is justifiable, part of its justification stems from the fact that "many people *want* to be married, where this desire to marry is typically a serious desire that deserves to be respected."[72] For political liberals, this could not be part of the justification of marriage. Rawls notes that for political liberals, "desires and wants, however intense, are not by themselves reasons in matters of constitutional essentials and basic justice."[73] However, securing equal citizenship is a basis on which political liberals could ground legal marriage as a matter of basic justice. In accordance with this foundation, political liberals, we think, could recognize a variety of relationships as marital to the extent they fit with the essential elements of marriage as it is socially understood and to the extent that the essential social meaning does not itself degrade or undermine some persons' status as equal citizens. Legal marriage in a political liberal society would not carry with it all the benefits and entitlements currently associated with legal marriage—tax benefits, special entitlement to caretaking leave (as it should be recognized that all dependents are entitled to care), evidentiary privileges and many others; but the state could legitimately make certain assumptions having to do with emergency decision-making and inheritance, for example, that could be defeasible given a private contract to the contrary.

---

[70] Wedgwood, "The Fundamental Argument," p. 234.

[71] Wedgwood, "The Fundamental Argument," pp. 237–238.

[72] Wedgwood, "The Fundamental Argument," p. 235.

[73] PL, p. 190. See also Brake's discussion of Wedgwood's view ("Minimal Marriage," p. 326).

VI. Political Liberalism, Marriage, and Children

We have heretofore left unaddressed a commonly recognized rationale for marriage law, which is that state recognition of legal marriage is important for the proper care of children. Rawls certainly seemed to think that the connection of marriage to the family (specifically, the rearing of children) makes the institution of marriage part of the basic structure. As we noted, the family, Rawls says, is included as part of the basic structure because "one of its main roles is to be the basis of the orderly production and reproduction of society and its culture from one generation to the next."[74] He thinks the state's concern with the family, then, is the "reasonable and effective" care of children, which includes the "moral development and education" they need to be citizens; political liberalism is neutral among any family form that reasonably and effectively does this, provided it is consistent with or does not undermine any citizen's other basic entitlements of justice.[75] To the extent that marriage among consenting adults in whatever form (and consistent with citizens' other entitlements of justice) is necessary to or centrally supportive of political family forms that reasonably and effectively care for children, such forms of marriage are a matter of basic justice. In Rawls's discussion of the family, he assumes that marriage will be part of most or some families (as evidenced by his repeated reference to "wives" in his discussions of the family),[76] but, for political liberals, whether the political family as such brings marriage into the basic structure depends on the connection of marriage to the family's political function.

Brake's discussion of this issue is very helpful. Brake rejects the claim that "traditional" marriage (understood as monogamous, heterosexual marriage) or marriage in any form is *necessary* for caring for children. She is certainly right about this: children can be reasonably and effectively cared for outside of marriage. And she is right to stress that "society does not and cannot require that parents be ideally suited to maximize

---

[74] IPRR, p. 595.

[75] IPRR, p. 596 (noting fn. 60) and p. 587. However, Nussbaum stresses that institutions other than the family could effectively care for children and that "there need not even be a presumption that all functions we now associate with the family will be bundled under a single institution" ("The Future of Feminist Liberalism," pp. 118–119).

[76] IPRR, pp. 596, 597, 598, 600.

children's well-being."[77] Political liberals understand justice to concern the creation and maintenance of a society based on mutual respect among free and equal citizens. Citizens are entitled to certain basic goods relevant to their interests as citizens and to the distribution of those goods as specified by the fundamental principles of justice, but citizens' interests as free and equal persons do not include that as children their well-being will be *maximized*. This would intrusively interfere with the other basic freedoms of citizens. Moreover, judgments about the maximization of children's well-being would involve appeals to comprehensive doctrines, which are not permitted in public reason. But, as Rawls emphasizes, children are entitled to reasonable and effective care; this is a matter of basic justice.

Is some form of marriage conducive to the care of children? In our nonideal world, Brake says the evidence about traditional marriage is mixed.[78] Of course, studies about the effects of some forms of marriage on children in our society do not tell us whether some kind of marriage in a society structured by a politically liberal conception of justice would be conducive to the reasonable and effective rearing of children. Brake notes that empirical evidence shows that "what matters greatly to child psychological development is continuity of care, which is available in polygamous, same-sex, single-parent, and extended families."[79] Continuity of care is surely important and available in a wide variety of families. If, in a politically liberal society, the recognition of some form of legal marriage is not conducive to continuity of care and other factors relevant to the reasonable and effective care of children, then political liberals do not have a public reason tied to the care of children for the recognition of legal marriage.

Also, as Brake stresses, it is important to distinguish state support of marriage from state support of parenting frameworks.[80] One reason is that many children have parents who are not married; "focusing on marriage leaves out children of unmarried and divorced parents."[81] Certainly,

---

[77] Brake, "Minimal Marriage," p. 318. See also *Minimizing Marriage*, chapter 6, for Brake's discussion of the separation of parental and marital legal frameworks.

[78] Brake, "Minimal Marriage," p. 317.

[79] Brake, "Minimal Marriage," p. 318. Brake cites Alstott's *No Exit*, pp. 15–20.

[80] Brake, "Minimal Marriage," pp. 318–319.

[81] Brake, "Minimal Marriage," p. 319.

unmarried parents need recognition and support for the socially obligatory work they perform and, like married caretakers of children, should
not be disadvantaged relative to other citizens in their ability to participate
in all spheres of social life because they perform this work. Of course,
state support of some form of marriage on the grounds that it is conducive to the effective and reasonable care of children does not prevent the
state from enacting other laws and policies to recognize and support the
socially obligatory work all caretakers perform. One might respond that it
would be more effective to simply focus on recognizing and supporting
the caretakers of children. If so, that is one reason to favor that approach.
But it does not settle the matter, and it may not be the case.

Another reason, according to Brake, for distinguishing marriage and
parenting frameworks is that persons understand marriage to concern
goods other than the care of children. This is certainly true, but the fact
that the state recognizes legal marriage for a certain reason does not mean
that persons who are legally married (according to whatever form the state
recognizes) have to understand their marriage to be only or fundamentally
for that reason or that any persons cannot privately marry in order to recognize what social goods they think are essential to or available as part of
the kind of marriage they seek.

Brake, however, defends the thesis that "minimal marriage, and no
more extensive or restrictive law, is consistent with political liberalism."[82]
There are two ways to interpret this claim. One might think that Brake's
view is that there are no empirical conditions in which political liberals
can support a form of marriage more robust than her minimal marriage
in an ideal society. Or one might attribute to Brake the weaker claim that,
given the conditions likely to obtain in an ideal society, it does not seem
that political liberals can support a form of marriage more robust than her
minimal marriage. Even if one attributes to Brake the weaker claim, we do
not think that Brake's view can be defended. In the previous two sections,
we noted quite plausible circumstances under which political liberals
could defend a form of marriage more robust than minimal marriage in
an ideal society. When it comes to whether some form of marriage is conducive to the reasonable and effective care of children, we suspect that
Brake is right: in a practically realizable, ideal society, no particular form
of marriage will be conducive to this function of the family. But instead

---

[82] Brake, "Minimal Marriage," p. 312.

of making the claim that political liberals can defend no form of legal marriage on this ground, we prefer to stress the context-sensitive nature of political liberalism, as we have tried to do throughout this chapter. The reasonable and effective care of children is part of the family's political function, and whether political liberals can support a form (or forms) of marriage on the grounds that some form (or forms) of marriage is conducive to the care of children depends on the circumstances of the society as well as whether any public reasons can be given against recognizing that form (or forms) of marriage.

VII. Plural Marriage

In recent discussions of the legalization of same-sex marriage, some commentators claim that the same arguments that support the legal recognition of same-sex marriage support the legal recognition of polygamy. While some people take that to be a vice, others take it to be a virtue. In the introduction, we briefly stated the view we will defend here. In short, we claim that some forms of polygamy are simply incompatible with free and equal citizenship, while other forms, in certain contexts, cannot justly be denied the legal recognition and support offered to other types of legally recognized marital relationships. Of course, even the forms of polygamy that we think are not structurally incompatible with free and equal citizenship may be prohibited on other grounds, such as, for the sake of sex equality, given various contingent facts.

To begin, we need to specify how we will use some terms. By "plural marriage" or "polygamy" we simply mean a marriage of more than two people. By "polygyny" we mean a marriage in which one male marries two or more females, and by "polyandry" we mean a marriage in which one female marries two or more males. By "traditional polygamy" we have in mind the familiar and most prominently practiced type of polygamy in which one male marries two or more females, and each marital relation between the male and a female is such that the male has more power and fewer commitments or obligations than the female. As we explain below, Gregg Strauss argues that any marital relationship with this *inegalitarian structure*, regardless of the sex or gender of the parties, is morally objectionable.[83] But we also think it is objectionable on politically liberal

---

[83] Strauss, "Is Polygamy Inherently Unequal?"

grounds. We will argue that a politically liberal state can't legally recognize any form of polygamy with this structure because it is incompatible with free and equal citizenship. However, in his work, Strauss identifies two other forms of polygamy: polyfidelity and molecular polygamy. The former, polyfidelity, is a marriage of three or more persons in which all spouses marry each other and have the very same rights and obligations.[84] The latter, molecular polygamy, is a model in which persons can have multiple spouses who do not have to marry each other but who can marry others and in which the rights and obligations exchanged in a marital relation are the same for both spouses.[85] Political liberals, we will claim, can't object to the structure of these forms of polygamy.

Consider traditional polygamy. It is sexist and heterosexist, and, as practiced, it is correlated with the emotional, physical, and sexual abuse of women and girls as well as other forms of sex discrimination.[86] The structure of this form of marriage is that one person, whom Strauss calls the center spouse, has multiple marital relations, more power within each marital relation, and fewer commitments to each spouse than the other spouses possess. Only the center spouse can have multiple marital relations. Now imagine a form of polygamy that has the same structure as traditional polygamy but which is not sexist (a male or female can be the center spouse) or heterosexist (the center spouse can marry someone of the same sex), and let us suppose that this form of polygamy is not linked to the emotional, physical, and sexual abuse of women and girls or other forms of sex discrimination. Strauss perspicuously argues that the *structure* of this form of polygamy is inegalitarian. He says that no matter what one takes the moral nature of marriage to be (e.g., "sharing lives, love, or raising children"), this model of marriage is inherently unequal, and "an asymmetry in the kind or extent of moral demands in personal or intimate relationships is prima facie morally objectionable."[87]

Of course, in a politically liberal society, the mere fact that the structure of this form of polygamy may be morally objectionable according to

---

[84] Strauss, "Is Polygamy Inherently Unequal?," pp. 534–535.

[85] Strauss, "Is Polygamy Inherently Unequal?," pp. 540–542.

[86] For an overview of these problems with polygamy, see, e.g., Brooks, "The Problem with Polygamy." Stephen Macedo also includes a thoughtful discussion of some of these issues in his *Just Married*, pp. 161–178.

[87] Strauss, "Is Polygamy Inherently Unequal?," pp. 524–526, 523.

some views of morality is not a public reason argument for prohibiting this form of polygamy as a matter of basic justice. Reasonable people hold different views about the moral ideal of marriage, and a comprehensive doctrine that includes an ideal of marriage with unequal marital demands and power is not unreasonable simply due to this aspect of the view. A comprehensive doctrine is unreasonable if a reasonable person could not endorse the view. Reasonable people possess both "the willingness to propose fair terms of cooperation and to abide by them provided others do" and "the willingness to recognize the burdens of judgement" and its consequences for public reason.[88]

However, there is a strong public reason argument for prohibiting this form of polygamy. Consider that when a form of marriage is legally recognized, the state is involved in different ways at various points in the marital relationship. First, the state determines if individuals can marry given the state's laws, and then the state recognizes a marital relationship by conferring the status of married. Then, in accordance with its marriage laws, the state confers benefits and offers entitlements to those who enjoy a marital status. Finally, the state enforces its laws about the dissolution of marriage if an individual decides he or she wants to end the marital relationship. The state's role in the dissolution of marriage is incredibly important and concerns, for example, how assets will be divided as well as, in actual societies, matters of custody and financial responsibility for children. If there was a legal form of marriage in which one individual could be a center spouse with more power within each of his or her marital relations and fewer obligations to each spouse, then the state will have to enforce different and unequal rights and entitlements among spouses. The state will be an instrument of inequality. While we are supposing that those who marry the center spouse choose to enter a relationship in which they have less power and more commitments and in which they are legally unable to change their asymmetrical position with the center spouse absent a divorce, the fact of their agreement does not change their legal disadvantage, which would have to be enforced by the state.

Consider a case that raises some similar issues. In *Shelley v. Kramer*, the U.S. Supreme Court considered whether the Equal Protection Clause of the 14th Amendment prohibited judicial enforcement by state courts

---

[88] PL, p. 54.

of racially restrictive covenants.[89] In this case the issue was "private agreements entered into by property owners to restrict the sale and occupation of real property on a racial basis."[90] The Court held that despite the fact that the contracts themselves did not involve state action, the enforcement of the contracts necessarily involves state action, and any such enforcement would amount to a denial of equal protection of the laws on the basis of race. Thus, the state cannot enforce such contracts. This position itself does not depend upon a moral condemnation of racism apart from the political value of equal protection of the laws, as such a condemnation is not necessary for the ruling.

Similarly, with respect to the type of polygamy we are now considering, the state would license marital relations that are wholly based on structural inequality, grant rights and entitlements unequally, and enforce divorce laws premised on this inequality. Although such intimate relationships may be part of some comprehensive doctrines, the state's involvement in marital relations wholly based on structural inequality denies equal protection of the laws to all persons as free and equal citizens and undermines their equal standing as citizens. Of course, we have said that Brake's minimal marriage may be recognized in some politically liberal societies, and her view permits the asymmetrical and unbundled exchange of the rights and entitlements relevant to the social bases of adult caregiving relationships. Doesn't her view permit the same kind of disadvantage? What is the relevant difference? The legal structure of Brake's minimal marriage is not premised on the recognition of a center spouse who in virtue of occupying that role has more power and different rights and entitlements than other spouses. Rather, Brake's view simply permits persons to exchange the rights needed for supporting the social bases of adult caring relationships reciprocally or asymmetrically and altogether or unbundled. These rights are quite limited, as we discussed above. She stresses that "in an ideal liberal egalitarian society" a person's access to health care and a basic income is not through marriage and that there is no assumed economic dependency between spouses.[91] Her view is for a well-ordered society, and we have claimed, contra Brake, that marriage

---

[89] *Shelley v. Kraemer*, 334 U.S. 1 (1948).

[90] MacKinnon, *Sex Equality*, p. 78.

[91] Brake, "Minimal Marriage," p. 309.

laws can differ in well-ordered societies given different social contexts.[92] Here what is important, though, is that structurally Brake's view is not the same as the kind of polygamy we think there is a strong public reason argument to prohibit.

The two egalitarian forms of polygamy that Strauss proposes— polyfidelity and molecular polygamy—do not involve structural inequality among spouses. Again, polyfidelity is a marriage of three or more persons in which all spouse marry each other and have the very same rights and obligations, and molecular polygamy is a model in which persons can have multiple spouses who do not have to marry each other but who can marry others and in which the rights and obligations exchanged in a marital relation are the same for both spouses. There is no public reason argument against these forms of marriage based on structural inequality and the state's denial of equal protection of the laws to all persons as free and equal citizens. In each of these models, the legal rights and obligations exchanged are identical. There may be other reasons to object to either of these models in certain social contexts. Perhaps molecular polygamy, as practiced in a particular society, nearly always involves a male with multiple wives and, although the spouses exchange identical rights as a matter of a law, as a matter of fact the marital relations involve significant inequalities. In such societies, there may be public reason arguments against the legal recognition of this form of polygamy.

Stephen Macedo offers additional considerations against polygamy that merit attention. He claims that "polygamy as a widespread practice, or normative system, appears to be inconsistent with efforts to secure the preconditions of equal liberty and fair opportunity for all."[93] His argument for this claim is not based on a single factor but various factors taken together. First, he thinks that it is not "by nature or deep-seated nurture" that persons want multiple spouses; for most, polygamy is a preference, not an orientation.[94] It is, though, for some a matter of religious obligation. Second, he claims that "only in dyads do we get a perfect symmetry of reciprocal dependence"; hence, full reciprocity of marital relations is

---

[92] Brake revises her view somewhat in *Minimizing Marriage*, acknowledging that social context, in part, determines the rights one will need to support caregiving relationships (pp. 160–161).

[93] Macedo, *Just Married*, p. 161.

[94] Macedo, *Just Married*, pp. 162–163.

compromised in polygamy.[95] Third, Macedo claims that considerations of distributive justice support legalizing only monogamous marriage. Marriage is an important good, and allowing individuals to have multiple spouses will compromise fair opportunity for a spouse. And those with more spouses are likely to be privileged individuals in society.[96] Finally, Macedo claims that polygamy may "degrade" some of marriage's core functions. He says that marriage allows a person to "join with another person, settle parts of our lives together, and a build a joint future on that settled foundation." Spouses have "assurance of stability." For reasons that are not clear in his text, Macedo thinks that such "assurance of stability" is available only with the promise of exclusivity in twosomes.[97]

We do not think the considerations that Macedo raises—either alone or taken together—constitute a strong public reason argument to oppose forms of polygamy with egalitarian structures, *if* there are considerations in their favor. He says that polygamy is a preference and not an orientation. That may be, but if the state chooses to support the social bases of adult caregiving relationships by recognizing a variety of marriage options, such as minimal marriage and monogamous marriage with bundled marital rights, then it seems that, absent compelling considerations against them, the state should recognize structurally egalitarian forms of polygamy with bundled marital rights. This will offer citizens the option of having their needs met in the manner they prefer, and this promotes equal freedom for all. Macedo also says that full reciprocity in marital relations is compromised in polygamy. And this is especially important given modern marriage, which he says "is not just an alliance for pooling of property and other resources; it is unique (or nearly so) in the depth and breath of its commitments. Two people come to depend on each other deeply and across wide segments of their lives, making each other uniquely and deeply vulnerable to loss and betrayal."[98] However, in a politically liberal society, the state's interest in marriage is limited. The state may recognize marriage to support the social bases of adult caring relationships and in that context recognize various rights and entitlements that support adult caregiving. We argued that structurally inegalitarian marital relationships

---

[95] Macedo, *Just Married,* pp. 163–164.

[96] Macedo, *Just Married,* pp. 164–165.

[97] Macedo, *Just Married,* pp. 165–166.

[98] Macedo, *Just Married,* p. 163.

in which legal marital rights are based on positional inequality between spouses are problematic. However, "full reciprocity in marriage relations" in the "wide segments" of one's life that marital caring relations affect is beyond the state's interest. The promotion of such full reciprocity would be based on a particular view of a good marriage and goods that are not tied to political values or commitments. Moreover, Macedo claims that full reciprocal dependence is available only in dyadic marital relationships, but it is highly implausible that in any actual dyadic marital relationship there is full reciprocal dependence. In structurally egalitarian polygamous relationships spouses will exchange identical legal marital rights and may do just as well or well enough when it comes to any kind of reciprocal dependence that would matter given the state's limited interest in marriage. In any case, without strong empirical evidence to the contrary, there doesn't seem to be any reason to restrict freedom and permit two-person, structurally egalitarian marriages while prohibiting structurally egalitarian marriages of multiples.

Now recall Macedo's claim that allowing individuals to have multiple spouses will compromise fair equality of opportunity for a spouse and will disadvantage the less privileged, who are less likely to secure multiple spouses. Macedo has in mind a society that permits traditional polygamy and in which lower-class men will not be able to marry because privileged men have multiple wives. In a politically liberal society that recognized various forms of marriage, including egalitarian models of polygamy, it is unclear that this concern would arise. The kind of income inequality and the poverty that is characteristic of the societies that Macedo has in mind would not exist in a politically liberal society. Furthermore, on what grounds could the state justify regulating the marriage market so that everyone has fair equality of opportunity to marry? Although the state should guarantee to everyone the social bases of adult caring networks and itself provide care to dependents who do not have caretakers, for the state to enact policy on the grounds that it needs to make sure everyone has fair opportunity for intimate personal relationships is an objectionable infringement of freedom.

Finally, Macedo claims that the dyadic marriages offer the assurance of stability persons need in marital relations. He says that introducing a third person, or more persons, is likely to increase conflict, and conflict is destabilizing. Hence, he claims restricting marriages to dyads is more likely to promote the stability of particular marriages. Here, again, Macedo seems to have in mind the importance of reciprocal dependence. Indeed, in this discussion, Macedo remarks, "Obviously, when children become a part of the family, this complicates the twoness of family life. The important point is that *marriage* remains a fully reciprocal partnership between two spouses."[99] Again, equal marital rights do not guarantee a fully reciprocal partnership. But whether egalitarian polygamous relationships would fail to provide the "assurance of stability" is an empirical claim. Of course, we do agree that if legal marriage is meant to support the social bases of adult caregiving networks, then relationship security with respect to marital rights that support adult caregiving is important. We don't think that there is available empirical evidence to indicate how egalitarian polygamy would do in this regard.

So, although one might think that political liberals cannot support the recognition of any form of legal marriage given its account of public reason, we have shown that what political liberalism recommends when it comes to the legal recognition of marriage depends on circumstances of a particular society. It is not the case, in our view, that even if we imagine ideal societies that are practically realizable from our current location, political liberalism is compatible only with some particular form of marriage (like Brake's minimal marriage). Rather, the implications of political liberalism for marriage law cannot be determined in advance of information about a particular politically liberal society.

---

[99] Macedo, *Just Married*, p. 164, emphasis in original.

Conclusion

AT THE HEART of our defense of feminist political liberalism is a substantive account of free and equal citizenship. In fact, our defense of political liberalism *as a feminist liberalism* hinges on the claims we make about the substantive content of this conception of citizenship and how this conception limits and shapes what kinds of state action can be justified to others.

Political liberalism's feminist content is explicit in our account: central to political liberalism is the elimination of social class positions in which relationships of domination and subordination based on group membership frustrate the interests and standing of persons as free and equal citizens. Hence, when gender marks out such social positions, the aspects of it that maintain and perpetuate women's subordination must be eliminated.

This doesn't mean that political liberalism is incompatible with all conceptions of gender or even gender hierarchy in some institutions that are part of the background culture (if this hierarchy doesn't affect persons' interests as free and equal citizens); we claim in chapter 5 that, in some circumstances, religious institutions can discriminate in employment on the basis of sex, given beliefs about gender that are part of religious doctrine. It also doesn't follow that nonhierarchical gender differences are always compatible with the interests of persons as free and equal citizens, as we discuss with respect to work and gender specialization in chapter 8. While we think that gender specialization and gender hierarchy tend to go hand in hand, gender specialization even absent hierarchy could frustrate the interests of persons as free and equal citizens, if, for example, persons are effectively marginalized from spheres of life central to free and equal citizenship.

Much of our discussion of the feminist content of political liberalism, though, concerns examples of how aspects of gender function to subordinate women and frustrate or undermine their interests and standing as free and equal citizens. In chapter 8, we argue that caring for dependents is socially necessary work and that those who perform this work can't be disadvantaged relative to other members of society with respect to their ability to participate in spheres of life central to citizenship on a basis of equality; these spheres include the labor market, civil society, the political sphere, and the family. As such caring work is gendered, failure to address the ways in which gendered patterns of care labor sustain gender inequality is to deny women substantive equality. Political liberals can not only recognize this injustice but can also require that the state develop policies to ensure substantive equality for those who provide care labor.

Or, for example, in chapter 5 we argue claims to religious exemptions as grounds for denying women or gays and lesbians or others access to public goods or services is incompatible with the political liberal commitment to free and equal citizenship for all. Thus, we argue that wedding vendors can't refuse service and discriminate against same-sex couples in places of public accommodation, even when they claim religious grounds for doing so. Nor can pharmacists or doctors refuse to meet the medical needs of women, gays or lesbians, or trans persons on grounds of religious objections. Where substantive civil rights are at stake, free and equal citizenship requires that persons enjoy the same access to goods in places of public accommodation that their fellow citizens enjoy.

We admittedly, and purposively, argue that political liberalism's idea of free and equal citizenship and criterion of reciprocity have implications far beyond what Rawls imagined; this is both what makes our view distinct and what will be a source of concern for some. For example, we argue for an interpretation of the criterion of reciprocity in chapter 6 in which reciprocity demands both the eradication of social conditions of domination and subordination relevant to democratic deliberation and participation among equal citizens and the provision of the social conditions of recognition respect. We further claim that the sort of reasoning that Rawls employs to produce the list of features that any reasonable political conception of justice will have will actually generate a list with considerably more content than he realized. Consider: if we take the criterion of reciprocity as the "limiting feature" of reasonable political conceptions of justice,[1]

---

[1] IPRR, p. 581.

how could reasonable people recognize "reproductive labor" and the rearing of children as socially necessary work[2] and not protect caregivers from disadvantage relative to other citizens for their work? Rawls's list of the features of all reasonable political conceptions of justice does not include such protection, although he suggests sympathy for some of them in his discussion of the family in the "Idea of Public Reason Revisited."[3]

Some critics—even if they are sympathetic to our substantive account of citizenship—may charge that we have not defended a *political* liberalism but have offered, instead, a partially comprehensive liberalism. One way to develop this concern is to charge that we have, through our substantive account of the demands of reciprocity and the account of equal citizenship that follows, made the set of reasonable comprehensive doctrines too narrow. A defining characteristic of reasonable persons is that they possess "the willingness to propose fair terms of cooperation and to abide by them provided that others do."[4] As we note in chapter 2, reasonable persons accept the criterion of reciprocity. And, as we just stated, we interpret this to have significant substantive content. One might think that the set of reasonable comprehensive doctrines is much broader than our view allows. And so the conclusion to be drawn is that we, in effect, offer a partially comprehensive liberalism insofar as the set of views that count as reasonable is smaller than our critics might think warranted.

Another way in which one might begin to develop this objection to our view is by emphasizing the importance of neutrality to liberal political thought. A version of this criticism might look like this: political liberalism aims to be neutral among competing comprehensive doctrines in the sense that "the state is not to do anything intended to favor or promote any particular comprehensive doctrine rather than another, or to give greater assistance to those who pursue it."[5] One might worry that our substantive notion of citizenship exceeds any plausible account of the needs of persons as free and equal citizens and is a partially comprehensive liberalism. As such, the state is not neutral in aim and favors egalitarian doctrines.

---

[2] IPRR, pp. 595–596.

[3] IPRR, pp. 595–601.

[4] PL, p. 54.

[5] PL, p. 193.

Although each of these criticisms is expressed by emphasizing different features of political liberalism, they both come to the same point: our view is just too restrictive with regard to what kinds of reasonable comprehensive doctrines will be consistent with or accepting of the conception of free and equal citizenship and its demands as we have defended it. This is the worry that we will address in the closing of the book.

We begin by returning to the problem political liberalism aims to solve—namely, "how is it possible for there to exist over time a just and stable society of free and equal citizens, who remain profoundly divided by reasonable religious, philosophical, and moral doctrines?"[6] With Rawls, we agree that under conditions in which freedoms of thought and conscience are protected basic liberties—that is, under conditions of modern liberal democracies—reasonable pluralism is inevitable. It is neither desirable nor possible for any liberal state to expect agreement, among citizens, over any particular comprehensive doctrine. Moreover, "a second and related general fact is that a continuing shared understanding on one comprehensive religious, philosophical, or moral doctrine can be maintained only by the oppressive use of state power."[7] Rawls calls this "the fact of oppression."[8]

Political liberalism aims to solve the problem just posed while avoiding the oppressive use of state power. However, this does not mean that political liberalism is not a substantive political doctrine. It is. Political liberalism is a substantive doctrine based on moral ideas that are part of a particular view of a constitutional democracy in which citizens stand in a relation of freedom and equality.

The fundamental ideas of political liberalism are part of the history, tradition, and culture of liberal democratic theory and practice. We have drawn on the work of egalitarian social movements in democratic states, such as represented by feminist and antiracist theory and practice as well as movements for more egalitarian forms of gay, lesbian, and trans rights in developing the details of what is needed to secure genuine substantive equality for citizens. And while we have not defended any particular political conception of justice here, we developed an interpretation of the limiting features of any such conception based on the criterion of reciprocity

---

[6] PL, p. 4.

[7] PL, p. 37.

[8] PL, p. 37.

and the idea of persons as free and equal citizens engaged in social co-operation for the end of living on terms of mutual respect with fellow co-citizens.

As we stated in chapter 6, in our initial response to the worry that our view is, in fact, a partially comprehensive liberalism, political liberals are committed to the normative priority of citizenship. Ruth Abbey thinks this commitment brings more substance to political liberalism than the view can stand, as a strictly political liberalism. She makes this point in questioning how to interpret Rawls's claim that while the internal dynamics of family life are not governed by the principles of justice, the principles of justice constrain what families and other associations may do. She writes:

> It is unclear what remains of a strictly political conception of liberalism in light of passages like these [referring to Rawls's account of the way the principles of justice constrain nonpolitical institutions such as the family], for there is no domain or space immune from the principles of justice. What does a purely political liberalism demarcate if its principles penetrate all (or most) aspects of life?

And Abbey goes on, "Or, if it is not the case that political principles apply to the family's internal dynamics, one's status as a citizen of the just society takes normative priority over one's identity as a family member."[9] She directs a version of this criticism at our view: "They go further than previous feminist defenders of political liberalism by claiming that 'political liberalism is feminist liberalism.' They do not discuss, however, a key issue that arises from attempts like theirs . . . to recover a feminist position from political liberalism, namely, the limitations that this necessarily places on pluralism, which was, as noted above, the impetus to its creation in the first place."[10]

It is first worth underscoring that the claim that one's status as a citizen enjoys normative priority over other features of oneself isn't all that remarkable. In one sense, this just means that there are rights that citizens possess that can't be infringed upon by others or the state without adequate justification. After all, the whole basis for criminal law is the idea

---

[9] Abbey, "Back toward a Comprehensive Liberalism?," p. 16.

[10] Abbey, *Feminist Interpretations of Rawls*, p. 20.

that there are limits to what others can do to you as a citizen, a free and equal person. Criminal laws straightforwardly set limits on the actions one may undertake, and it doesn't matter whether the grounds any particular person appeals to for wanting to, say, own slaves or marry their daughters off at the age of 12 or force sex upon their wives lie in their comprehensive doctrines. The rights guaranteed to citizens prohibit such practices, and laws punish those who violate them, and this just reflects the view that one's standing as a citizen has normative priority over other features of social life.

So Abbey's concern can't simply be about the mere fact of the normative priority of citizenship. Rather, the worry must be about the substance and range of constraints our account places on the set of doctrines that count as reasonable. We have defended the substantive content of our view of citizenship throughout the book. As should be clear, we think that interests of persons as free and equal citizens go beyond those that liberals have traditionally recognized, that understanding the interests of persons as free and equal citizens requires paying attention to the material conditions of persons and persistent inequalities, and that, ultimately, some doctrines perhaps traditionally thought of as reasonable are not so. We do not think this undermines the impetus to develop political liberalism in the first place. Rather, it underscores that substantive equality is a precondition to many of the freedoms that liberals prize.

While our view does rest on a substantive interpretation of the kind of equality required to realize liberal ideals, it does not extend beyond the domain of the political. We do not offer a defense of egalitarianism as a value across all domains of life. Nor does our defense of substantive equality entail any particular view about how persons should arrange their relationships with others (friends, family, strangers) outside of respecting their rights as citizens. Nor does our view have implications about one's priorities and values as a person independent of one's role as a citizen. It respects the fact of reasonable pluralism about all these matters.

Finally, we should note what we think political liberalism cannot deliver concerning feminist arguments and values. Political liberalism is a feminist liberalism, yet there is a gap between the equality delivered by political liberals as a matter of equal citizenship and the vision of egalitarian gender relations that some feminist comprehensive views demand. Susan M. Okin famously claims, "A just future would be one without gender. In its social structures and practices, one's sex would have no more relevance than one's eye color or the length of one's toes."[11] Not all notions or aspects of gender are incompatible with the interests of persons as free and equal citizens. Hence, it is not the aim of political liberalism to achieve a social world in which gender or sex has no more social importance than eye color. Political liberals are concerned to eliminate those aspects of gender that undermine or frustrate persons' interests and standing as free and equal citizens. We all care deeply about certain moral and social issues, and we sometimes think that the world would be a better place if others shared our view, too. Our work here has stressed the way in which persons, their beliefs and desires, practices, and institutions take shape in the background culture. While we have focused on how power works to shape social life in a way that sometimes undermines persons' standing as free and equal citizens, we should not forget how we can affect the background culture in numerous ways to bring about a world that we think is better and more egalitarian given our feminist visions. So, for example, if children's toys and programming perpetuate and reinforce views about gender that we think are objectionable, we can campaign against this and try to effect change. Not all issues of equality are matters for state intervention.

We think we have shown that political liberalism offers an especially attractive account of political morality that demands substantive equality for all persons as free and equal citizens. The promise of a feminist political liberalism lies in its vision of liberal democracies as a shared project among persons who aim to live on terms of mutual respect with others as free and equal citizens. We hope to have made a contribution to that project here.

---

[11] Okin, *Justice, Gender and the Family*, p. 171.

Bibliography

Abbey, Ruth. "Back toward a Comprehensive Liberalism? Justice as Fairness, Gender and Families." *Political Theory* 35 (2007): 5–28.

———. *The Return of Feminist Liberalism*. Durham, UK: Acumen, 2011.

———, ed. *Feminist Interpretations of John Rawls*. University Park: Pennsylvania State University Press, 2013.

Aboriginal Women's Action Network. "Aboriginal Women's Statement on Legal Prostitution." 2007. http://www.prostitutionresearch.com/aboriginal%20 statement%20on%20legal%20prostitution.pdf.

Ahrens, Deborah. "Not in Front of the Children: Prohibition on Child Custody as Civil Branding for Criminal Activity." *New York University Law Review* 75 (2000): 737–774.

Akers, Naomi, and Cathryn Evans, eds. *Occupational Health and Safety Handbook*. 3rd ed. San Francisco: St. James Infirmary, 2013. http://perma.cc/ 02CetqGsJMU?type=live.

All-Party Parliamentary Group on Prostitution and the Global Sex Trade. "Shifting the Burden: Inquiry to Assess the Operation of the Current Legal Settlement on Prostitution in England and Wales." March 2014. http://appgprostitution.files. wordpress.com/2014/04/shifting-the-burden1.pdf.

Alstott, Anne L. *No Exit: What Parents Owe Their Children and What Society Owes Parents*. Oxford: Oxford University Press, 2004.

Amnesty International. "Amnesty International Publishes Policy and Research on Protection of Sex Workers' Rights." May 26, 2016. https://www.amnesty.org/en/ latest/news/2016/05/amnesty-international-publishes-policy-and-research-on- protection-of-sex-workers-rights/.

Anderson, Elizabeth. *Value in Ethics and Economics*. Cambridge, MA: Harvard University Press, 1995.

———. "What's the Point of Equality?," *Ethics* 109 (1999): 287–337.

———. "Toward a Non-Ideal, Relational Methodology for Political Philosophy: Comments on Schwartzman's *Challenging Liberalism*." *Hypatia* 24 (2009): 130–145.

———. *The Imperative of Integration*. Princeton, NJ: Princeton University Press, 2010.

Anderson, Scott. "Prostitution and Sexual Autonomy: Making Sense of Prohibition and Prostitution." In *Prostitution and Pornography: Philosophical Debate about the Sex Industry*. Ed. Jessica Spector, 358–393. Stanford, CA: Stanford University Press, 2006.

Arneson, Richard. "Against Freedom of Conscience." *San Diego Law Review* 47 (2010): 1015–1040.

Baehr, Amy R., ed. *Varieties of Feminist Liberalism*. Lanham, MD: Rowman & Littlefield, 2004.

———. "Perfectionism, Feminism and Public Reason." *Law and Philosophy* 27 (2008): 193–222.

———. "Feminist Receptions of the Original Position." In *The Original Position*. Ed. Timothy Hinton, 119–138. Cambridge, UK: Cambridge University Press, 2015.

Barnett, Laura, and Lyne Casavant. "Prostitution: A Review of Legislation in Selected Countries." Background Paper. Occupational Safety and Health Service, Department of Labour, New Zealand. https://lop.parl.ca/Content/LOP/ResearchPublications/2011-115-e.pdf.

Barrett Enterprises Group. "Moonlite Bunny Ranch: Independent Contractor Hiring Package." January 5, 2012. http://tmz.vo.llnwd.net/o28/newsdesk/tmz_documents/1222-jimi-lynn-bunnyranch.pdf.

Barry, Brian. *Culture and Equality*. Cambridge, MA: Harvard University Press, 2001.

Blum, Brian A. *Contracts*. 6th ed. New York: Walters and Kluwer, 2013.

Boettcher, James W. "Respect, Recognition, and Public Reason." *Social Theory and Practice* 33 (2007): 223–249.

Bonham, James, and Henry Richardson. "Liberalism, Deliberative Democracy, and 'Reasons That All Can Accept.'" *Journal of Political Philosophy* 17 (2009): 253–274.

Brake, Elizabeth. "Minimal Marriage: What Political Liberalism Implies for Marriage Law." *Ethics* 120 (2010): 302–337.

———. *Minimizing Marriage: Marriage, Morality and the Law*. Oxford: Oxford University Press, 2012.

Brooks, Thom. "The Problem with Polygamy." *Philosophical Topics* 37 (2009): 109–122.

Budig, Michelle J. "The Fatherhood Bonus and the Motherhood Penalty: Parenthood and the Gender Gap in Pay." *Third Way*, September 2, 2014. http://www.thirdway.org/report/the-fatherhood-bonus-and-the-motherhood-penalty-parenthood-and-the-gender-gap-in-pay.

Calhoun, Cheshire. "Standing for Something." *Journal of Philosophy* 92 (1995): 235–260.

———. *Feminism, The Family, and the Politics of the Closet: Lesbian and Gay Displacement*. New York: Oxford University Press, 2000.

Card, Claudia. "Against Marriage and Motherhood." *Hypatia* 11 (1996): 1–23.

———. "Gay Divorce: Thoughts on the Legal Regulation of Marriage." *Hypatia* 22 (2007): 24–38.

Catalyst. *Pyramid: Women in S&P 500 Companies.* New York: Catalyst, 2017.

Chambers, Clare. *Sex, Culture and Justice: The Limits of Choice.* University Park: Pennsylvania State University Press, 2008.

———. "The Marriage-Free State." *Proceedings of the Aristotelian Society* 113 (2013): 123–143.

———. "The Limitations of Contract: Regulating Personal Relationships in the Marriage-Free State." In *After Marriage: Rethinking Marital Relationships.* Ed. Elizabeth Brake, 51–83. Oxford: Oxford University Press, 2016.

———. *Against Marriage: An Egalitarian Defense of the Marriage-Free State.* Oxford: Oxford University Press, 2017.

Chateauvert, Melinda. *Sex Workers Unite: A History of the Movement from Stonewall to Slut Walk.* Boston: Beacon Press, 2013.

Chicken Ranch. "The 'Girlfriend Experience.'" *Brothel Blog*, March 21, 2017. https://chickenranchbrothel.com/index.php/blog/the-girlfriend-experience.

Collins, Patricia Hill. *Black Feminist Thought: Knowledge, Consciousness and the Politics of Empowerment.* Revised 10th anniversary ed. New York: Routledge, 1999.

———. *Black Sexual Politics: African Americans, Gender and the New Racism.* Routledge, 2005.

Committee on Gynecologic Practice, "Vaginal 'Rejuvenation' and Cosmetic Vaginal Procedures: ACOG Committee Opinion No. 378." American College of Obstetricians and Gynecologists. (2007, reaffirmed 2017). https://www.acog.org/Clinical-Guidance-and-Publications/Committee-Opinions/Committee-on-Gynecologic-Practice/Vaginal-Rejuvenation-and-Cosmetic-Vaginal-Procedures.

Corvino, John. "Homosexuality and the PIB Argument." *Ethics* 115 (2005): 501–534.

Corvino, John, Ryan T. Anderson, and Sherif Girgis. *Debating Religious Liberty and Discrimination.* Oxford: Oxford University Press, 2017.

Crenshaw, Kimberlé. "Race, Gender, and Sexual Harassment." *Southern California Law Review* 65 (1992): 1467–1476.

Crittenden, Ann. *The Price of Motherhood: Why the Most Important Job in the World Is Still the Least Valued.* New York: Henry Holt, 2001.

Darwall, Stephen. *The Second-Person Standpoint: Morality, Respect, and Accountability.* Cambridge, MA: Harvard University Press, 2006.

Davis, Adrienne D. "Slavery and the Roots of Sexual Harassment." In *Directions in Sexual Harassment Law.* Ed. Catharine A. MacKinnon and Reva B. Siegel, 457–478. New Haven, CT: Yale University Press, 2004.

de Marneffe, Peter. "Liberalism, Liberty and Neutrality." *Philosophy & Public Affairs* 19 (1990): 253–274.

———. *Liberalism and Prostitution.* New York: Oxford University Press, 2010.

Duncan, Richard. "Free Exercise under Current Doctrine." In *The First Amendment: The Free Exercise of Religion Clause.* Ed. Thomas C. Berg, 183–196. New York: Prometheus Books, 2008.

Eichner, Maxine. *The Supportive State: Families, Government, and America's Political Ideals.* Oxford: Oxford University Press, 2010.

Equality Now. "What Is the Nordic Model?" N.d. https://www.equalitynow.org/sites/default/files/Nordic%20Model%20Fact%20Sheet_0.pdf.

Esbeck, Carl H. "The Lemon Test: Should It Be Retained, Reformulated or Rejected." *Notre Dame Journal of Law, Ethics & Public Policy* 4 (1990): 513–548.

European Parliament, Directorate-General for Internal Policies. "Sexual Exploitation and Prostitution and Its Impact on Gender Equality." January 2014. http://www.europarl.europa.eu/RegData/etudes/etudes/join/2014/493040/IPOL-FEMM_ET(2014)493040_EN.pdf.

European Parliament. "European Parliament Resolution of 26 February 2014 on Sexual Exploitation and Prostitution and Its Impact on Gender Equality." February 26, 2014. http://www.europarl.europa.eu/sides/getDoc.do?pubRef=-//EP//TEXT+TA+P7-TA-2014-0162+0+DOC+XML+V0//EN.

Family Caregiver Alliance. "Women and Caregiving: Facts and Figures." N.d. https://www.caregiver.org/women-and-caregiving-facts-and-figures.

Farley, Melissa. *Prostitution, Trafficking, and Traumatic Stress.* New York: Routledge, 2003.

———. "'Bad for the Body, Bad for the Heart': Prostitution Harms Women Even If Legalized or Decriminalized." *Violence against Women* 10 (2004): 1087–1125.

———. *Prostitution and Trafficking in Nevada.* San Francisco, CA: Prostitution Research & Education, 2007.

Farley, Melissa, Jacqueline Golding, Emily Schuckman, Neil M. Malamuth, and Laura Jarrett. "Comparing Sex Buyers with Men Who Do Not Buy Sex: New Data on Prostitution and Trafficking." *Journal of Interpersonal Violence,* August 31, 2015, https://doi.org/10.1177/0886260515600874.

Farley, Melissa, Nicole Matthews, Sarah Deer, Guadalupe Lopez, Christine Stark, and Eileen Hudson. "Garden of Truth: The Prostitution and Trafficking of Native Women in Minnesota." A project of Minnesota Indian Women's Sexual Assault Coalition and Prostitution Research & Education. October 27, 2011. http://www.prostitutionresearch.com/Garden_of_Truth_The%20Prostitution%20and%20Trafficking%20of%20Native%20Women.pdf.

Fraser, Nancy. *Justice Interruptus: Critical Reflections on the "Postsocialist" Condition.* New York: Routledge, 1997.

Freeman, Samuel. *Justice and the Social Contract: Essays on Rawlsian Political Philosophy.* New York: Oxford University Press, 2007.

———. *Rawls.* New York: Routledge, 2007.

Fricker, Miranda. *Epistemic Injustice: Power and Ethics of Knowing.* New York: Oxford University Press, 2007.

————. "Epistemic Justice as a Condition of Political Freedom." *Synthese* 190 (2013): 1317–1332.

Gaus, Gerald. *The Order of Public Reason: A Theory of Freedom and Morality in a Diverse and Bounded World.* Cambridge, UK: Cambridge University Press, 2011.

————. "Moral Constitutions." *Harvard Review of Philosophy* 19 (2013): 5–22.

————. "Public Reason Liberalism." In *The Cambridge Companion to Liberalism.* Ed. Stephen Wall and Chandran Kukathas, 1–22. Cambridge, UK: Cambridge University Press, 2015.

————. *The Tyranny of the Ideal: Justice in a Diverse Society.* Princeton, NJ: Princeton University Press, 2016.

Gaus, Gerald, and Kevin Vallier. "The Roles of Religious Conviction in a Publicly Justified Polity: The Implications of Convergence, Asymmetry and Political Institutions." *Philosophy & Social Criticism* 35 (2009): 51–76.

Germany, Federal Ministry for Family Affairs, Senior Citizens, Women and Youth. "Report by the Federal Government on the Impact of the Act Regulating the Legal Situation of Prostitutes (Prostitution Act)." July 2007. https://www.bmfsfj. de/blob/93346/f81fb6d56073e3a0a80c442439b6495e/bericht-der-br-zum-prostg-englisch-data.pdf.

Grant, Melissa Gira. "Let's Call Sex Work What It Is: Work." *The Nation*, March 5, 2014. https://www.thenation.com/article/lets-call-sex-work-what-it-work/.

Greenawalt, Kent. *Religious Convictions and Political Choice.* Oxford: Oxford University Press, 1988.

Halloway, Kali. "The Search for the Perfect Vagina: Why Labiaplasty Is Suddenly Booming." *Salon*, February 21, 2015. http://www.salon.com/2015/02/22/the_search_for_the_perfect_vagina_why_labiaplasty_is_suddenly_booming_partner.

Hartley, Christie. Review of Vallier's *Liberal Politics and Public Faith: Beyond Separation. Ethics* 127 (2016): 315–319.

————. "Political Liberalism and Children." *Philosophical Studies* 175 (2018): 1095–1112.

Hartley, Christie, and Lori Watson. "Feminism, Religion, and Shared Reasons: A Defense of Exclusive Public Reason." *Law and Philosophy* 28 (2009): 493–536.

————. "Is a Feminist Political Liberalism Possible?" *Journal of Ethics & Social Philosophy* 5 (2010): 1–21.

————. "Political Liberalism, Marriage and the Family." *Law and Philosophy* 31 (2012): 185–212.

————. "Civic Virtue and Political Thought: On Civic Virtue and Political Liberalism." In *Virtues and Their Vices.* Ed. Kevin Timpe and Craig Boyd, 415–434. Oxford: Oxford University Press, 2014.

————. "Political Liberalism and Religious Exemptions." In *Religious Exemptions.* Ed. Kevin Vallier and Michael Weber, 91–119. Oxford: Oxford University Press, 2018.

Hay, Carol. *Kantianism, Liberalism and Feminism: Resisting Oppression.* London: Palgrave Macmillan, 2013.

Hernández, Tanya Katerí. "The Racism of Sexual Harassment." In *Directions in Sexual Harassment Law.* Ed. Catharine A. MacKinnon and Reva B. Siegel, 479–495. New Haven, CT: Yale University Press, 2004.

Heymann, Jody. *The Widening Gap: Why America's Working Families Are in Jeopardy and What Can Be Done about It.* New York: Basic Books, 2000.

Horton, Karen. "Stats Show Labiaplasty Is Becoming More Popular." American Society of Plastic Surgeons, April 25, 2017. https://www.plasticsurgery.org/news/blog/stats-show-labiaplasty-is-becoming-more-popular.

Hubert Blackman v. Las Vegas Exclusive Personals. U.S. District Court, Southern District of New York. January 3, 2011. http://www.abajournal.com/files/escort_suit_filing.pdf.

Institute for Women's Policy Research. "Mothers Earn Just 71 Percent of What Fathers Earn." IWPR #Q062, May 2017. https://iwpr.org/publications/mothers-earn-just-71-percent-fathers-earn/

International Labor Organization. "C155: Occupational Health and Safety Convention." 1981. http://www.ilo.org/dyn/normlex/en/f?p=NORMLEXPUB:1 2100:0::NO::P12100_ILO_CODE:C155.

Jakobsson, Niklas, and Andreas Kotsdam. "The Law and Economics of International Sex Slavery: Prostitution Laws and Trafficking for Sexual Exploitation." *European Journal of Law and Economics* 35 (2013): 87–107.

James, Sarah. "What Happens during a Girlfriend Experience with a Sex Worker?" *Bunny Ranch Blog,* November 17, 2016. https://www.bunnyranch.com/blog/girlfriend-experience/.

Jeffreys, Shelia. *The Idea of Prostitution.* North Melbourne, Vic., AU: Spinifex Press, 1997.

Kittay, Eva. *Love's Labor: Essays on Women, Equality and Dependency.* New York: Routledge, 1999.

Koppelman, Andrew. *Defending American Religious Neutrality.* Cambridge, MA: Harvard University Press, 2013.

———. "Gay Rights, Religious Accommodations, and the Purposes of Antidiscrimination Law." *Southern California Law Review* 88 (2015): 619–660.

Krakauer, Jon. *Missoula: Rape and the Justice System in a College Town.* New York: Doubleday, 2015.

Laden, Anthony Simon. *Reasonably Radical: Deliberative Liberalism and the Politics of Identity.* Ithaca, NY: Cornell University Press, 2001.

Larmore, Charles. "The Moral Basis of Political Liberalism." *Journal of Philosophy* 96 (1999): 599–625.

———. *The Autonomy of Morality.* Cambridge, UK: Cambridge University Press, 2008.

Leidholdt, Dorchen A. "Prostitution and Trafficking in Women: An Intimate Relationship." In *Prostitution Trafficking and Traumatic Stress*. Ed. Melissa Farley, 167–183. New York: Routledge, 2003.

Liberto, Hallie. "Normalizing Prostitution versus Normalizing the Alienability of Sexual Rights: A Response to Scott A. Anderson." *Ethics* 120 (2009): 138–145.

Lloyd, S. A. "Family Justice and Social Justice." *Pacific Philosophical Quarterly* 75 (1994): 353–371.

———. "Toward a Liberal Theory of Sexual Equality." In *Varieties of Feminist Liberalism*. Ed. Amy R. Baehr, 63–84. Lanham, MD: Rowman & Littlefield, 2004.

Locke, John. "An Essay Concerning Toleration" (1667). In *Locke: Political Essays*. Ed. Mark Goldie, 135–159. New York: Cambridge University Press, 1997.

Macedo, Stephen. *Just Married: Same-Sex Couples, Monogamy and the Future of Marriage*. Princeton, NJ: Princeton University Press, 2015.

MacKinnon, Catharine A. "Disputing Male Sovereignty: On *United States v. Morrison*." *Harvard Law Review* 144 (2000): 135–177.

———. *Women's Lives, Men's Laws*. Cambridge, MA: Harvard University Press, 2005.

———. "Trafficking, Prostitution, and Inequality." *Harvard Civil Rights–Civil Liberties Law Review* 46 (2011): 271–309.

———. *Sex Equality*. 3rd. ed. St Paul, MN: Foundation Press, 2016.

"Man Sues Dominatrix for Hitting Him Too Hard." *The Local*, October 10, 2012. https://www.thelocal.de/20121010/45473.

Markel, Dan, Jennifer M. Collins, and Ethan J. Leib. *Privilege or Punish: Criminal Justice and the Challenge of Family Ties*. Oxford: Oxford University Press, 2009.

Matthews, Roger. *Prostitution, Politics and Policy*. New York: Routledge-Cavendish, 2008.

Matthews, R., H. Easton, L. Reynolds, J. Bindel, and Lisa Young. *Exiting Prostitution: A Study in Female Desistance*. New York: Palgrave Macmillan, 2014.

May, Simon Căbulea. "Liberal Neutrality and Civil Marriage." In *After Marriage: Rethinking Marital Relationships*. Ed. Elizabeth Brake, 9–28. Oxford: Oxford University Press, 2016.

———. "Exemptions for Conscience." In *Religion in Liberal Political Philosophy*. Ed. Cécile Laborde and Aurélia Bardon, 191–203. Oxford: Oxford University Press, 2017.

McGregor, Jean. "The Number of Women CEOs in the Fortune 500s Is at an All-Time-High—of 32." *Washington Post*, June 7, 2017.

Metz, Tamara. *Untying the Knot: Marriage, the State and the Case for Their Divorce*. Princeton, NJ: Princeton University Press, 2010.

Miller, Claire Cain. "It's Not Just Fox: Why Women Don't Report Sexual Harassment." *New York Times*. April 10, 2017. https://www.nytimes.com/2017/04/10/upshot/its-not-just-fox-why-women-dont-report-sexual-harassment.html.

Mills, Charles. *The Racial Contract*. Ithaca, NY: Cornell University Press, 1997.

———. "'Ideal Theory' as Ideology." *Hypatia* 20 (2005): 165–184.

———. "The Domination Contract." In *Contract and Domination*. Ed. Carole Pateman and Charles W. Mills, 79–105. Cambridge, UK: Polity, 2007.

———. "Schwartzman vs. Okin: Some Comments on Challenging Liberalism." *Hypatia* 24 (2009): 164–176.

Moran, Rachel. *Paid For: My Journey through Prostitution*. Dublin: Gill & Macmillan, 2013.

National Domestic Violence Hotline. "Get the Facts and Figures." N.d. http://www. thehotline.org/resources/statistics.

Netherlands, Scientific Research and Documentation Center. "Prostitution in the Netherlands since the Lifting the Brothel Ban." 2007. https://repository.tudelft. nl/view/wodc/uuid:a0ca309e-9739-49a9-a803-9820a8deofa5/.

Neufeld, Blain. "Civic Respect, Political Liberalism, and Non-Liberal Societies." *Politics, Philosophy & Economics* 4 (2005): 275–299.

———. "Coercion, the Basic Structure and the Family." *Journal of Social Philosophy* 40 (2009): 37–54.

———. "Why Public Reasoning Involves Ideal Theorizing." In *Political Utopias: Contemporary Debates*. Ed. Michael Weber and Kevin Vallier, 73–93. Oxford: Oxford University Press, 2017.

Neufeld, Blain, and Lori Watson. "The Tyranny—or the Democracy—of the Ideal?" *Cosmos + Taxis* 5, no. 2 (2018): 47–61.

New Zealand Department of Labour, Occupational Safety and Health Service. "A Guide to Occupational Health and Safety in the New Zealand Sex Industry." June 2004. http://espu-usa.com/espu-ca/wp-content/uploads/2008/02/nz-health-and-safety-handbook.pdf.

New Zealand Lawsuit. http://time.com/36603/prostitute-sued-by-nz-man/.

New Zealand Parliamentary Counsel Office. Prostitution Reform Act of 2003. http:// www.legislation.govt.nz/act/public/2003/0028/latest/DLM197815.html.

NSW Parliamentary Research Service. "Brothel Regulation in NSW." *Issues Backgrounder* 1 (August 2015). https://www.parliament.nsw.gov.au/researchpapers/Documents/ brothel-regulation-in-nsw/Brothel%20Regulation%20in%20NSW%20Aug%20 2015.pdf.

Nussbaum, Martha. *Sex and Social Justice*. Oxford: Oxford University Press, 2000.

———. *Women and Human Development*. Cambridge, UK: Cambridge University Press, 2000.

———. "Rawls and Feminism." In *The Cambridge Companion to Rawls*. Ed. Samuel Freeman, 488–520. Cambridge, UK: Cambridge University Press, 2003.

———. "The Future of Feminist Liberalism." In *Varieties of Feminist Liberalism*. Ed. Amy R. Baehr, 103–132. Lanham, MD: Rowman & Littlefield, 2004.

———. *Frontiers of Justice: Disability, Nationality, Species Membership*. Cambridge, MA: Belknap Press of Harvard University Press, 2006.

———. "'Whether from Reason or Prejudice': Taking Money for Bodily Services." In *Prostitution and Pornography: Philosophical Debate about the Sex Industry*. Ed. Jessica Spector, 175–208. Stanford, CA: Stanford University Press, 2006.

———. *Liberty of Conscience: In Defense of America's Tradition of Religious Equality*. New York: Basic Books, 2008.

———. "Veiled Threats?" *New York Times*, July 11, 2010. http://opinator.blogs. nytimes.com/2010/07/11/veiled-threats/.

Okin, Susan M. *Justice, Gender and the Family*. New York: Basic Books, 1989.

———. "Political Liberalism, Justice and Gender." *Ethics* 105 (1994): 23–43.

———. "Justice and Gender: An Unfinished Debate." *Fordham Law Review* 72 (2004): 1537–1567.

———. "'Forty Acres and a Mule' for Women: Rawls and Feminism." *Politics, Philosophy & Economics* 4 (2005): 233–248.

Olson, Elizabeth. "A Bleak Picture for Women Trying to Rise at Law Firms." *New York Times*, July 24, 2017.

Outshoorn, Joyce. "Policy Change in Prostitution in the Netherlands: From Legalization to Strict Control." *Sexuality Research and Social Policy* 9, no. 3 (2012): 233–243.

Parker, Kim. "Women More Than Men Adjust Their Careers for Family Life." *Pew Research Center*. October 1, 2015. http://www.pewresearch.org/fact-tank/2015/10/01/women-more-than-men-adjust-their-careers-for-family-life/.

Pateman, Carole. *The Sexual Contract*. Stanford, CA: Stanford University Press, 1998.

Pateman, Carole, and Charles Mills. *Contract and Domination*. New York: Polity Press, 2007.

Pegula, Stephen, and Jill Janocha. "Death on the Job: Fatal Work Injuries in 2011." *Beyond the Numbers* 2, no. 22 (2013). http://www.bls.gov/opub/btn/volume-2/death-on-the-job-fatal-work-injuries-in-2011.htm.

Perry, Michael. "From Religious Freedom to Moral Freedom." *San Diego Law Review* 47 (2010): 993–1013.

Pheterson, Gail, ed. *A Vindication of the Rights of Whores*. Seattle, WA: Seal Press, 1989.

Potterat, J.J. et al. "Morality in a Long-Term Open Cohort of Prostitute Women." *American Journal of Epidemiology* 159, no. 8 (2004): 778–785.

Quinn, Philip L. "Political Liberalisms and Their Exclusions of the Religious." In *Religion and Contemporary Liberalism*. Ed. Paul A. Weithman, 138–161. South Bend, IN: University of Notre Dame Press, 1997.

Quong, Jonathan. *Liberalism without Perfectionism*. Oxford: Oxford University Press, 2011.

———. "On the Idea of Public Reason." In *A Companion to Rawls*. Ed. Jon Mandel and David A. Reidy, 265–280. Oxford: Wiley Blackwell, 2014.

Raymond, Janice G. *Not a Choice, Not a Job: Exposing the Myths about Prostitution and the Global Sex Trade*. Washington, DC: Potomac Books, 2013.

Rawls, John. "The Idea of Public Reason Revisited." In *John Rawls: Collected Papers.* Ed. Samuel Freeman, 573–615. Cambridge, MA: Harvard University Press, 1999.

———. *The Law of Peoples.* Cambridge, MA: Harvard University Press, 1999.

———. *A Theory of Justice.* Revised ed. Cambridge, MA: Harvard University Press, 1999.

———. *Justice as Fairness: A Restatement.* Ed. Erin Kelly. Cambridge, MA: Harvard University Press, 2001.

———. *Political Liberalism.* Expanded ed. New York: Columbia University Press, 2005.

———. "Reply to Habermas." In *Political Liberalism,* 373–434. Expanded ed. New York: Columbia University Press, 2005.

Reidy, David. "Rawls's Wide View of Public Reason: Not Wide Enough." *Res Publica* 6 (2000): 49–72.

Satz, Debra. "Markets in Women's Sexual Labor." In *Why Some Things Should Not Be for Sale,* 135–153. Oxford: Oxford University Press, 2010.

———. *Why Some Things Should Not Be for Sale.* Oxford: Oxford University Press, 2010.

Schmidtz, David. "Nonideal Theory: What It Is and What It Needs to Be." *Ethics* 121 (2011): 772–796.

Schouten, Gina. "Does the Gendered Division of Labor Undermine Citizenship?" In *The Good Society.* Ed. George Hull, 291–309. Lanham, MD: Rowman and Littlefield, 2015.

———. "Is the Gendered Division of Labor a Problem of Distribution?" In *Oxford Studies in Political Philosophy.* Vol. 2. Ed. Peter Vallentyne, David Sobel, and Steven Wall, 185–206. Oxford: Oxford University Press, 2016.

———. "Citizenship, Reciprocity, and the Gendered Division of Labor: A Stability Argument for Gender Egalitarian Political Interventions." *Politics, Philosophy & Economics* 16 (2017): 174–209.

Schwartzman, Lisa H. *Challenging Liberalism: Feminism as Political Critique.* University Park: Pennsylvania State University Press, 2006.

———. "Feminism, Method, and Rawlsian Abstraction." In *Feminist Interpretations of John Rawls.* Ed. Ruth Abbey, 40–56. University Park: Pennsylvania State University Press, 2006.

———. "Non-Ideal Theorizing, Social Groups and Knowledge of Oppression: A Response." *Hypatia* 24 (2009): 177–164.

Schwartzman, Micah. "The Completeness of Public Reason." *Politics, Philosophy & Economics* 3 (2004): 191–220.

———. "The Sincerity of Public Reason." *Journal of Political Philosophy* 19 (2011): 375–398.

———. "What If Religion Is Not Special?" *University of Chicago Law Review* 79 (2012): 1351–1427.

———. "Religion, Equality, and Anarchy." In *Religion in Liberal Political Philosophy*. Ed. Cécile Laborde and Aurélia Bardon, 15–30. Oxford: Oxford University Press, 2017.

Sen, Amartya. *The Idea of Justice*. Cambridge, MA: Harvard University Press, 2009.

Seo-Young, Cho, Axel Dreher, and Eric Neumayer. "Does Legalized Prostitution Increase Human Trafficking?" *World Development* 41, no. 1 (2013): 67–82.

Shanley, Mary Lyndon. "Just Marriage." In *Just Marriage*. Ed. Joshua Cohen and Deborah Chasman, 3–30. Oxford: Oxford University Press, 2004.

Shelby, Tommie. "Racial Realities and Corrective Justice: A Reply to Charles Mill." *Critical Philosophy of Race* 1 (2013): 145–162.

Shrage, Laurie. "Prostitution and the Case for Decriminalization." *Dissent* 43 (1996): 41–45.

———. "Feminist Perspectives on Sex Markets." In *The Stanford Encyclopedia of Philosophy*. Ed. Edward N. Zalta. Fall 2016. https://plato.stanford.edu/archives/fall2016/entries/feminist-sex-markets/.

Simmons, John. "Ideal and Nonideal Theory." *Philosophy & Public Affairs* 38 (2010): 5–36.

Slaughter, Anne-Marie. "Why Women Still Can't Have It All." *The Atlantic*, July/August 2012.

Solum, Lawrence B. "Inclusive Public Reason." *Pacific Philosophical Quarterly* 75 (1994): 217–231.

Spector, Jessica, ed. *Prostitution and Pornography: Philosophical Debate about the Sex Industry*. Stanford, CA: Stanford University Press, 2006.

Stemplowska, Zofia, and Adam Swift. "Ideal Theory and Nonideal Theory." In *The Oxford Handbook of Political Philosophy*. Ed. David Estlund, 373–389. Oxford: Oxford University Press, 2012.

Strauss, Gregg. "Is Polygamy Inherently Unequal?" *Ethics* 122 (2012): 516–544.

Sullivan, Mary. "What Happens When Prostitution Becomes Work?" *Turn Off the Red Light*, n.d. http://www.feministes-radicales.org/wp-content/uploads/2012/03/Mary-Sullivan-CATW-What-Happens-When-Prostitution-Becomes-Work...-An-Update-on-Legalisation-of-Prostitution-in-Australia.pdf.

———. *Making Sex Work: A Failed Experiment with Legalized Prostitution*. North Melbourne, Australia: Spinifex Press, 2007.

Sunstein, Cass. "Should Sex Equality Law Apply to Religious Institutions?" In *Is Multiculturalism Bad for Women*. Ed. Joshua Cohen, Matthew Howard, and Martha C. Nussbaum, 85–94. Princeton, NJ: Princeton University Press, 1999.

Sunstein, Cass, and Richard H. Thaler. "Privatizing Marriage." *The Monist* 91 (2008): 377–387.

Swedish Institute. "Selected Extracts of the Swedish Government Report SOU 2010:49: The Ban against the Purchase of Sexual Services. An Evaluation 1999–2008." November 2010. https://ec.europa.eu/anti-trafficking/publications/ban-against-purchase-sexual-services-evaluation-1999-2008_en.

Taylor, Harriet. "Early Essays on Marriage and Divorce." In *Essays on Sex Equality: John Stuart Mill and Harriet Taylor Mill.* Ed. Alice S. Rossi, 65–88. Chicago: University of Chicago Press, 1970.

Thukral, Juhu, Melissa Ditmore, and Alexandra Murphy. "Behind Closed Doors: An Analysis of Indoor Sex Work in New York City." Sex Workers Project at the Urban Justice Center. 2005. http://sexworkersproject.org/downloads/BehindClosedDoors.pdf.

Tucker, Jasmine, and Caitlin Lowell. "National Snapshot: Poverty among Women and Families, 2015." Fact Sheet. Washington, DC: National Women's Law Center, September 2016.

United Nations. "Protocol to Prevent, Suppress and Punish Trafficking in Persons, Especially Women and Children, Supplementing the United Nations Convention against Transnational Organized Crime." 2000. https://ec.europa.eu/anti-trafficking/sites/antitrafficking/files/united_nations_protocol_on_thb_en_4.pdf.

U.S. Bureau of Labor Statistics. "Unpaid Eldercare in the United States: 2011–2012 Summary." Washington, DC: Department of Labor. https://www.bls.gov/news.release/archives/elcare_09182013.pdf.

———. "American Time Use Survey, 2015." Washington, DC: Department of Labor. https://www.bls.gov/news.release/archives/atus_06242016.pdf.

———. "American Time Use Survey, 2016." Washington, DC: Department of Labor. https://www.bls.gov/news.release/pdf/atus.pdf.

———. "Women in the Labor Force: A Databook." Report 1065. Washington, DC: Department of Labor. https://www.bls.gov/opub/reports/womens-databook/2016/home.htm.

U.S. Centers for Disease Control and Prevention. "Sexual Violence: Facts at a Glance." 2012. https://www.cdc.gov/ViolencePrevention/pdf/SV-DataSheet-a.pdf.

U.S. Congress. "Victims of Trafficking and Violence Protection Act of 2000." https://www.congress.gov/bill/106th-congress/house-bill/3244/text?r=1.

U.S. Department of Labor. "Occupational Health and Safety Act of 1970." https://www.osha.gov/law-regs.html.

Vallier, Kevin. "Liberalism, Religion and Integrity." *Australasian Journal of Philosophy* 90 (2012): 149–165.

———. *Liberal Politics and Public Faith, Beyond Separation.* New York: Routledge, 2014.

———. "Public Justification versus Public Deliberation: The Case for Divorce." *Canadian Journal of Philosophy* 45 (2015): 139–158.

Watson, Lori. "Constituting Politics: Power, Reciprocity, and Identity." *Hypatia* 22 (2007): 96–112.

———. "Pornography and Public Reason." *Social Theory and Practice* 33, no. 3: (2007) 467–488.

———. "Why Sex Work Isn't Work." *Logos: A Journal of Modern Culture* 16, nos. 1–2 (2017). http://logosjournal.com/2014/watson/.

Watson, Lori, and Jessica Flannigan. *Debating Sex Work*. Oxford: Oxford University Press, forthcoming.

Wedgwood, Ralph. "The Fundamental Argument for Same-Sex Marriage." *Journal of Political Philosophy* 7 (1999): 225–242.

———. "Is Civil Marriage Illiberal?" In *After Marriage: Rethinking Marital Relationships*. Ed. Elizabeth Brake, 29–50. Oxford: Oxford University Press, 2016.

Weithman, Paul. *Religion and the Obligations of Citizenship*. New York: Cambridge University Press, 2002.

———. *Why Political Liberalism: On John Rawls's Political Turn*. New York: Oxford University Press, 2010.

———. "Convergence and Political Autonomy." *Public Affairs Quarterly* 25 (2011): 327–348.

———. *Rawls, Political Liberalism and Reasonable Faith*. Cambridge, UK: Cambridge University Press, 2016.

Weitzer, Ronald. *Legalizing Prostitution: From Illicit Vice to Lawful Business*. New York: New York University Press, 2012.

Williams, Joan. *Unbending Gender: Why Family and Work Conflict and What to Do about It*. Oxford: Oxford University Press, 2000.

Wood, Allison. "'Get Home Safe,' My Rapist Said." *New York Times*, December 12, 2015. http://www.nytimes.com/2015/12/13/opinion/get-home-safe-my-rapist-said.html.

World Health Organization. "Eliminating Female Genital Mutilation: An Interagency Statement." 2008. www.un.org/womenwatch/daw/csw/csw52/statements_missions/Interagency_Statement_on_Eliminating_FGM.pdf.

Index

children. *See also* caretaking work;
 families
 marriage, importance for care of,
  237–240
 moral power development in,
  139–140n12
 religious indoctrination of,
  122–123, 125
 removal from families, 213
choice. *See also* freedom
 as determinant of justice, 122–123, 193
 in gendered division of labor, 192–196,
  201, 210
 gender norms and, 195
 hypothetical choice situations, 25,
  30–31, 82n49
 institutional influences on, 61, 195
 as normative transformer, 193, 197
 political, 142
 religious, 122, 125
 social construction of, 10, 123, 124,
  192–194, 208
citizens and citizenship
 autonomy of (*see* autonomy)
 basic interests of, 70–71
 deliberation among (*see* democratic
  deliberation; public deliberation)
 democratic, 45, 77, 97, 103
 education for (*see* education)
 free and equal (*see* equal citizenship)
 fundamental interests of, 157n62,
  202, 218–219, 218n25
 integrity of (*see* integrity)
 normative priority of, 9, 161–162,
  161n73, 252–253
 political relationships among, 68, 83,
  152–153
 public reason and (*see* public reason)
 realization of, 100–103
 reasonable (*see* reasonable persons)
 religious (*see* persons of faith)
 respect for (*see* respect)
 second-class, 117–118, 154, 232–233
 as self-authenticating sources of valid
  claims, 161
 substantive account of, 248–250, 253

civic education, 49n19, 125, 155, 199
civic friendship, 68
civic respect, 151n47
civil disobedience, 23–24
civility. *See* duty of civility
civil rights
 for persons with disabilities, 179
 equal citizenship and, 67, 116–117
 legislative protections, 124, 153
 prostitution and, 178, 200
 realization of citizenship and, 101, 249
 religious claims for exemptions
  from, 120
 violations of, 84, 101, 178
 violence against women as issue
  of, 159
Civil Rights Act of 1964, 153
civil rights movements, 78, 162
civil society
 background culture of, 99
 equality in, 116, 153, 159
 full justification in, 91n5
 gender inequality in, 157, 202
 participation in, 155, 203, 228n55
civil unions, 83–84
clean-hands view of integrity, 95, 98
coercion
 female genital mutilation and, 198
 of natural freedom, 55
 into prostitution, 182, 183
 public justification of, 60–61
 in restructuring of religious doctrine,
  125–126
coercion-centric account of public
  justification, 47n10
coercive power, 42, 54, 56, 60–61
collective enterprise view of liberal
  democracies, 42, 61, 62
compensatory justice, 23
comprehensive doctrines
 in background culture, 36–38, 159
 equal citizenship in, 142
 families in, 203, 213, 214
 marriage in, 215, 222, 242
 overlapping consensus of, 47, 50, 59,
  60, 77, 150

CPSIA information can be obtained
at www.ICGtesting.com
Printed in the USA
BVHW031529300120
570904BV00004B/17